THE AMERICAN EXPRESS POCKET GUIDE TO WASHINGTON DC

Christopher McIntosh

with contributions by
Nancy Rayburn and Bernard Burt

Acknowledgments

The author and publishers thank the following for their invaluable help: Lois Brooks, the staff of the Washington DC Convention and Visitors Bureau, the staff of the International Visitors Service Center, Antoine Hamilton and Jean Gordon, editors of the original edition.

Quotations

Extracts have been taken from the following publications: *In 2 and 3 Out of Africa* by Washington *Story* by Angela McGinty (Doubleday, New York 1977) pp.5 and p.101 (page). *Roots-Anon* by France's *Parkinson Keyes* (Horace incident New York 1930) (p.25) *index* and Go down by Allen Drury (Doubleday, New York 1979) (p.89 and p.98). *Washington* *1954 by Frank Baldwin* etc. & schmuck and Inc. New York 1952, 1973) (p.11 and p.92) (the Easy of the Southern crush by Willie Morris, Alfred A. Knopf, New York 1971)

General Editor   David Townsend Jones
Art Editor   Nigel D Gorman
Designer   Christopher Howson
Illustrator   Karen Cochrane
Managing Editor   David Haslam
Production   Hilary Bird
Indexer   Sue McKinley

© American Express Publishing
Corporation Inc 1987, Out dated 1987
text and text of American Express
Publishing Corporation Inc, 1987
All rights reserved no portion of this
work in any manner or in part of in
this section

Published by Prentice Hall Press
Division

A division of Simon & Schuster Inc
One Gulf & Western Building
New York, New York 10023

PRENTICE HALL is a trademark of
Simon & Schuster
Any maps or index published by J.P. Oxford, England, based on
cartographic material of ...
Typeset by ...
Printed in Great ...
Originated in Great ...
Photoset produced through ...
Printed by Mandate Ofset ...

Library of Congress
Cataloging-in-Publication Data
(paperback). Christopher
McIntosh and Amex pocket
guide to Washington D.
Co-operation McIntosh Amex
contributions by Nancy Rayburn
and Bernard Burt
ISBN 0-13-025297-5 : $7.95
1. Washington (D.C.)—
Description—Guide-books. I.
McIntosh, Nancy. II. Burt,
Bernard. III. American Express
Co. IV. Title. V. Title:
Pocket guide to Washington DC.
F192.3.M39 1987 917.53—dc19
917.53

PRENTICE HALL PRESS
NEW YORK

The Author and Contributors
Christopher McIntosh is the author of many books and
articles on subjects ranging from travel to biography. After a
career in writing and publishing, he recently entered the
academic world. His other works include *The Swan King*, a
biography of Ludwig II of Bavaria, and *The American Express
Pocket Guide to Paris*. Contributors to the first edition were
Bernard Burt, on hotels and restaurants, and Nancy Rayburn,
on nightlife, the arts and shopping. The guide was revised in
1989 by Herbert Bailey Livesey, author of *New York* and *Spain*
in the same series.

Acknowledgments
The author and publisher thank the following for their
invaluable help and advice: Andrew Gray, Elisavietta Ritchie,
Clyde Farnsworth, Mila Brooks, the staff of the Washington
DC Convention and Visitors Association, the staff of the
International Visitor Information Center, and Leonie Hamilton
and Jean Gordon, editors of the original edition.

Quotations
Extracts have been taken from the following publications:
(p.7 and p.98) *Circles: A Washington Story* by Abigail
McCarthy (Doubleday, New York 1977); (p.9 and p.66) *Queen
Anne's Lace* by Frances Parkinson Keyes (Horace Liveright,
New York 1930); (p.23) *Advise and Consent* by Allen Drury
(Doubleday, New York 1959); (p.49 and p.88) *Washington,
USA* by Faith Baldwin (Farrar & Rhinehart Inc., New York
1942, 1943); (p.60 and p.92) *The Last of the Southern Girls* by
Willie Morris (Alfred A. Knopf, New York 1973).

General Editor David Townsend Jones
Art Editor Nigel O'Gorman
Designer Christopher Howson
Illustrator Karen Cochrane
Map Editor David Haslam
Jacket illustration Pierre Marie Valat
Indexer and gazetteer Hilary Bird
Proof-reader Sue McKinstry

Edited and designed by
Mitchell Beazley International Limited,
Artists House, 14-15 Manette Street,
London W1V 5LB

© American Express Publishing
Corporation Inc. 1987 (reprinted 1987)
New edition © American Express
Publishing Corporation Inc. 1990
All rights reserved including the right
of reproduction in whole or in part in
any form
Published by Prentice Hall Trade
Division
A Division of Simon & Schuster, Inc.
Gulf & Western Building
One Gulf & Western Plaza
New York, New York 10023
PRENTICE HALL is a trademark of
Simon & Schuster, Inc.

**Library of Congress
Cataloging-in-Publication Data**
McIntosh, Christopher
  The American Express pocket
  guide to Washington, DC /
  Christopher McIntosh: with
  contributions by Nancy Rayburn
  and Bernard Burt.
    p. cm.
  ISBN 0-13-025297-2 : $10.95
  1. Washington (D.C.)—
  Description—1981—Guide-books.
  I. Rayburn, Nancy. II. Burt,
  Bernard. III. American Express
  Company. IV. Title. V. Title:
  Pocket guide to Washington, DC.
F192.3.M36 1990
917.5304'4—dc20   89-36973
                              CIP

Maps in 2-color and 4-color by Lovell Johns Ltd, Oxford, England, based on
copyrighted material of Rand McNally & Company.
Typeset by Castle House Press, Llantrisant, Wales.
Typeset in Garamond and Univers.
Linotronic output through Microstar DTP Studio, Cardiff, Wales.
Produced by Mandarin Offset. Printed and bound in Malaysia.

Contents

How to use this book

The American Express Pocket Guide to Washington, DC is an encyclopedia of travel information, organized in the sections listed on the previous page. There is also a comprehensive *Index* (pages 155-162) and a *Gazetteer of street names* (pages 162-164), and there are full-color *Maps* at the end of the book.

For easy reference, all major sections (*Sights and places of interest, Hotels, Restaurants*), and other sections where possible, are arranged alphabetically. For the organization of the book as a whole, see *Contents*. For individual places that do not have separate entries in *Sights and places of interest*, see the *Index*.

Abbreviations

As a rule only standard abbreviations have been used, such as days of the week and months, points of the compass (N, S, E and W), street names (Ave., Blvd., Pl., Sq., Rd., St.), Saint (St), rms (rooms), C for century, and measurements.

Bold type

Bold type is used in the text mainly for emphasis, to draw attention to something of special interest or importance. It is also used in this way to pick out places — shops or minor museums, for example — that do not have full entries of their own. In such cases it is usually followed in brackets by the address, telephone number, details of opening times etc., which are printed in *italics*.

Cross-references

A special type has been used for cross-references. Whenever a place or section title is printed in *sans serif italics* (for example *Library of Congress* or *Basic information*) in the text, this indicates that you can turn to the appropriate heading in the book for further information.

Cross-references in this typeface always refer either to

How entries are organized

Frederick Douglass House *(Cedar Hill)*
1411 W St. SE, DC 20020 ☎ 426-5960 (house), 426-5961 (group tour reservations). Map 8J11 ▣ ✗ Open Apr-Labor Day 9am-5pm; rest of year 9am-4pm. Closed Christmas, New Year's Day. Tourmobile.

Frederick Douglass (1817-95) was the leading spokesman for American blacks in their struggle for freedom and justice during the 19thC. He lectured and wrote books about his own early life under slavery, campaigned tirelessly for abolition, helped recruit blacks for the Union army during the Civil War and finally settled down to a distinguished old age in Washington. He lived first in A St. (see *National Museum of African Art*), then bought Cedar Hill, this elegant white house on a height overlooking the Anacostia River. All the furnishings, except for curtains and wallpaper, are original. Douglass' library and other belongings are still *in situ*, and the whole house is redolent of the spirit of a very remarkable man. On arrival you are directed to the **Visitors' Center** at the foot of the hill where a film is shown about Douglass' life; books about black liberation, including Douglass' own, are on sale.

sections of the book — *Basic information*, *Planning and walks*, *Hotels* — or to individual entries in *Sights and places of interest*, such as *Library of Congress* or *Old Downtown*.

For easy reference, use the running heads printed at the top corner of the page (see, for example, **Capitol** on page 49 or **Hotels** on page 100).

Map references

Each of the full-color maps at the end of the book is divided into a grid of squares, identified vertically by letters (A, B, C, D, etc.) and horizontally by numbers (1, 2, 3, 4, etc.). A map reference identifies the page and square in which the street or place can be found — thus *Library of Congress* is located in Map **8**G10.

Price categories

Price categories are denoted by the symbols ☐ ▯☐ ▯▯☐ ▯▯▯▯ and ▮▮▮▮, which signify cheap, inexpensive, moderately priced, expensive and very expensive, respectively. In the cases of hotels and restaurants these correspond approximately with the following actual prices, which give a guideline at the time of printing. Although actual prices will inevitably increase, in most cases the relative price category — for example expensive or cheap — is likely to remain more or less the same.

Price categories	Corresponding to approximate prices	
	for **hotels**	for **restaurants**
	double room with bath; singles are slightly cheaper	*meal for one with service, taxes and house wine*
☐ cheap	under $50	under $10
▯☐ inexpensive	$50-75	$10-20
▯▯☐ moderate	$75-100	$20-40
▮▮▮▮ expensive	$100-150	$40-50
▮▮▮▮ very expensive	over $150	over $50

Bold blue type for entry headings.

Blue italics for address, practical information and symbols.
For list of symbols see page 6 or back flap of jacket.

Black text for description.

Sans serif italics used for cross-references to other entries or sections.

Bold type used for emphasis.

Entries for hotels, restaurants, shops, etc. follow the same organization, and are usually printed across a half column.

In hotels, symbols indicating special facilities appear at the end of the entry, in black.

Watergate
2600 Virginia Ave. NW, DC 20037 ☎ 298-4450 ☻904994. Map 2F4 ▮▮▮▮ *238 rms* ◄ 〓 *AE* CB ○ ○ *visa Metro: Foggy Bottom.*
Location: Foggy Bottom, near the Kennedy Center. Part of a large conglomeration of buildings overlooking the Potomac (see *Watergate Complex*), this luxurious hotel, set in attractively landscaped grounds, is run with tremendous style and polish. It has two restaurants, one of which is the well-known **Jean-Louis**.
& ❀ 〈〈 ⚮ ♈

Key to symbols

☎	Telephone	▦	Air conditioning
⊚	Telex	AE	American Express
★	Recommended sight	CB	Carte Blanche
⇌	Parking	◉	Diners Club
☒	Free entrance	◉	MasterCard
☒	Entrance fee payable	VISA	Visa
📷	Photography forbidden	⅋	Facilities for disabled people
⥀	Guided tour	☙	Garden
▬	Cafeteria	⋘	Good view
⁂	Special interest for children	⪡	Swimming pool
✤	Hotel	⅋	Tennis
▫	Cheap	ʬ	Gym/fitness facilities
▨	Inexpensive	⇌	Restaurant
▨	Moderately priced	⬛	Good wines
▨	Expensive		
▨	Very expensive		

An introduction to Washington

Washington in the 1980s is entering a golden age. Never before has the city been so vibrant, lively, cosmopolitan and civilized. Washington retains her Classical dignity, but has suddenly learned how to have fun. She still has her exquisite monuments and majestic perspectives, but she has grown sprightly of late, acquiring chic tastes, international habits and a new *joie de vivre*.

This new lease on life that Washington has assumed in the past decade or so has taken many people by surprise. Not long ago the US capital was a Cinderella among American cities, scorned by her big sisters — New York, Chicago and Los Angeles — as a "company town" dominated by the federal government and markedly lacking in culture, refinement and most of the good things in life. Now the tables have turned; Washington has become one of the most desirable American cities in which to live and one of the country's top tourist destinations.

It has taken surprisingly long for the city to achieve this transformation. The reasons lie in the multiple conflicts, anomalies and paradoxes that have marked the city's history from the beginning.

The choice of site was the outcome of a deal between the northern and southern states. In the War of Independence, the North, which had incurred bigger debts than the South, asked Congress to bail them out. Secretary of State Thomas Jefferson — a Southerner — struck a bargain with his northern rival Alexander Hamilton, Secretary of the Treasury, whereby the South would yield in the matter of the debts if the North would agree to a new national capital being located in the South. In due course President Washington himself chose the site, a diamond of territory 10 miles square (26 square kilometers) taken from Virginia and Maryland. Subsequently the area west of the Potomac seceded back to Virginia, spoiling the symmetry of the diamond.

The weather of April has been a little raw and winds had whipped the cherry blossoms early from the trees around the Tidal Basin and a week later from the sturdy trees of Kenwood in the northwest suburbs. It was a late spring, everyone agreed, but when Jeff got out of the cab that morning on the corner of C Street, the weather was Washington at its finest. A warm sun shone on the tourists streaming across the crosswalk to the Capitol, and on those standing in little groups eyeing the limousines along the curb and the secret service men already deployed at the entrance to the Old Senate Office Building on the south side.

Abigail McCarthy, *Circles: A Washington Story*

Washington appointed three Commissioners to administer this territory and to oversee the creation of the city within it, and it was they who decided to name the city Washington, after him. The man chosen by the President to lay out the city was a brilliant, irascible Frenchman called Pierre Charles L'Enfant, an army engineer who had fought for the Americans in the War of Independence. Taking his inspiration from the best examples of European town planning, L'Enfant designed a city that he considered worthy of the lofty ideals of the new nation: triumphal avenues radiating out from the President's mansion and the Capitol on its hilltop, broad streets laid out on a grid pattern, circles, squares, generous parks and imposing vistas. He drew the plan on a grand, ambitious scale, foreseeing that as the United States grew in prosperity it would be able gradually to flesh out his scheme and eventually achieve a really impressive capital. As L'Enfant put it in a letter to Washington: "It will be obvious that the plan should be drawn on such a scale as to leave room for the aggrandizement and embellishment which the increase of the wealth of the nation will permit it to pursue at any period however remote."

For its time L'Enfant's plan was astonishingly bold. He insisted, for example, on very wide streets. At that time 50 feet (15 meters) would have been more than generous, but L'Enfant wanted 90-130 feet (27-40 meters) for ordinary thoroughfares and 180-400 feet (55-122 meters) for the grander ones. The capital of the United States deserved no less.

Unfortunately L'Enfant's vision was not matched by the Commissioners, nor by the local landowners, and there were bitter quarrels over the implementation of the plan. Daniel Carroll of Duddingston, nephew of one of the Commissioners, built a farmhouse on a site that had been earmarked to become what is now Garfield Park to the southeast of the Capitol. After writing twice to Carroll and receiving no reply, L'Enfant had the building carefully dismantled and moved away. In the ensuing outcry, L'Enfant prevailed, but in the end opposition to him became so fierce that Washington felt obliged to dismiss him a year after he had been appointed. It was the first of many setbacks suffered by the city as a result of pettiness and lack of imagination.

L'Enfant's basic scheme, however, was retained, and the construction of the city limped along. By 1800 it was sufficiently far advanced for Congress to move there, but for decades Washington remained a sorry sight. The Capitol and the White House stood out amid the chaos of sporadic housing development, farmyards and areas of swamp. The city had no proper sidewalks, street lighting or sanitation. To add insult to injury, the District of Columbia was made a politically neutral federal district, residence of which did not carry the privilege of a vote in congressional or presidential elections; the idea was to protect the Government from local interference. Belonging to no state, it was given short shrift by Congress, which was preoccupied with other matters.

The miserliness with which the city was treated was astounding. Oil lamps were installed in the vicinity of the Capitol and the White House, but not enough money was allocated for oil, and so the lamps became mere ornaments. Meanwhile planning control was lax. It was not until 1820 that the government ordered farmers to stop fencing in and planting areas that had been designated as streets. Periodically congressmen would agitate for the removal of the nation's capital to a more westerly location, but nothing came of it.

The city languished without proper amenities until the 1870s, when a dynamic city administrator named Alexander ("Boss") Shepherd forced through a vast scheme of public works without worrying about where the money would come from. Sidewalks were laid, sewers and street lights installed and thousands of trees planted. Although he bankrupted the city, posterity should be grateful to Shepherd. The response of Congress, however, was to dissolve the city council and take over the government of the District through congressional committees, thus leaving the citizens with neither federal nor local representation — an extraordinary state of affairs for the capital of a great democracy.

During the late 19th and early 20thC the situation improved, partly owing to a steady influx of wealthy people who colonized areas such as Cleveland Heights in the northwest, so-called because President Cleveland lived there. The city gained some fine buildings such as the Library of Congress and Union Station, and in the same period the Mall was laid out more or less in its present form. With World War I, the New Deal and World War II, the ranks of Washington's bureaucracy swelled, but as late as 1960 it still felt like a company town.

In that year it became a black majority city, and achieved another turning point with the election of John F. Kennedy as President. Kennedy appointed his own adviser on Washington, preserved threatened historic houses, had a new code for public buildings drawn up, approved the plan for the Metro and presided over the rebuilding of the old slum area in the southwest. As Kennedy put it: "The Nation's capital should represent the finest in living environment which America can plan and build."

The trip to Washington had been everything that they both had dreamed of and hoped for and more...to them it seemed as beautiful as a vision of a white-pillared Paradise.

Frances Parkinson Keyes, *Queen Anne's Lace*

Washington since then has undergone rapid and accelerating change. Today it has its own elected mayor and city council, drawn largely from the black areas, and DC residents can at last vote in presidential elections, although they still have no full representation in Congress. The Kennedy Center, opened in 1971, has helped to fuel a cultural boom in the city. The Smithsonian Institution has expanded its already vast museum facilities. The building of the Metro, still being extended, has triggered the dramatic growth of suburban business centers such as Bethesda, Rosslyn and Crystal City, where large corporations have been rushing to set up their headquarters, bringing affluent and discriminating new customers to Washington's restaurants and night spots, which have consequently blossomed.

All over the District itself splendid new luxury hotels, office buildings and shopping malls are mushrooming, while glorious historic buildings such as the Old Post Office have been beautifully restored. At the same time a strict ban on high-rise buildings has kept the city's delicate skyline intact. However, not all the news is good, for large areas of deprivation and poverty remain in the predominantly black northeast and southeast sectors, and there are strident contrasts between rich and poor neighborhoods — one of the contradictions that Washington has yet to overcome.

The capital of the United States is one of the most European of American cities. Its scale is human; its streets invite you to stroll rather than rush; and its unfolding vistas of townscape and its mixture of grandeur and intimacy have a distinctly European feel. Washington appropriately has been dubbed "Paris on the Potomac."

Pierre L'Enfant, whose grave is in Arlington Cemetery, would be pleased if he could see his city now, for Washington has become the gracious capital that he wanted it to be — even if it has taken nearly two centuries. For today's visitor, Washington is a rich feast.

Before you go

Documents required

You must show a valid driver's license in order to rent a car. If you are driving your own car from another state (or country), you should bring a certificate of insurance. Most car rental companies will offer to sell you short-term insurance and it is wise to get it, unless your own policy has adequate coverage.

Senior citizens are eligible for discounts in some hotels and museums, but must bring proper identification in order to claim it.

Travel and medical insurance

Medical care is good to excellent, but expensive. Be sure your own medical coverage is up to date; if not, you may want to take out medical insurance. Since theft is common, baggage insurance is recommended. American Express offers baggage insurance to card members, and so do automobile clubs.

Money

It is wise to carry cash in small amounts only, keeping the remainder in travelers cheques. Travelers cheques issued by American Express, Bank of America, Barclays, Citibank and Thomas Cook are widely recognized, and MasterCard and Visa have also introduced them. Make sure you read the instructions included with your travelers cheques. It is important to note separately the serial numbers of your cheques and the telephone number to call in case of loss. Specialist travelers cheque companies such as American Express provide extensive local refund facilities through their own offices or agents. Many stores accept dollar travelers cheques. Credit cards are welcomed by nearly all hotels, airlines and car rental agencies, most restaurants and garages, and many stores. American Express, Diners Club, MasterCard and Visa are the major cards in common use. Carte Blanche has less comprehensive coverage. While personal checks drawing on out-of-town banks are not normally accepted, many hotels will cash small amounts in conjunction with a credit card.

Write a letter

As far in advance as possible, drop a note to your senator or representative if you would like to receive free passes for VIP tours of the White House, the Capitol, the FBI and Kennedy Center. Give exact dates of your visit. Address your senator at US Senate, DC 20510, and your congressperson at US House of Representatives, DC 20515.

Getting there

Three airports serve the Washington area. National, the closest to the center (15-20mins), is restricted to domestic flights of less than 1,000 miles (1,600km). International flights and additional domestic routes are served by the other two airports: Dulles (40mins to the W) and Baltimore-Washington (45mins-1hr to the NE), which lies between the two cities.

Long-distance and commuter trains arrive at Union Station, on the eastern edge of the central area at Massachusetts Ave. and North Capitol St. Many trains also stop at suburban stations, such as the Capital Beltway and Alexandria.

Two long-distance bus companies serve Washington. The

Greyhound bus terminal is at 1110 New York Ave. NW
(☎ 289-5145), and the Trailways terminal is at 1005 1st St.
NE (☎ 284-5155).

Washington is easily accessible by car. From New York you
can go via Baltimore and then take Interstate 95 or the
Baltimore-Washington Parkway; or go s from Wilmington,
Delaware on US 301, across the Chesapeake Bay and on to
the capital via Annapolis. From the NW you approach by
Interstate 270, from the w by Interstate 66 and from the sw by
Interstate 95/395. The city is encircled by the Capital Beltway
at a radius of about 10 miles (16km) from the center.

Climate
Apr, May, early June, Sept and Oct are the most pleasant
months to visit Washington. The winters range from mild to
bitterly cold, the average Jan temperature being 3˚C (37˚F).
The summers are hot, humid and enervating, with an average
July temperature of 28˚C (82.5˚F).

Clothes
However warm it is in Washington, always have something
extra to put on indoors, as the almost universal air
conditioning can make buildings seem positively arctic. In
winter the central heating is equally extreme, so be prepared
to peel off.

Washington is an informal city, and sightseers can dress as
casually as they wish. In most restaurants a tie is not needed
during the day, but in the evening a tie should be worn at the
smarter restaurants.

General Delivery
A letter marked "General Delivery" c/o the Central Post Office
(*2 Massachusetts Ave. NE, Washington, DC 20066*) should be
held until collected. The office is right next to Union Station
at Massachusetts Ave. and North Capitol St.

Getting around

From the airport to the city
Washington National Airport is the closest to the District. The
taxi fare is reasonable, but it's very simple to take a courtesy
van from the airport terminal to the Metro station; National
Airport is on the Blue and Yellow Metro lines and it's a short
trip from here to anywhere in Washington. From
Baltimore-Washington Airport, the taxi fare is expensive
because of the distance. But there is a bus from the airport to
the Capitol and Washington Hilton hotels courtesy of the
Airport Connection, which departs roughly every 45mins
(☎ 261-1091 for exact schedules). From Dulles International
Airport, the taxi fare is also fairly expensive. A bus service is
provided by the Washington Flyer, with departures about
every 45mins, to the Capitol and Washington Hiltons, the
Omni Shoreham and J. W. Marriott hotels (☎ (703) 685-1400).

Public transportation
The Washington Metropolitan Area Transit Authority
(WMATA) runs the Metrobus system and a superb new

11

subway system, the Metro, opened in 1973 and still being extended, with well-designed stations and sleek, quiet, comfortable trains. There are four subway lines: Blue, running from National Airport in the s to the e suburbs; Orange, running roughly e and w; Red, forming a loop to the n; and Yellow, running from Gallery Place via National Airport to Huntington station in Alexandria. A Green line is also projected and should begin running in about 1990. The trains run 6am-midnight Mon-Fri, 8am-midnight Sat, and 10am-6pm Sun.

Fares depend on distance traveled, and during rush hours (6-9.30am and 3-6.30pm) they are higher. Tickets ("fare cards") are bought from a machine (there are no ticket offices); insert one-, five- and ten-dollar bills and get change. A fare card valid for several journeys can be bought. Season tickets ("flash passes") are also available. When leaving the station insert your card in a machine, which deducts the fare and prints out the value remaining in the card. Fares vary depending upon distance, and there are discounts for many stops during non-rush hours. You can change to, but not from, the buses without extra charge in DC and for a small extra charge outside. To do this, pick up a "transfer ticket," which can be obtained free from a separate machine at your station of entry.

The Metrobus system is efficient and comprehensive, but can be baffling in its size and complexity. It has about 400 city and suburban routes, many of which operate only in rush hours. Most routes run from about 5am to midnight, and a few continue until about 2am. There is one flat fare for the city and another for suburban journeys; both cost more during rush hours. If you plan to use the buses frequently a map is indispensable. Maps of each bus route and a general subway map are, at least in theory, available from any Metro station.

In addition two comprehensive maps, for DC and Virginia and for DC and Maryland, can be bought from one of the special Metro sales outlets, for example at WMATA headquarters (*600 5th St. NW*), as well as at certain stores. Be prepared to wait some time for an answer when telephoning for bus and subway information (☎ *637-1234*).

Taxis

Cabs are plentiful, and can usually be hailed quite easily, except in bad weather or during rush hours. Their rooftop lights have no significant purpose, as the cabs may be occupied or available whether or not they are illuminated. They can also be ordered by phone: check the *Yellow Pages* or try Diamond Cab Company (☎ *387-6200*), Yellow Cab (☎ *544-1212*) or Capitol Cab (☎ *546-2400*). City cabs have no meters; fares are based on a zone system. When you take a cab from one point to another in the same zone, the fare is standard, no matter how many miles are traveled. Fortunately, most of the major sightseeing attractions are within Zone 1. If you journey into a second or third zone, the fare increases slightly. There is also a small charge for each additional passenger after the first, a rush-hour surcharge per trip between 4 and 6.30pm weekdays, and usually a luggage charge. Be prepared to share, as cabs often stop to pick up extra passengers en route. Suburban cabs' metered rates are reasonable; tip 15 percent of the fare.

Getting around by car

With such good public transportation a visitor has little need for a car in Washington. However, for trips outside the city a car is often indispensable. In Maryland and Virginia remember that there is a strictly enforced maximum speed limit of 55mph (90kph) on the freeways. In DC the limit is 25mph (40kph) unless otherwise indicated.

If you cannot avoid driving in the city try to keep clear of rush hours (7-9.30am and 4-6pm) when congestion is heavy and changes in traffic regulations can be perplexing: for example, certain streets become one-way, and at many intersections left turns are forbidden. Remember that, unless otherwise indicated, you are permitted to turn "right on red" when you come to a traffic light, but you must give pedestrians the right of way.

Parking too is a severe problem. Some areas have meters, which operate from 9.30am to 6.30pm. Most have a two-hour limit. In areas with resident-only parking you may park for 2hrs, and in an unrestricted area for up to 72hrs. Visitors staying in a private house (but not a hotel) can obtain free-of-charge from the nearest police station a permit allowing 15 days' parking provided the car does not remain in one place for more than 72hrs.

Renting a car

There are many car-rental firms operating in Washington, and it is worth shopping around for the best deal. Rates vary widely, and proportional discounts are offered at different times of year. Certain airlines also have special-rate agreements with particular rental companies. Rent-it-here-leave-it-there arrangements are available, as well as unlimited-mileage, weekend and other packages. Comprehensive insurance is compulsory in Virginia and Maryland but optional in DC, so make sure you are covered against accidents with uninsured drivers.

Getting around on foot

It's easy. Washington is a pleasant city to walk in, more suited to the pedestrian than many other American cities. It is little more than 10 miles (16km) across at its widest point, and the main tourist attractions are concentrated in a relatively small area.

The Mall, for example, home to the Smithsonian Institution complex of museums, can keep the visitor engrossed for days. All within walking distance of one another are the National Air and Space Museum, the National Museum of American History, the National Museum of Natural History, the Arts and Industries Building, the National Gallery of Art, the Hirshhorn Museum and Sculpture Garden and the Freer Gallery of Art.

Finding your way

It's simple to find your way around Washington once you get the hang of it, although it can be daunting at first. The city is laid out on a grid-like plan and divided into four quadrants, NW, NE, SW and SE (see p.36 of *Planning and walks*). Lettered streets run E to W and numbered streets run N to S. Finding an address is quite simple. On lettered streets, the first two digits indicate the nearest streets; for example, 2112 R St. NW is between 21st and 22nd St. On numbered streets, count the letters of the alphabet; no. 511 10th St. NW, for example, is between E and F St. There is no J St., so K becomes the 10th letter.

Railroad services

Washington has only one main rail terminal, Union Station, which is well served by bus routes and the Metro subway. A small center at the station run by Travelers Aid provides tourist information and guidance in finding accommodations. AMTRAK (the Federal rail system) handles passenger inquiries (☎ 484-7450).

Domestic airlines

Domestic flights leave from all three airports. National is mainly for East Coast, Southern and Midwest routes. Other routes are served by Dulles and Baltimore-Washington. The following domestic and North American airlines, among others, serve the Washington area; telephone numbers in most cases are for central inquiry and reservation offices, and the addresses are those of ticket offices.

Air Canada   1000 16th St. NW ☎ 638-3348
American   Capital Hilton and Washington hotels
☎ 393-2345
Braniff   Dulles Airport ☎ (800) 272-6433
Continental   1830 K St. NW ☎ 478-9700 and Dulles Airport
☎ 471-7056
Delta   1605 K St. NW and 1800 N Kent St., Arlington, Va.
☎ 468-2282
Eastern   Capital Hilton hotel ☎ 393-4000
Northwest   Capital Hilton hotel ☎ 737-7333
Piedmont   12500 Commerce Pkwy ☎ 620-0400
Presidential Airways   Dulles Airport ☎ 478-9700
TWA   1825 J St. NW ☎ 737-7404
United   Offices include Capital Hilton hotel and 1725 K St.
NW ☎ 893-3400
US Air   Dulles Airport ☎ 661-8102
World Airways   13873 Park Center Rd., Reston, Va.
☎ 834-9200

Other transportation

Private limousines are a de luxe way to travel but affordable if you shop around for competitive rates and special reductions, with such luxuries as a bar and color TV available at moderate extra cost. Reputable firms include the following:
Admiral Limousine Service   1243 1st St. SE ☎ 270-3233
Carey Limousine   768 S 23rd St., Arlington, Va. ☎ 892-2000
Manhattan DC Executive Transportation   2500 Calvert St.
NW ☎ 775-1888

Sightseeing companies are numerous (see *Useful addresses*, p.18). One of them, Tourmobile Sightseeing (☎ 554-5100), offers three routes covering Washington and Arlington Cemetery, with optional visits to Mount Vernon and the Frederick Douglass House. Fares vary according to distance, and there are discounts for students, senior citizens and children under 12. A similar service is provided by Old Town Trolley Tours of Washington (☎ 269-3020), which can be joined at any of 17 major hotels and sites.

River cruises on the Potomac are operated by Washington Boat Lines (*Potomac River Cruises, Pier 4, 6th and Water St. SW* ☎ 554-8000).

One of the most agreeable ways to see Washington is by
bicycle. For general information contact the Washington Area
Bicyclist Association (*1332 I St. NW* ☎ *544-5349*). The
following firms rent bicycles:
Big Wheel Bikes   1004 Vermont Ave. NW ☎ 638-3301 and
1034 33rd St. NW ☎ 337-0254
Fletcher's Boat House   4940 Canal Rd. NW ☎ 244-0461
Thompson Boat Center   Rock Creek Parkway and Virginia
Ave. NW ☎ 333-4861

On-the-spot information

Public holidays
Jan 1; Martin Luther King Day, third Mon in Jan; President's
Day, a three-day weekend in mid-Feb; Memorial Day, a
three-day weekend at the end of May; Independence Day,
July 4; Labor Day, first Mon in Sept; Columbus Day, second
Mon in Oct; Election Day, first Tues in Nov; Veterans Day,
Nov 11; Thanksgiving, last Thurs in Nov; Dec 25.

A number of other special days are observed, some of them
particular to Washington, with parades, gift-giving, religious
or other celebrations. These include Chinese New Year, late
Feb; St Patrick's Day, Mar 17; blooming of Japanese cherry
trees, late Mar/early Apr; Easter; Thomas Jefferson's birthday,
Apr 13; Passover, Apr; Asian Pacific American Heritage
Festival, Sat in early May; Smithsonian Institution's Festival of
American Folklife, late June/early July; Hispanic Festival, last
week of July; Rosh Hashanah, Sept; Halloween, Oct 31;
Hanukkah, Dec; Christmas Pageant of Peace/National Tree
Lighting, second Thurs in Dec. See also *Calendar of events* in
Planning and walks.

Time zones
Washington is in the US Eastern Time Zone, 1hr ahead of
Central Time Zone, 2hrs ahead of Mountain Time Zone and
3hrs ahead of Pacific Time Zone. All zones observing
Daylight Saving Time put their clocks forward one hour
Apr-Oct.

Banks
Banking hours vary widely, but average from 9am to 3pm
Mon-Fri. A few are open Sat mornings. Travelers cheques can
be cashed at all banks.

Shopping hours
Big department stores generally open at 10am and close at
6pm, 7pm, 8pm or 9pm, depending on the day of the week
and the season. Some are open on Sun afternoon. Otherwise,
shopping hours vary widely. Many shops, especially in smart
areas such as Georgetown's Wisconsin Ave., are open on Sun.
Some large food stores are even open 24hrs all week.

Rush hours
It's much easier to drive or ride the subways and buses if you
can avoid the periods 7-9.30am and 4-6.30pm. Rush-hour
fares on the subway and buses are in effect Mon-Fri 6-9.30am
and 3-6.30pm.

Post and telephone services

Post offices are open 8am-5pm Mon-Fri and 8am-noon Sat, with the notable exception of the main Post Office (*N Capitol St. and Massachusetts Ave. NE*), which is open around the clock.

Telephones are everywhere, on the street, in public buildings and in stores and restaurants. Generally they are in working order. The area code for DC is 202. If your are dialing within DC simply use the 7-digit number. This also applies to most locations in suburban Virginia and Maryland, but for some suburban numbers use area code 703 for Virginia and 301 for Maryland.

Some numbers are "toll-free"; they are always preceded by the code 800.

Public rest rooms

Washington has almost no public rest rooms, except for a few in some of the parks. But there are plenty in museums, and restaurants are required to have them by law, so there will usually be one not far away.

Laws, regulations and safety

Although Washington is no more dangerous than many other American cities, certain precautions should be taken in any major tourist area, where pickpockets and thieves are on the lookout for easy prey. Women will find it safer to be accompanied by another person when walking at night, especially outside the main thoroughfares. Keep a tight hold on cameras, handbags and other valuable personal items. Carry the minimum amount of cash and use travelers cheques whenever possible. If you have valuables, carry them with you, or lock them in the hotel's safe; do not leave them in your room. Always count your change carefully, especially at souvenir stalls. In a crowd of tourists or on a crowded bus or subway, be alert for pickpockets. Keep your doors locked when driving; many snatch thefts occur at traffic lights. When leaving your car, take your valuables with you, or at least lock them in your trunk.

In the unlikely event that you are actually attacked or robbed, do not try to resist. Try to memorize the appearance of the criminal and contact the police immediately (☎ *911 — this is a toll-free emergency number*).

Laws relating to drug use are strict and getting stricter. Those caught even with marijuana could face up to a year in prison.

Smoking is allowed in most public buildings and offices, but you cannot light up in elevators, nor on the subways and buses. Private and public restrictions on smoking are increasing, as in many taxicabs and parts of restaurants.

Tipping

In hotels and restaurants, tip 15-20 percent. Taxi tips should be 15 percent. Airport, railroad and hotel porters should be tipped at your discretion; 50¢ to $1 per bag, depending on distance and service, is a fair guideline.

Disabled travelers

Provisions for disabled travelers are better in Washington than in many other US cities, since the federal government, which passed architectural accessibility regulations here in the

16

1970s, controls so many of the museums, monuments, and sightseeing attractions. Much of the terrain is flat, and curbs are well ramped along such major sightseeing areas as the Capitol Building and the Mall. Many of the higher-priced hotels have specially converted rooms, as do a number of the motels in close-in Arlington, Va. Metrorail, the subway system, has superb facilities for those with impairments of sight, hearing, or mobility, including elevator access from the street entrance and between platforms. Wheelchair lifts on Metrobuses are not too reliable; Tourmobile is excellent for those who can handle four steps. When a wheelchair-lift van is required, for example to go to the airport, contact Murray's Non-Emergency Transportation Service (*2001 16th St NE* ☎ *269-0865*).

For further information, contact the nonprofit Information Protection Advocacy for Handicapped Individuals (IPACHI) (*300 I St. NW, suite 202, DC 20002* ☎ *547-8081*), which publishes a special guide for handicapped people, *Access Washington*, available for a modest fee. You may also contact Rehabilitation International USA (*1123 Broadway, NY 10010*).

Note also the following numbers in Washington: Paralyzed Veterans of America Association (☎ *872-1300*); Easter Seal Society for Disabled Children and Adults (☎ *232-2342*); Travelers Aid Society (*Central Office* ☎ *347-0101; National Airport* ☎ *684-3472; Dulles Airport* ☎ *661-8636*).

Local publications

The main Washington paper, the famous *Washington Post*, appears daily and has a multi-supplement Sunday edition. Another, more recently founded, daily newspaper is the *Washington Times*. *USA Today*, a colorful newcomer, concentrates on pictures rather than editorial. The *Weekend* section of the *Washington Post* on Fri is a good source of information for coming events and entertainment. The monthly magazine *Washington* also has a bulletin of events, advice on dining out, and feature articles about the capital. Similar bulletins are published in a number of free magazines handed out in hotels.

There are also a number of very lively free newspapers appearing every two or three weeks; these include *The Uptown Citizen*, the *City Paper*, the *Georgetowner* and the *Northwest Current*.

Out-of-town publications

Newspapers and magazines from just about everywhere and on just about any subject can be found at World News (*International Sq., 1825 I St. NW at the Farragut West Metro* ☎ *223-2526*).

Useful addresses

Tourist information

The Washington DC Convention and Visitors Association aims to promote the city as a convention and tourist destination. Their Tourist Information Center (*1455 Pennsylvania Ave. NW* ☎ *737-8866 for recorded information* ☎ *789-7000 for specific inquiries*) will provide information on sightseeing, hotels, restaurants, convention facilities and tourist matters.

Basic information

The International Visitor Information Center (IVIS) provides a comprehensive service for tourists. Their main office and reception center (*733 15th St. NW, Suite 300* ☎ *783-6540*) has a multilingual staff.

American Express Travel Service (*1150 Connecticut Ave. NW* ☎ *457-1300*) is a valuable source of information for any traveler in need of help, advice or emergency services.

The Travelers Aid Society (*1015 12th St. NW* ☎ *347-0101*) provides emergency help and advice to visitors in need, or lacking accommodations. Their Union Station office (☎ *347-0101*) will also give tourist information. They have offices also at National Airport (☎ *684-3472*) and Dulles Airport (☎ *661-8636*).

The Bob Hope USO Building (*601 Indiana Ave. ☎ 783-8117*) is Washington USO headquarters for servicepeople on active duty. They provide help with all travel-related problems, as well as free tickets for theater and sporting events, discounts on hotels, restaurants and tours, and a friendly place to relax. They also sponsor many recreational and cultural events for service families. Other USO facilities are at the North Terminal of National Airport and at Baltimore-Washington International Airport.

Telephone services

Congresspersons   You can locate your congressional representative or senator through the Capitol switchboard ☎ 224-3121.

DC Department of Recreation   Events, activities ☎ 673-7671

Dial-a-Museum   Smithsonian activities ☎ 357-2020

Dial-a-Park   National Capital Parks daily events ☎ 426-6975

Dial-a-Phenomenon   The night sky ☎ 357-2000

General Tourist Information ☎ 737-8866

Metrobus/Metrorail Information   How to get from here to there via bus or subway, in DC, suburban Maryland, or suburban Virginia (operates weekdays 6am-midnight, Sat 8am-midnight, Sun 10am-6pm) ☎ 637-7000.

Time   ☎ 844-1212

Voice of the Naturalist   Audubon Society information on birds seen in Washington ☎ 652-1088

Weather   ☎ 936-1212

Main post office

900 Brentwood Rd. NE ☎ 682-9595 (open 24hrs)

Tour operators

Tourmobile Sightseeing (*1000 Ohio Dr. SW* ☎ *554-7950*) operate the Tourmobile, a shuttle bus service, with running commentary, connecting the major sights of Capitol Hill, the Mall and Arlington National Cemetery. It operates continuously mid-June to Labor Day 9am-6.30pm and the rest of the year 9.30am-4.30pm. After purchasing a daily ticket from the driver or at one of the Tourmobile booths, you can break your journey as often as you like. Also available are excursions to Mount Vernon and the Frederick Douglass House and a tour of Arlington Cemetery itself.

Old Town Trolley Tours (*3150 V St. NE* ☎ *269-3020*) run motorized replicas of electric streetcars, stopping at or near all major museums and monuments. Leave or re-board at will throughout the day at a single fare. Students and senior citizens receive discounts and children under 12 ride free with adults. The trolleys follow a regular route at 30min intervals. They operate Labor Day (Sept)-Memorial Day (May) 9am-4pm, the rest of the year 9am-8pm.

Other tour operators include:

All About Town Sightseeing   519 6th St. NW ☎393-1618
DC Tours   PO Box 7028, Alexandria, Va. 22307 ☎768-5252
East Coast Parlor Car Tours   1730 K St. NW ☎783-0077
Eyre Bus Service   13600 Triadelphia Rd., Glenelg, Md. 21737
☎854-6600
Gray Line   30 Massachusetts Ave. NE ☎289-1995
Spirit of '76 Tours   6229 87th Ave., New Carrollton, Md.
20784 ☎731-4050
Washington Airways   Helicopter tours, National Airport
☎765-4200
Washington Boat Lines   Pier 4, 6th and Water St. SW
☎554-8000

Major libraries
Folger Shakespeare Library   201 E Capitol St. SE ☎544-4600
Library of Congress   1st St., between E Capitol St. and
Independence Ave. SE ☎707-5000
Martin Luther King Memorial Library   901 G St. NW
☎727-1111

Major places of worship
Christian
Church of the Epiphany (Episcopal)   1317 G St. NW
☎347-2635
Church of St John the Baptist (Russian Orthodox)   4001 17th
St. NW ☎726-3000
First Baptist Church   16th and O St. NW ☎387-2206
First Church of Christ Scientist   1770 Euclid St. NW ☎265-1390
Franciscan Monastery (Roman Catholic)   1400 Quincy St.
NE ☎526-6800
Friends Meeting House   2111 Florida Ave. NW ☎483-3310
Metropolitan African Methodist Episcopal Church   1518 M
St. NW ☎331-1426
Mormon Temple (Church of Jesus Christ of Latter Day Saints)
9900 Stoneybrook Dr., Kensington, Md. 20895 ☎587-0144
*National Shrine of the Immaculate Conception (Roman
Catholic)*   4th St. and Michigan Ave. NE ☎526-8300
New York Avenue Presbyterian Church   1313 New York
Ave. NW ☎393-3700
St John's Lafayette Square (Episcopal)   16th and H St. NW
☎347-8766
St Matthew's Cathedral (Roman Catholic)   1725 Rhode
Island Ave. NW ☎347-3215
Saint Sophia's Cathedral (Greek Orthodox)   36th St. and
Massachusetts Ave. NW ☎333-4730
Washington National Cathedral (Episcopal)   Massachusetts
and Wisconsin Ave. NW ☎537-6200
Jewish
Adas Israel Synagogue   Connecticut Ave. and Porter St. NW
☎362-4433
Washington Hebrew Congregation   Massachusetts Ave. and
Macomb St. NW ☎362-7100
Muslim
Islamic Mosque and Cultural Center   2551 Massachusetts
Ave. NW ☎332-8343

Emergency information

Emergency services

Police/fire/ambulance ☎911
Medical referral service ☎466-1880
Dental referral service ☎547-7613

Hospitals with emergency departments

Ambulances called on 911 carry the patient to the nearest municipal hospital. If you wish to go directly to a hospital, the following are the main ones:
Adams-Morgan: Children's Hosp. National Med. Center, 111 Michigan Ave. NW ☎745-4066. *Capitol Hill*: Capitol Hill Hosp., 700 Constitution Ave. NE ☎269-8000. *Georgetown*: Georgetown University Hosp., 3800 Reservoir Rd. NW ☎625-0100. *Northwest*: George Washington University Hosp., 901 23rd St. NW ☎994-1000; Sibley Memorial Hosp., 5255 Loughboro Rd. NW ☎537-4000. *Southeast*: DC General Hosp., 19th St. and Massachusetts Ave. SE ☎675-5416; Greater Southeast Community Hosp., 1310 Southern Ave. SE ☎574-6000. For minor emergencies, treatment is available at clinics, listed in the *Yellow Pages* under "Clinics."

All-night pharmacy

Peoples Drug Store 14th St. and Thomas Circle NW ☎628-0721

Help lines

Suicide Prevention and Emergency Mental Health ☎362-8100 (24hrs)
Travelers Aid Society ☎347-0101
Poison Control Center ☎625-3333 (24hr hotline)

Motoring accidents

— Call the police immediately.
— If car is rented, call number in rental agreement.
— Do not admit liability or incriminate yourself.
— Ask witnesses to stay and give statements.
— Exchange names, addresses, car details, insurance companies and three-digit insurance company codes.
— Remain to give your statement to the police.

Car breakdowns

Call one of the following from nearest telephone.
— Number indicated in car rental agreement.
— Local office of AAA (if you are a member).
— Nearest garage or towing service.

Lost travelers cheques

Notify the police immediately, then follow the instructions provided with your travelers cheques, or contact the issuing company's nearest office. Contact your consulate or American Express if you are stranded with no money.

Lost property

Rail ☎484-7540 (AMTRAK at Union Station)
Subway ☎962-1195
In the street ☎727-4326 (Police Communications)

Time chart

1608	English adventurer Captain John Smith explored the Potomac. His enthusiastic descriptions of the spot encouraged settlement.
1634	Colonization of Maryland was begun.
1749	The town of Alexandria was created on the Virginia shore of the Potomac.
1751	Georgetown was founded.
1775	American Revolutionary War (the War of American Independence) began.
1789	George Washington became the first President of the United States. Georgetown University was founded.
1790	A southern location was agreed upon for the new federal capital, and President Washington was asked by Congress to choose a site on the Potomac.
1791	Pierre Charles L'Enfant began planning the city.
1792	L'Enfant was dismissed. Work on the White House, then called the President's House, began.
1793	Work began on the construction of the Capitol.
1800	The Government moved to Washington from Philadelphia. President John Adams took up residence in the unfinished White House.
1801	Thomas Jefferson became the first president to be inaugurated in the new capital.
1802	A local government, consisting of a mayor and an elected council, was established.
1814	British forces raided Washington, burning the White House, the Capitol and other public buildings. President Madison moved temporarily to the Octagon. Congress was housed in a brick building while the original Capitol was restored.
1820	Washington residents were given the right to elect the city's mayor.
1835	The USA came into possession of the fortune bequeathed by James Smithson, which led ultimately to the creation of the Smithsonian Institution.
1846	The portion of the District of Columbia sw of the Potomac seceded back to Virginia, reducing the District to approximately 69sq.miles (179sq.km) instead of its original 100sq.miles (259sq.km).
1848	Work began on the construction of the Washington Monument on the Mall.
1861–65	American Civil War. Washington found itself the focal point of the war effort.
1863	President Lincoln signed the Emancipation Proclamation.
1864	Arlington National Cemetery was established.
1865	President Lincoln was assassinated during a performance at Ford's Theatre.
1867	Blacks voted for the first time in local elections.
1868	President Andrew Johnson was impeached by the House of Representatives, but was narrowly acquitted by the Senate.
1871	Congress established a new form of city administration under a governor appointed by the President.
1871–74	A public works program under Alexander ("Boss") Shepherd turned Washington for the first time into a city with proper urban amenities.
1878	Government of DC by Commissioners appointed by

the President was re-established, leaving residents with no say in the running of the city.

1884 The Washington Monument was completed.

1896 For the first time a motor car was driven down Pennsylvania Ave.

1902 A large-scale program of city beautification was implemented.

1909 L'Enfant's remains were transferred to Arlington Cemetery.

1910 Height restrictions were imposed on buildings in the city.

1917 The USA entered World War I. In a few months the population of Washington increased by about 50 percent.

1921 The first bathing beauty contest in America was held beside the Tidal Basin. Miss Washington DC was elected Miss America in Atlantic City.

1924 Washington Senators baseball team defeated the New York Giants to win the World Series.

1929 Beginning of the Great Depression.

1931 Hunger March on Washington.

1932 Washington invaded by Bonus Marchers, veterans seeking immediate payment of their war bonuses. The marchers were dispersed by the army.

1933 Election of Franklin D. Roosevelt as President. Roosevelt introduced the New Deal, and the country began to recover from the Depression. The city population swelled as federal jobs multiplied and people were drawn to Washington by New Deal activity and lobbying.

1941 The USA entered World War II, following the Japanese attack on Pearl Harbor. War activity swelled Washington's population further.

1943 The Pentagon was completed.

1950- The black population of Washington rose from 35
60 percent to 54 percent.

1954 Washington became the first major American city to introduce racial integration in schools.

1964 Washingtonians voted for the first time in a presidential election.

1968 The assassination of Martin Luther King Jr sparked off violent riots, blighting many areas of the city, especially Old Downtown. DC residents voted in a presidential election for the first time since 1800.

1971 Walter Fauntroy was elected DC's first representative in Congress for a century. His seat carries no vote except in committee. The John F. Kennedy Center for the Performing Arts was opened.

1974 Resignation of President Richard Nixon, following the Watergate scandal.

1975 Washington regained an elected city council, and Walter Washington, a black, was elected the first Mayor for over a century.

1976 The first stretch of the Metro subway was opened.

1980 Building of the Convention Center was begun as a key element in the revitalization of Old Downtown, a process that is now coming to fruition.

1983 The Washington Redskins football team won Superbowl XVII, watched by a record TV audience.

1987 Bicentennial of the enactment of the US Constitution.

Political Washington

Politics is the *raison d'être* of Washington, and to understand the city it is necessary to known something of the complex web of power that underlies it.

The map of Washington converges symbolically on two points: the White House and the Capitol. Between them, like a rope in a tug-of-war contest, stretches Pennsylvania Ave., as though to represent the curious link of both tension and partnership that exists between the executive and legislative branches of the government. Since the USA came into existence, power has alternated between the two, depending on the relative force and prestige of the President and Congress.

The President controls the day-to-day business of running the country's domestic and foreign affairs. He does so with the aid of a Cabinet, made up of the appointed heads of the various executive departments, and an Executive Office consisting of a large number of aides, special advisers and advisory councils. There is much coming and going between the White House and the neighboring Executive Office Building, which is used by many of the President's advisory staff.

The President can initiate bills in Congress and veto legislation coming from Congress; but Congress can vote to override a presidential veto. Furthermore it can (and frequently does) block legislation emanating from the White House. There is a passage in Gore Vidal's novel *Washington D.C.* where a senator expresses the way Congress jealously guards the right to curb excessive presidential power: " 'You see, I think our kind of government is the best ever devised. At least originally. So whenever a President draws too much power to himself, the Congress must stop him by restoring the balance. Let him reach too far and...we shall...' The Senator's other hand, rigid as a knife, made as if to chop the tyrant's hand from its wrist." Thus Congress blocked Kennedy's Civil Rights legislation in the 1960s, and it was Kennedy's successor Johnson, the wily catcher of Congressional votes, who was able to push the legislation through.

Now in the moments before the Senate was about to begin the chamber resembled a sort of tan, marble-paneled fishbowl in which pageboys in their white shirts and black pants darted about like minnows distributing bills and copies of the legislative calendar to all the desks, whisking off stray specks of dust, shoving the spittoons carefully out of sight, checking the snuff boxes to make sure they were full, joking and calling to one another across the big brown room.

Allen Drury, *Advise and Consent*

Behind the Congress on Capitol Hill sits the gleaming marble palace of the Supreme Court, representing the third branch of government. the Judiciary. The Court, which upholds the US Constitution, has on occasions opposed both President and Congress. Some of its decisions have had epoch-making consequences, such as its famous 1954 ruling that racial segregation in the public schools was unconstitutional.

These three institutions are the most conspicuous pinnacles in the citadel of federal power, but a glance at the map of Washington reveals the extent of the government's presence. Central Washington is dominated by the names of the great departments and agencies, such as the State Department, the

Treasury, the Department of Commerce, the Internal Revenue Service, the National Aeronautics and Space Administration, the Department of Justice and its offshoot the Federal Bureau of Investigation. Across in Virginia is the Pentagon, housing the Department of Defense, and the Langley headquarters of the Central Intelligence Agency, which, unlike the FBI, is not open to the public. These and the other government organizations employ a total of more than 300,000 people in Washington alone — a far cry from the 130 clerks who made up the total federal workforce in 1800 when the government first moved to Washington.

There is much more to this vortex of power than the government itself, however. Take, for example, the lobbyists. Washington is continually besieged by special-interest groups seeking to make the government receptive to their needs. They may be companies angling for contracts, farmers seeking bigger subsidies, environmental groups agitating for stricter pollution controls or foreign governments looking for financial aid. These groups generally employ professional lobbyists — often lawyers, former civil servants or public relations men — who frequently earn large sums of money for pleading their clients' causes over lunch or cocktails or at lavish receptions.

Another important element in Washington political life is the media: the syndicated columnists, investigative journalists and television interviewers who both reflect and monitor current events in the political sphere. The media can also influence events directly and crucially — an obvious instance was the *Washington Post*'s investigations into the Watergate scandal, which led to President Nixon's resignation.

Social life too has its part to play in the political drama. Power and prestige go hand in hand, and Washington's social world acts as one barometer of prestige. Washingtonians covet invitations to White House receptions, embassy functions and private parties in the fashionable suburbs. At these events alliances are forged, deals made, gossip exchanged and reputations enhanced or diminished.

Much of America resents the size of the federal government and the growing dominance of Washington. Every so often a president, capitalizing on this resentment, sets out to reduce the federal bureaucracy, but invariably with little result. The government continues to grow in size and power, and the lure of Washington grows ever stronger.

The arts in Washington

There was a time when the cultural diet of Washington was as meager and monotonous as its cuisine. This is no longer the case. From grand opera at the Kennedy Center to poetry readings at the Library of Congress, there is a rich menu to satisfy the culture-hungry visitor. Yet for many decades the only art that flourished in Washington was the art of politics. While the city was going through the long, slow process of transforming itself from a glorified shanty town into an effective capital, its inhabitants had little time or inclination for cultural refinements. The opening of the National Theater in 1835 at least brought regular theatrical performances, and later came Ford's Theatre (until Lincoln's assassination in 1865, after which it was closed for about a century); but still the theatrical fare was hardly impressive, and the musical fare even less so, although by the 1850s certain federal buildings were being used after office hours for concerts. Until recently, however, facilities for large musical performances were very limited.

Lovers of painting and sculpture were less deprived. In 1869 the Corcoran Gallery opened, and numerous other galleries followed, finally making Washington one of the richest cities in the world for the visual arts. Yet it was a long time before Washington had anything approaching an artists' colony; and the same was true in the literary field. It was left to Henry Adams and a tiny handful of other writers to carry the torch for literature in the US capital.

The fact is that for the first century and a half of its existence, Washington lacked the kind of social and urban fabric that makes for a thriving cultural life. In Paris and Vienna there were cafés where artists, writers and composers could gather and exchange ideas in a heady atmosphere, fueled by the feverish energy of a great metropolis with centuries of cultural history behind it. Washington had no such milieu. Its steak-and-potatoes eating houses were no substitute for the cafés of Montmartre or the Ringstrasse.

Washingtonians eager for cultural nourishment were acutely aware of these deficiencies. One of them wrote in 1902: "What is capital life after all? Small talk and lots to eat, an infinite series of teas and dinners. Art? There is none." These were the words of the painter and society hostess Alice Pike Barney, whose Studio House on Sheridan Circle (see p.42) was, in the early years of the 20thC, one of the few centers of real cultural exchange in the city. Until she moved to Los Angeles in 1924, the house was the scene of continuous artistic activity. She herself not only painted but also taught art, wrote and produced plays, and promoted the cultural life of the city as a whole. In 1917 she was instrumental in creating the Sylvan Theater in the Washington Monument grounds, the first federally supported outdoor theater in the USA.

Apart from valiant efforts on the part of individuals such as Mrs Barney, Washington remained culturally undernourished until long after World War II — one of the reasons why it was considered a hardship post by foreign embassy staff. The world's great orchestras and opera and ballet companies were reluctant to include Washington on their tours, mainly because the facilities for performances were so poor. The only large auditorium suitable for musical events was the Constitution Hall of the Daughters of the American Revolution. Otherwise performances had to be held in various small auditoriums dotted around the city in museums, galleries, libraries and churches. It was ironic that a city, so far ahead of its European counterparts in the grandeur and sophistication of its urban design, should lag so far behind them in its cultural life.

Clearly such a situation could not be allowed to continue, as President Eisenhower realized when in 1955 he appointed a commission to examine the feasibility of building a new auditorium in the capital. Three years later he signed the legislation for the creation of a National Cultural Center, which, after a further 13 years and much heroic battling on the part of its supporters, finally opened as the Kennedy Center in 1971. Now Washington had, under one roof, an opera house, a concert hall and a theater, all of them large and superb in their acoustics and facilities.

The Kennedy Center has moved Washington into the top

league of world cities for the performing arts, and today it features very firmly on the itinerary of the great touring companies and orchestras. Its opening was therefore a major turning-point. But it is not the only factor in the cultural efflorescence that has taken place in the capital in recent years. Before the appearance of the Kennedy, Arena Stage was already winning a reputation as one of the most vital and innovative theaters in the country, drawing audiences with its imaginative productions ranging from Shakespeare to Tom Stoppard; and a host of other small experimental theaters, such as New Playwrights and The Source, offer a consistently exciting range of drama.

Washington's small theaters have not been smothered by the Kennedy Center. On the contrary, they have benefited from the heightened cultural atmosphere that the Kennedy has created. Much the same is true in the field of music. Besides the National Symphony Orchestra, there are numerous other orchestras, large and small, performing regularly in Washington and its environs. Today Washington is possibly the richest city in the world for chamber music. Gone is the climate of musical philistinism in which President Grant could say proudly: "I know two tunes; one of them is *Yankee Doodle* and the other isn't." Likewise in opera, where in addition to the Washington Opera at the Kennedy, numerous smaller opera companies operate in less imposing premises.

The same healthy balance of great and small can be seen in the visual arts. Washington has not only the great galleries around the Mall but also a host of small private galleries, many of which can be found near Dupont Circle and in the Old Downtown area, where the work of black artists is much in evidence.

An article by Joseph McLellan in the *Washington Post Magazine* in February 1986 attributed Washington's cultural vitality partly to its lively, well-educated audiences made up of "thought-and-word people" — civil servants, lobbyists, officials of national associations, journalists, university professors and students. "The special qualities of the Washington population," McLellan says, "may account for the fact that this city has been building a major league symphony orchestra and opera company while it lacked a major league baseball team. Washington may not be the only American city where more tickets are sold for performing arts events than for sporting events, but it is certainly one of them."

The diplomatic community is an important ingredient in the cultural alchemy of Washington. As McLellan writes: "Embassies are still among the brightest cultural spots in the Washington scene. Most embassies will engage in some discreet promotion and offer a gala reception when one of their native stars is appearing in the Washington area. Quite a few embassies have also given substantial aid to Washington museums or performing arts of their countries — not necessarily financial aid, but mailing lists, refreshments and an elegant room for a reception, sometimes publicity and sometimes performing space."

One outstanding feature of Washington's culture is that so much of it is free. It would be possible to go to an exhibition, a concert and a lecture every day without paying a cent. It is no wonder that other American cities have grown envious of the capital, and little wonder that cultured diplomats no longer find Washington a hardship post.

Architecture

Few cities as young as Washington have spawned such an astonishingly rich variety of architecture. Included here are examples of all the great architectural styles inherited from Europe, a multiplicity of home-grown and hybrid forms, as well as buildings, such as the Islamic Mosque, which reflect an Eastern influence. In the history of Washington's architecture there are two strands, the domestic and the public, which are sometimes separate, sometimes intertwined.

18thC

Before Washington was even a twinkle in L'Enfant's eye there was already a well-established vernacular architectural tradition in Georgetown and Alexandria. The oldest house in the District, Old Stone House in Georgetown's M St., built in 1766, is a good example of the solid, unpretentious building style of the Colonial period.

The period immediately after the American Revolution is known as the Federal period and was greatly influenced by the modified Georgian style created in Scotland by the Adam brothers. It brought an increased though careful use of ornamentation to the Georgian mode, with the result that interior decorative plasterwork became a common feature of Federal houses. A striking example of this style is the Octagon, designed by William Thornton and built in 1797-1800. It is typically Federal in its beautifully balanced

Old Stone House, Georgetown, a rare example of pre-Revolutionary vernacular architecture, dating from before the founding of Washington.

The Octagon, built in the late 18thC to a design by William Thornton in the Federal style, a modified version of the Georgian idiom.

The White House, a graceful example of Federal architecture, designed by James Hoban in 1792 and lived in by every president except Washington.

27

proportions and elegant but restrained decorative features, such as the delicate wrought-iron balconies at the second-floor level.

Official buildings of the Federal period include the graceful residence designed by James Hoban as the President's mansion and now known as the White House. The Capitol, originally designed by Thornton, began in the Federal idiom, which can still be detected in the central portion of the w front, but in the hands of later architects the building developed a more grandiose aspect.

1800-50

While the Federal style continued well into the 19thC, especially for private houses, architects of public and commercial buildings increasingly favored a Greek revival style, which made every other church, bank and courthouse look as if it had been taken from the Acropolis. A typical example is the Old Patent Office (now the National Portrait Gallery and National Gallery of American Art), designed by William P. Elliott and Robert Mills and built in the years 1836-67. The s portico is a direct copy of the Parthenon in Athens. This style was in keeping with the widespread notion that, in its democratic ideals, the USA was the spiritual heir of ancient Greece.

1850-1900

This was a period of romanticism, eclecticism and experimentation in architecture. By the 1850s the growth of

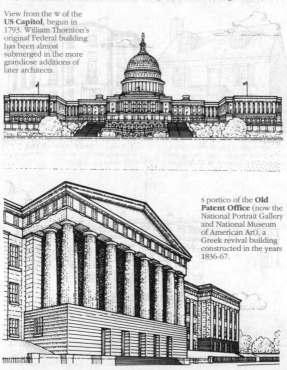

View from the w of the **US Capitol**, begun in 1793. William Thornton's original Federal building has been almost submerged in the more grandiose additions of later architects.

s portico of the **Old Patent Office** (now the National Portrait Gallery and National Museum of American Art), a Greek revival building constructed in the years 1836-67.

the nation required so many post offices, customs houses and federal courthouses that a special authority called the Office of the Supervising Architect was set up within the Treasury Department to design and administer the construction of all federal buildings. It was not afraid to experiment with many different styles, provided the end results were sufficiently imposing. Examples of its work include the astounding Old Pension Building (now the National Building Museum), completed in 1885, the Old Post Office, built in the following decade in the form of a Romanesque castle, and the State, War and Navy Building (now called the Executive Office Building), completed in 1888 in the French Second Empire style, with mansard roofs, high chimneys and tier upon tier of windows, balustrades and columns. Overlapping with the Second Empire style was the Beaux-Arts style, examples of which are the Library of Congress and Corcoran Gallery. The Beaux-Arts designers developed a grandiose sensuality, using bulges, curves and wedding-cake ornamentation.

Many other styles were employed during this period. Gothic was favored for churches, while private houses displayed a vast range of influences. The Italianate idiom had become a national craze by the 1850s. Its houses had low-pitched roofs with markedly overhanging eaves and large decorative brackets. Then, in the last quarter of the 19thC, a style known as Queen Anne became popular, which had very little to do with the architecture of the Queen Anne era in England. This

The Neo-Romanesque **Old Post Office** on Pennsylvania Ave., built in the 1890s and typical of the romantic eclecticism of the period. Several times threatened with demolition, it has now been beautifully restored and turned into a complex of offices, shops and restaurants.

The **Renwick Gallery**, which was designed by James Renwick and originally housed the Corcoran Gallery. The style is an early example of what was called Second Empire, the high mansard roofs being a characteristic feature.

was a highly eclectic idiom, grafting together such disparate features as medieval-type gables and chimneys, Romanesque arches, turrets and heavily accented stonework. Houses built in this style can be found in many residential districts.

1900-45

The early part of the 20thC saw a continuation of Beaux-Arts exuberance apparent in such buildings as Union Station, completed in 1908. There was, however, a general return to more sober Classical forms, especially in public government buildings. Victorian eclecticism was replaced with what has been termed Late Classical Revival, epitomized by the huge Federal Triangle complex, built between 1928 and 1938, with its monumental colonnades and porticoes. A leading architect of this style was John Russell Pope, designer of the National Gallery's West Building, completed in 1941, and of the Jefferson Memorial, completed in 1943.

In domestic architecture a similar trend can be seen. The great houses built in the early 20thC in what is today the Embassy Row area (for example the Everett House, now the Turkish Embassy) still have the opulent Beaux-Arts look. But as the century progressed a Georgian revival took hold and indeed has continued to the present day. An example is the Woodrow Wilson House, designed in 1915.

More eclectic were the hotels, apartment houses and office buildings erected during this period, ranging in style from Art Deco to Neo-Romanesque.

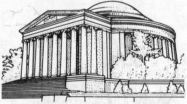

The **Jefferson Memorial**, designed by the Neoclassical architect John Russell Pope and completed in 1943.

The **Christian Heurich Memorial Mansion** (headquarters of the Columbia Historical Society), completed in 1894. Its style can loosely be called Romanesque revival, but, like many houses of its period, it shows many different influences.

1945 to the present day

In the postwar years the faceless "international" style of
architecture has made its mark on Washington, especially on
the New Downtown business area in K St. and its environs,
where glass and concrete monotony reigns supreme. The
redeveloped SW has fared better with its rows of gracious
new townhouses and its Arena Stage theater, opened in 1960.
A memorable example of the so-called "New Brutalist" style is
the FBI headquarters, the J. Edgar Hoover Building on
Pennsylvania Ave., opened in 1975. Although grim, it is not
without a certain cyclopean stature. Mies van der Rohe's
Martin Luther King Memorial Library, completed in 1972, has
been hailed as a masterpiece, but many find it dull. By
contrast, Edward Durrell Stone's Kennedy Center, which was
widely vilified when it opened in 1971, has since grown in
appeal. Another building which shows that modern
architecture need not be boring is I. M. Pei's East Building of
the National Gallery, completed in 1978.

Recently, an ongoing Post-Modernist reaction against the
stark functionalism that has dominated architecture for so
long is evident. An exciting example of Post-Modernism in
Washington is Arthur Cotton Moore's design for the huge
Washington Harbour residential, commercial and leisure
complex on the shore of the Potomac at Georgetown. With its
profusion of domes, columns and pitched roofs, it is a
dynamic combination of bold modernity and traditional forms.

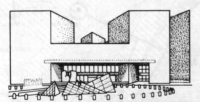

Edward Durrell Stone's
controversial **Kennedy
Center**, opened in 1971.

The **East Building** of
the National Gallery of
Art, designed by I.M. Pei
and opened in 1978.

Post-Modernism with a
vengeance: Arthur
Cotton Moore's
**Washington Harbour
complex**.

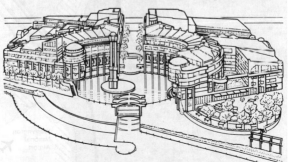

31

Orientation map

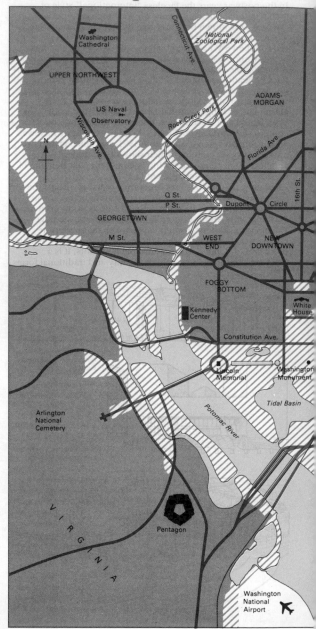

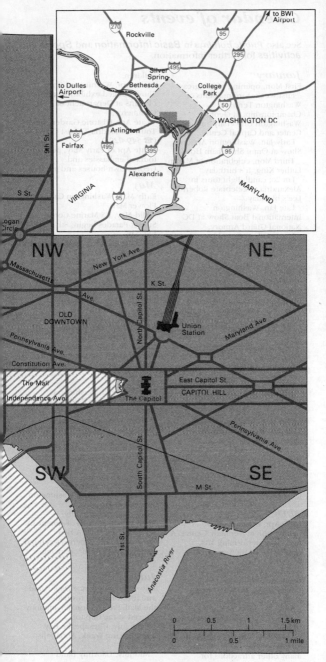

Calendar of events

See also *Public holidays* in **Basic information** and **Sports and activities** for further information.

January

First Mon, opening of Congress.

First week, Virginia Slims of Washington Tennis Championship, at George Washington University Smith Center and Capital Centre.

Early Jan, Washington Antique Show at Omni Shoreham Hotel.

Third Mon, celebration of Martin Luther King, Jr's birthday.

Jan 26, candlelight tours in Alexandria to celebrate Robert E. Lee's birthday.

Late Jan, Washington International Boat Show at DC National Guard Armory.

Jan or Feb every odd year, biennial exhibition of contemporary American art at Corcoran Gallery.

February

Feb 12, celebration of Lincoln's birthday at Lincoln Memorial.

Mid-Feb, Ice Capades. Family ice-skating show at Capital Centre.

Feb 22, Washington's birthday. Festivities at Washington Monument and huge parade in Alexandria.

Late Feb, Chinese New Year celebrations in Chinatown.

March

Mar 17, St Patrick's Day Parade, Constitution Ave.

Late Mar, Smithsonian Kite Carnival in the Mall and Kite Festival at Gunston Hall, Va.

Late Mar or early Apr, Cherry Blossom Festival, Easter Egg Roll on White House Lawn and Easter sunrise services in Arlington National Cemetery and other locations.

April

Early Apr, Imagination Celebration at Kennedy Center. A festival of performing arts, especially for the young, with many free events.

Early Apr, Ringling Brothers/Barnum and Bailey Circus at DC National Guard Armory.

Apr 13, Jefferson's birthday celebrated at Jefferson Memorial.

Late Apr, Smithsonian Institution's Spring Celebration including clowns, mimes and many other attractions for children.

Late Apr, Washington Craft Show. Judged exhibition and sale of crafts at Department of Commerce.

Late Apr, Historic Garden Week Tour, Alexandria Tourist Council (☎ 549-0205).

Late Apr or early May, public tours of embassies and Georgetown houses and gardens.

May

Early May, Washington Cathedral Flower Mart.

Mid-May, US Marine Corps Sunset Parades begin, 8th and I St. SW.

Mid-May, Cherry Blossom Rugby Tournament, the Mall.

Late May, Boat Show, Annapolis Harbor, Annapolis, Md.

Late May, Kemper Open PGA Golf Tournament, Tournament Players Club, Avenel, Md. (☎ (301) 983-4052).

Last Mon, Memorial Day. Free National Symphony concert in Capitol grounds, jazz festival at Alexandria, and wreath laid by President at Tomb of the Unknown Soldier.

June

First weekend, Washington International Arts Fair. Series of exhibitions of contemporary work in many private galleries throughout the city (☎ 547-1080 for details).

Early June, President's Cup Regatta, off Hains Point.

Mid-June, Smithsonian Institution Children's Day.

Mid-June, Smithsonian Boomerang Festival, Washington Monument grounds.

Late June or early July, Smithsonian Festival of American Folk Life, the Mall. A rich cross-section of America's cultural heritage, with music, dancing, crafts and food.

July

July 4, Independence Day. Parade and fireworks and festivities in the Mall. Free National Symphony concert at the Capitol.

Early July, Chesapeake Bay Yacht Racing Week, Annapolis, Md.

Mid-July, US Army Band

performs *1812 Overture* at Washington Monument.

Third week in July, DC National Bank Volvo Tennis Classic, Rock Creek Tennis Stadium, 16th and Kennedy St. NW.

Late July, Hispanic Festival in Adams-Morgan district.

August

Mid-Aug to early Sept, Shakespeare Festival. Free performances in grounds of Sylvan Theater, near Washington Monument.

Mid-Aug, Middleburg Wine Festival, Middleburg, Va. (☎ (703) 687-5528).

Late Aug, Potomac Ramblin' Raft Race, sponsored by the WPGC radio station. A race down the Potomac on a variety of crazy crafts.

Early Aug, Redskins football exhibition season begins.

September

First Mon, Labor Day. Free National Symphony concert in Capitol grounds.

Preceding Sat and Sun, Labor Day weekend, International Children's Festival, Wolf Trap Farm Park. Performances and workshops of all kinds.

Early Sept, daylong Arts Festival in downtown DC.

Early Sept, Maryland Seafood Festival, Annapolis, Md.

Mid-Sept, Adams-Morgan Days. Ethnic festival of arts, crafts, music and foods.

Mid-Sept, Greek Festival at St Sophia's Church.

Mid-Sept, Constitution Day, band concert at National Archives.

October

First Mon, Opening of Supreme Court.

Early Oct, US Navy Band Birthday Concert, DAR Constitution Hall.

Early Oct, Washington Cathedral Open House, including extensive tours of the cathedral, organ recitals, antique merry-go-round rides and other activities for children.

Late Oct, Washington International Horse Show, Capital Centre.

Each Sun, jousting on the Mall.

November

Early Nov, Washington's Review of the Troops. Re-enactment of first commander's and president's final review of loyal colonial

troops, Gadsby's Tavern, Old Town Alexandria.

Early Nov, Marine Corps Marathon. Thousands of entrants race a 26.2-mile (39.3km) course, beginning at Iwo Jima Statue.

Early Nov, Junior League Christmas shop, Mayflower Hotel. Fashionable charity sale annually opens the Capitol's vacation season.

Early Nov, Washington International Horse Race at Laurel Race Track, Md.

Nov 11, Veterans Day ceremony, Arlington National Cemetery.

Mid Nov, DC Antiques Show, Sheraton-Washington Hotel.

Late Nov to Dec, numerous Christmas craft fairs.

December

Early Dec, YMCA International Fair including folk performances and sale of gifts from many countries, on 624 9th St. NW.

Early to mid-Dec, *Nutcracker Suite* ballet at Kennedy Center.

Mid-Dec, lighting of the national Christmas tree at the Capitol. The White House Christmas tree is lit by the President.

Mid to late Dec, open house at the Corcoran.

Mid-Dec, to Jan 1. Pageant of Peace. Nightly festivities and choral performances on the Ellipse and the Mall.

Late Dec, candlelight tours of the White House.

Throughout Dec, candlelight tours and caroling at many historic houses in the area.

Regular summer events

Sat and Sun in summer, artists at work, mimes, musicians and dancers performing along the Mall by the National Gallery of Art.

Every other Sun afternoon, folk and popular music concerts on C&O Canal at 30th and Jefferson St. NW.

Fri eve, Marine Corps Parade at 8th and I St. SW (*reservations necessary* ☎ 433-6060 ☎).

Tues, parade and musical tribute by the Marine Drum and Bugle Corps and silent drill team at Iwo Jima Statue.

Concerts by US Navy, Air Force, Marine and Army bands Mon, Tues, Wed and Fri eves on W Terrace of Capitol, and Sun, Tues, Thurs and Fri at Sylvan Theater in Washington Monument grounds.

When and where to go

Each season in Washington has its own individual appeal, advantages and drawbacks. Spring, a pleasant but crowded time for sightseeing, comes to the city with a burst of cherry blossoms around the Tidal Basin, bringing a fresh gaiety to the capital. The summer is slightly less crowded. The often exhausting high temperatures and humidity are mitigated by universal air conditioning, and many special events take place during the summer months: festivals, sporting contests, open-air concerts, and, of course, the Fourth of July Independence Day celebrations. During the fall, the crowds diminish still further, the weather is pleasantly cool, and the high cultural life of the city intensifies. The winter, however, is the richest time for the pleasures of theater, music, opera and ballet, and is also the quietest season for visitors, with correspondingly low hotel prices. Its main disadvantage is unpredictable, often bitterly cold weather.

The Washington metropolitan area is a cluster of communities with the District of Columbia at its center. The District itself is an area of about 69 sq. miles (177 sq.km) stretching along the NE side of the Potomac river and incorporating a slice of land to the SE of the Anacostia river. But the main core of Washington is the area nestling in the fork of the two rivers. Originally the District was a regular diamond-shaped area straddling the Potomac, but in 1846 the inhabitants of the territory to the SW of the river opted to return to Virginia, and even a current map will show that the county boundaries on the Virginia side are still based on the old District line. Metropolitan Washington is encircled by a beltway called the Capital Beltway.

The street plan of central Washington is essentially a grid with the Capitol at its center. To the N and S of the Capitol, the sequence of streets runs in both directions alphabetically (but there are no J, X, Y or Z streets), while to the E and W they are numbered, again in both directions. This divides the whole city into four quadrants: Northwest (NW), Northeast (NE), Southwest (SW) and Southeast (SE). Addresses must always bear these designations or confusion will result, as there are four 1st streets, four A streets and so on. Avenues, named after states (Connecticut, Wisconsin, Massachusetts, etc.) cut diagonally across the street grid. Once you grasp the system, this is an easy city in which to find your way around.

The four quadrants are fairly distinct in character. NW is where the President of the United States lives, along with most of the city's middle-class population, black and white. It has the largest share of tourist attractions, hotels, restaurants and places of entertainment.

The Mall, with its numerous museums and public buildings, straddles the NW and SW sections. The small SW area, formerly a slum district, has been redeveloped on a large scale and now contains a new middle-class community. SE and NE are predominantly poor areas with a mainly black population, apart from the middle-class enclave of Capitol Hill. The suburbs contain a number of burgeoning commercial and shopping centers and many good-quality hotels. Otherwise the immediate environs have little of interest to visitors, except for isolated places such as *Arlington National Cemetery*, the old town of Alexandria and Mount Vernon (see *Excursions*).

Area planners

Washington, unlike Paris, London or Boston, is not a city of small, distinct "villages," but it does have neighborhoods of widely differing character. The following main areas are those most likely to come within a visitor's itinerary.

The Mall (*Maps 6 &7 G7-8*). The heart of the city, a 2-mile (3km) stretch of park from the *Capitol* to the *Lincoln Memorial*, flanked by museums and government buildings.

West End/Foggy Bottom (*Maps 2 &3 E-F4-5*). The area to the N, S and W of Washington Circle. A commercial, government, residential and academic district, it includes George Washington University, the *Kennedy Center* and the *Watergate Complex*. These surround a neighborhood called Foggy Bottom, so named because of the miasmic fogs that once engulfed this low-lying, formerly swampy ground. The West End area to the N of Washington Circle incorporates a cluster of big new luxury hotels.

New Downtown (*Map 3 E-F5-6*). The district to the NW of the *White House*, bounded roughly by N St., 16th St., Pennsylvania Ave. and New Hampshire Ave. This is now the focus of commercial life in Washington, and boasts many new office buildings, smart shops and expensive restaurants, but not a great deal of charm.

Old Downtown (*Map 6 &7 F*). This district runs E from the White House to within a couple of blocks of *Union Station*. After a period of decay it has undergone a remarkable revival. It contains department stores, museums, theaters, restaurants, smart shops, small galleries, luxury hotels and some fine old buildings that have been restored. On its N side is the *Washington Convention Center* and the emerging Techworld Trade Center.

Capitol Hill (*Maps 7 &8*). This comprises the Capitol complex and the residential area to the E almost as far as Lincoln Park and extending roughly from E St. in the S to E St. in the N. An area of charming, tree-lined streets, much of it is still poor and crime-ridden, but is increasingly being colonized by young middle-class professional people.

Southwest (*Maps 6 &7*). The entire area S of the Mall, dominated by government departments, high-rise apartment blocks and new town houses. There is little to interest the visitor here, except for the Mall itself and the colorful Waterfront area.

Georgetown (*Map 2*). Between *Rock Creek Park* and Georgetown University. On the one hand Georgetown has picturesque charm and inflated real-estate values; on the other it is a rendezvous for young pleasure-seekers, with discos, jazz clubs, cafés and boutiques.

Dupont Circle (*Map 3 D5*). This district and Georgetown are the closest that Washington has to a Left Bank. As well as a relaxed atmosphere and a youngish residential population, Dupont Circle has some fine architecture and many small businesses: bookstores, art galleries, cafés, small bars and restaurants. This is a lively and enjoyable neighborhood. Just to the NW of Dupont Circle is a dense colony of embassies, many occupying gracious former patrician houses along Massachusetts Ave., now nicknamed "Embassy Row."

Adams-Morgan (*Map 3 C-D5*). In NW Washington in the fork between Connecticut and Florida Ave., Adams-Morgan is a colorful Hispanic enclave with a mixture of other ethnic elements and a correspondingly wide variety of restaurants.

Upper Northwest (*Map 2*). Most of the city above Georgetown and NW of Rock Creek Park. Here can be found the *National Zoological Park*, *Washington Cathedral*, the *US Naval Observatory*, some pleasant leafy suburbs and many interesting restaurants.

Northeast of the White House (*Maps 3 D-E6-7, 6 F6*). The area stretching NE from the White House to Logan Circle contains a rich pot-pourri of fine architecture in various styles. Bordering a poor district to the E, it is becoming less dilapidated as more affluent families move in and renovate, and there are now a number of recommended hotels in the area. For years 14th St. and its environs were rife with prostitution and pornography, but currently big business is redeveloping 14th St., and the sex industry is on the decline, although prostitutes still operate in the area.

When visiting Washington, it is wise, as in any other city, to plan a schedule in advance. The city's main sights are mostly concentrated in a relatively small area, and this makes sightseeing flexible. The following are suggested schedules for a two-day and a four-day visit.

Two-day visit
Day 1   Climb the *Washington Monument* for an introductory bird's-eye view of the city in the morning. Have lunch in the Old Post Office Building and possibly go up the tower for another panoramic view. Spend the afternoon in Georgetown and take a boat trip on the *Chesapeake and Ohio Canal* if the season is right. Have dinner at one of Georgetown's numerous restaurants, concentrated along M St. and Wisconsin Ave.
Day 2   First visit the Capitol, then take a Tourmobile tour of the Mall, stopping off at any number of museums. After visiting the *National Gallery of Art*, try to take in the *National Archives*, immediately to the NW, then have an early supper followed by a bus tour of Washington after dark, or perhaps go to the theater or a nightclub (see *Nightlife and the arts*).

Four-day visit
Day 1   As for two-day visit.
Day 2   In the morning, see the Capitol and the *Supreme Court*. In the afternoon, visit the *Library of Congress*, then take a Tourmobile to the National Gallery of Art, National Archives and any other museums on the N Mall. In the evening, take a Washington tour by night.
Day 3   Spend the morning at the *National Air and Space Museum* and perhaps a few of the other museums on the S Mall. In the afternoon walk S to Pier 4 (at 6th and Water St. SW) and take the boat down to Mount Vernon; check beforehand if and when the boat is sailing (*Washington Boat Lines* ☎ 554-8000). For dinner afterward, there are a number of recommended seafood restaurants on the waterfront.
Day 4   In the morning, take the Tourmobile to *Arlington National Cemetery* and visit *Arlington House*. Make sure you are out of the cemetery by lunchtime as no eating is allowed there. Spend the afternoon exploring the quaint old town of Alexandria, and finish up with dinner in one of its many good restaurants.

Walks in Washington

Washington stimulates and encourages the walker as many American cities do not. For all its leafy open spaces and grand boulevards, it is relatively compact. A single outing of a few square blocks can take in several museums and monuments or entire residential neighborhoods, with frequent opportunities to rest. Since no structure is permitted to be higher than the Capitol dome, streets are not thrown into shadow by intimidating ranks of faceless skyscrapers. Public transportation is excellent, with bus stops and Metro stations readily available when a stroll starts to become a chore. Far from being regarded as eccentric, walking is a favored form of recreation. Among countless possible routes, here are three, diverse in character and taking in both interesting and attractive parts of the city.

Walk 1/Getting to know central Washington
Allow 2-3hrs. Maps 6&7. Metro: Gallery Place.

This walk will introduce the visitor to four different aspects of the city: the *Old Downtown* area, the Federal Triangle, the environs of the *White House*, and finally the *Mall* and the *Washington Monument*.

Leave the Metro subway at Gallery Place, exiting at the intersection of 9th and G St. by the Old Patent Office Building, now housing the *National Museum of American Art* and the *National Portrait Gallery*. Walk w along the pedestrian mall past the Martin Luther King Memorial Library at 901 G St. NW. This is the main public library of the District of Columbia, and its comprehensive collection of books, including a Washington section, can be used by any visitor for reference purposes (☎ *727-1111*).

Turn left down 10th St. past *Ford's Theatre* at no. 511, the scene of Lincoln's assassination. Across the road at 516 is *Petersen House*, where he died. At E St. turn E past the

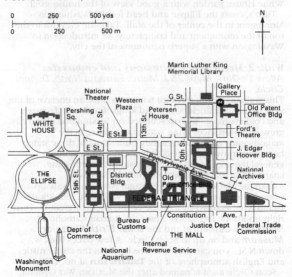

39

rather forbidding, cyclopean facade of the J. Edgar Hoover Building, headquarters of the FBI, then go down 9th St. leading into Pennsylvania Ave. Across the avenue and slightly to the left you will see the *National Archives*.

Now cross the avenue into what is known as the Federal Triangle. This massive government building project dates from the years 1928-38 when the triangle bounded by Pennsylvania Ave., Constitution Ave. and 15th St. was filled with a series of matching Federal buildings in an Italian Renaissance style of red-tiled roofs and imposing colonnades and porticoes. After the Department of Justice and the Internal Revenue Service, the Old Post Office Building is a welcome change of style, blending Neuschwanstein Castle with the Palazzo Vecchio in Florence, its massive clock tower vying with the Washington Monument for height. Pause inside, in one of the most staggering interiors in the city — a huge, glass-covered atrium, with shops, cafés and a performance stage — for coffee or a meal. Take an elevator to the top of the tower for a superb view.

Continue up the avenue to 13th St., crossing over to Western Plaza opposite the National Theater. Set into the white paving of the plaza is a map of central Washington laid out in black stone, with the floor plan of the White House and *Capitol* in brass. There are also plaques inscribed with memorable quotations about Washington, such as Henry Adams' back-handed compliment: "One of these days this will be a very great city if nothing happens to it." Looking SE from here, another great chunk of the Federal Triangle, occupied by the Bureau of Customs, is visible. Immediately to the s across the road is the smaller but still imposing District Building, headquarters of the DC administration. Just to the w of this is the Department of Commerce, which also houses the *National Aquarium*. Immediately w of the plaza is Pershing Sq., a pleasant little oasis of greenery with an open-air café by a pool. Continue w, passing on your right the railings of the White House garden with a good view of the house itself.

Turn s, cross the Ellipse and head for the Washington Monument in the center of the Mall. Take the elevator to the top of the monument and complete your introduction to Washington with a superb panorama of the city.

Walk 2/Monuments, mansions and embassies
Allow 1½-2hrs. Maps 2&3. Metro: Farragut North, Dupont Circle.

This walk takes you through what was once an enclave of the very rich: the financiers, railroad kings, food manufacturers and coal magnates who descended on Washington as the city grew in importance, vying with one another in the magnificence of the houses they built. Most of these stately homes are now embassies, clubs or institutions, but in general the area is still strongly residential with some charming streets ànd a real neighborhood flavor.

Take the Metro subway to Farragut North and walk up Connecticut Ave. to the intersection with M St. and Rhode Island Ave., marked by a statue of the poet Longfellow. Turn right up Rhode Island Ave., past the Roman Catholic *St Matthew's Cathedral* and the *B'nai B'rith Klutznick Museum* and on up to Scott Circle. A few paces back w, down N St., you can take a coffee break in the cozily rustic and English atmosphere of the **Tabard Inn** at no. 1739.

Scott Circle itself is named after the Mexican War General,

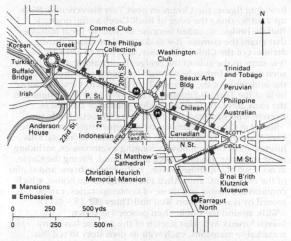

Winfield Scott, who sits astride a horse in the center. After the statue was completed it was felt indecorous that the General should be riding a mare, so the sculptor obediently added male parts to the animal. On the W side of the Circle is a monument to the 19thC statesman Daniel Webster, while on the E is one to Samuel Hahnemann, the founder of homeopathy, whose principle, *Similia similibus curentur* (like is cured by like) is inscribed on the monument.

Now turn and walk NW up Massachusetts Ave. known as "Embassy Row." The Australian Embassy is the first, a rather unmemorable modern building on the N side, by the Circle. Next to it is the Embassy of the Philippines, and, a little farther down, on the opposite side, are the embassies of Peru, Trinidad and Tobago, and Chile. The Chilean one at no. 1732 is a rather austere red-brick building by the architect Glenn Brown. A little farther on is the Canadian Embassy at no. 1746, the work of a prestigious architect of French origin, Jules Henri de Sibour. Completed in 1906, it was built in the fashionable Beaux Arts style for the coal magnate and financier Clarence Moore, who died in the *Titanic* disaster after only six years of residence. On the other side at no. 1785 is another handsome Beaux Arts building, now occupied by the National Trust for Historic Preservation.

A few steps on is Dupont Circle. Of the elegant mansions that once ringed the Circle, only two remain: 1801 Massachusetts Ave., now the Sulgrave Club, and 15 Dupont Circle, which houses the Washington Club. Both date from the turn of the century. The center of the Circle is marked by a graceful white fountain commemorating Rear Admiral Samuel Francis Dupont (1803-65), with a bowl supported by four allegorical figures suggestive of the sea and navigation. In the surrounding little park are chess tables, used on fine days. Now follow New Hampshire Ave. to no. 1307, a sumptuous *fin-de-siècle* mansion, currently the headquarters of the **Columbia Historical Society** with a delightful garden, entered from Sunderland Place.

From here go N up 20th St. and turn left down P St. Near the bridge to **Georgetown** is a large bronze statue of that

41

brooding figure, the Ukrainian poet Tara Shevchenko. Walk up 23rd St. along the edge of Rock Creek to the dramatic Buffalo Bridge, so called because of the four great buffaloes that guard the corners. It was designed by Glenn Brown, architect of the Chilean Embassy, and built in 1912-15. Just a few steps to the side of the bridge, facing along it, can be seen a row of Indian heads with feathered headdresses along the underside of the parapet. Turn around to view the ornate bulk of the Turkish Embassy at no. 1606 23rd St., designed in the early 20thC by George Oakley Totten for Edward H. Everett, who had made his fortune out of metal bottle tops.

Sheridan Circle, dominated by the equestrian statue of the Civil War hero, General Philip Sheridan, has more gracious houses, most of them now belonging to embassies, including those of Korea, Egypt, Greece and Ireland. Facing the Circle, at no. 2306 Massachusetts Ave., is the former home and studio of the early 20thC artist Alice Pike Barney. The house, which contains her works and those of contemporaries, can be toured by reservation on Wed and Thurs (☎ 357-3111).

Walk around the Circle, then proceed SE down Massachusetts Ave. This stretch of the avenue has many remarkable mansions, each with its own story to tell. No. 2121 was built in the style of the Petit Trianon for the railroad magnate Richard Townsend, whose wife insisted, for superstitious reasons, that the building should incorporate an existing house. Sadly, this did not prevent Mr Townsend from dying of a riding injury soon after the house was completed. The building now houses the elegant and exclusive Cosmos Club. Just around the corner at no. 1600 21st St. is the mansion housing the *Phillips Collection*, austere outside but delightfully intimate inside. Across the road at no. 2118 Massachusetts Ave. is the amazing *Anderson House*, headquarters of the elite Society of the Cincinnati. Open to the public, the even more lavish interior is worth a visit.

A little farther down at no. 2020 is the Indonesian Embassy, a building of well-fed appearance, bulging out at the corners. Like the Townsend house, its story is marked by tragedy. It was built just after the turn of the century by Thomas F. Walsh, an Irishman who had struck gold in Colorado. His son and grandson were both killed in automobile accidents, and he died a sad recluse in 1910.

Continue down the avenue to return to the neighborhood of Dupont Circle, where there is a Metro subway station. Before leaving the area a snack or meal can be had in one of the many lively cafés and restaurants along Connecticut Ave. by going NW from the Circle. At no. 1517, for example, is **Kramer Books and Afterwords**, a delightful bookstore-cum-café, while at no. 1521 is the **Café Splendide**, which has an Austro-Hungarian character.

Walk 3/Capitol Hill
Allow 2-3hrs. Maps 7&8. Metro: Union Station, Eastern Market.

This route includes not only the *Capitol* itself and the imposing buildings surrounding it, but also the charming and less well-known area to the E. As on the other walks, you will pass some striking outdoor sculptures, such as the figures on the facade of *Union Station*, where the walk begins, and the Columbus fountain in the station plaza.

From the station, walk down Louisiana Ave. to the

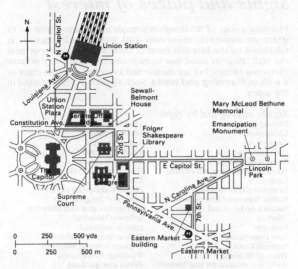

intersection of N Capitol St. Turn s toward the Capitol, passing through a park which has an elegant fountain (which is turned off in cold months). From here, either continue down to the Capitol and return to the route after your visit, or turn up Constitution Ave., passing the two Senate office buildings. At the NW corner of 2nd St. NE stands Sewall-Belmont House at no. 144 Constitution Ave., a well-proportioned, red-brick town house built in 1800 and now the headquarters of the National Women's Party. It has been well restored and is open to the public (*open Tues-Fri 10am-3pm, Sat, Sun and hols noon-4pm ☎ 546-1210*).

From here continue along 2nd St. past the rear of the **Supreme Court**, as far as the intersection with E Capitol St. Ahead is the **Library of Congress** on the SW corner and the **Folger Shakespeare Library** on the SE corner. Notice the reliefs on the Folger depicting scenes from Shakespeare.

Down E Capitol St. is Lincoln Park, past many attractive 19thC houses in a great variety of styles. Two monuments of interest in the park are the Emancipation Monument, showing Abraham Lincoln bidding a slave rise to freedom, and a memorial to the black educator Mary McLeod Bethune (1875-1955).

Return SW along N Carolina Ave. and turn s down 7th St. Here, in the first block to the right, is the red-brick building housing Eastern Market, one of the few genuine farmers' markets left in the city, where anything from a side of Virginia ham to a piece of ripe Stilton cheese may be bought. There is also a potters' studio upstairs in the market and at the N end is an auditorium where art exhibitions and dance performances are held. The market (*open Tues-Thurs 7am-6pm, Fri-Sat 6am-7pm*) is liveliest on Sat mornings. Nearby are boutiques, shops and small restaurants. At the next corner, 7th St. and Pennsylvania Ave., a fresh pastry and espresso coffee can be had at **Bread & Chocolate**. The Metro is diagonally across the street.

Sights and places of interest

Planning a tour of Washington's major tourist attractions — its great monuments, museums and public buildings — is facilitated by the fact that most of them are located on or near the Mall. Bear in mind that certain smaller sights do not have their own entries, but are mentioned as part of a district entry or a walk in *Planning and walks*. Such sights can still be found in the index.

Sights classified by type

Districts
Chinatown
Georgetown
Old Downtown
Federal buildings
Bureau of Engraving and Printing
Capitol
Executive Office Building
Federal Bureau of Investigation
National Archives and Records
  Service
Pentagon
State Department
Supreme Court
Treasury Building
Galleries, museums and historic houses
Anacostia Neighborhood Museum
Anderson House
Arlington House
Arthur M. Sackler Gallery
Arts Club of Washington
Arts and Industries Building
Blair and Lee Houses
B'nai B'rith Klutznick Museum
Capital Children's Museum
Columbia Historical Society
Corcoran Gallery of Art
Daughters of the American
  Revolution
Decatur House
Department of the Interior Museum
Doll's House and Toy Museum
Dumbarton Oaks
Frederick Douglass House
Freer Gallery of Art
Hillwood
Hirshhorn Museum
House of the Temple
Islamic Center
Lillian and Albert Small Jewish
  Museum
National Air and Space Museum
National Gallery of Art
National Geographic Society
Explorers Hall
National Museum of African Art
National Museum of American Art
National Museum of Natural History
National Museum of Women In The
  Arts
National Portrait Gallery
National Rifle Association of America
The Octagon
Old Pension Building
Petersen House

The Phillips Collection
Renwick Gallery
Textile Museum
Truxtun-Decatur Naval Museum
The White House
Woodrow Wilson House
Libraries
Folger Shakespeare Library
Library of Congress
Memorials and monuments
Jefferson Memorial
Lincoln Memorial
Marine Corps War Memorial
Vietnam Veterans Memorial
Washington Monument
Parks and gardens
Dumbarton Oaks
Kenilworth Aquatic Garden
Lady Bird Johnson Park and Lyndon
  Baines Johnson Memorial Grove
Lafayette Square
The Mall
Meridian Hill Park
National Arboretum
Potomac Park
Rock Creek Park
Theodore Roosevelt Island
United States Botanic Garden
Religious buildings
Church of the Epiphany
Franciscan Monastery
Mormon Temple
National Shrine of the Immaculate
  Conception
St Matthew's Cathedral
Washington Cathedral
Theaters
Ford's Theatre
Kennedy Center for the Performing
  Arts
Other sights
Arlington National Cemetery
Chesapeake and Ohio Canal
Fort Leslie J. McNair
National Aquarium
National Zoological Park
Navy Yard
Pierce Mill
Rock Creek Cemetery
Smithsonian Institution Building
Union Station
United States Naval Observatory
Voice of America
Washington Convention Center
Washington Post
Watergate Complex

Anacostia Neighborhood Museum

1901 Fort Place SE, DC 20560 ☎ 287-3369. Map 8K11▣ 🏛
for certain exhibitions. Open 10am-5pm. Closed Christmas.
Located in a black district on the SE side of the Anacostia
River, this lively museum has temporary exhibitions by black
artists or ones that reflect the culture and history of the area.
Established in 1967 as part of the Smithsonian Institution, the
museum has gained wide respect.

Anderson House

*2118 Massachusetts Ave. NW, DC 20008 ☎ 785-0540. Map
3D5▣ 𝒦 by appt. Open 1-4pm. Closed Sat in Aug, Sun,
Mon, hols. Library open Mon-Fri 10am-4pm. Metro:
Dupont Circle.*
Anderson House is home to the Society of the Cincinnati,
which was founded in 1783 by a group of Washington's
officers and has remained a strictly hereditary body, with
membership restricted to male descendants of officers who
fought for three years in the Revolutionary War. It exists to
perpetuate the fraternal spirit of the original founders, to
foster American ideals and to support educational, cultural
and literary activities related to the society's aims. The name
alludes to the parallel between George Washington and the
Roman statesman Lucius Quinctius Cincinnatus, who twice
returned from his farm to assume emergency powers of
rulership — just as Washington returned from Mount Vernon
— and finally retired there declining all honors.

The house itself was built between 1902 and 1905 for Mr
and Mrs Larz Anderson with the intention that it should
eventually be given to the society. Anderson, a member of the
society, was a distinguished diplomat. The building, with its
front courtyard protected from the hoi polloi by a screening
wall, reflects the exclusive nature of the society. Both
externally and internally it is lavish and imposing.

The interior boasts a patrician elegance exemplified by the
vast **ballroom**, with its musicians' gallery. It also houses the
society's **museum** with portraits of the founders, military
relics, documents and personal memorabilia. The second
floor still has most of its original furnishings and *objets d'art*,
including an impressive collection of 18thC paintings by
Hoppner, Raeburn, Reynolds and others. The basement has a
13,000-volume **library** of works on the American
Revolutionary period (*open Mon-Fri 10am-4pm*).

A pleasant way to enjoy the house in leisured fashion is to
attend one of the concerts held regularly on Sat afternoons.

Arlington House

*Arlington National Cemetery, Arlington, Va. 22211
☎ 557-0613. Map 4H2▣ 𝒦 Oct-Mar by reservation ⬅
Open Apr-Sept 9.30am-6pm; Oct-Mar 9.30am-5pm. Metro:
Arlington Cemetery.*
Also known as **Custis-Lee Mansion**, this house is
dramatically set on a hill within *Arlington National
Cemetery* and since 1955 has been a permanent memorial to
Robert E. Lee, a Civil War Confederate commander widely
admired both N and S of the Mason-Dixon line.

The house, with its massive Doric-columned portico, was
built between 1802 and 1817 by George Washington Parke
Custis, stepson of George Washington. Custis was a
many-faceted man: agriculturalist, painter, playwright, orator.

His portrait hangs over the fireplace in the **family dining room**, and some of his own paintings are also on view; for example, his dark hunting scenes in the **center hall**.

Custis' daughter, Mary, married Robert E. Lee in the **family parlor** in 1831, and the house was the Lee family home from then until the Civil War. Here, wrote Lee, "my affections and attachments are more strongly placed than at any other place in the world." It was here that he took his painful decision in 1861 to leave the US Army and offer his services to Virginia. After that he never returned to the house.

During the Civil War the house was occupied by the US Army. It was later confiscated in lieu of property taxes, won back by Lee's son through the Supreme Court and finally sold by him to the Federal Government.

The original atmosphere of a gracious Virginia family home has been painstakingly re-created, complete with staff dressed in 19thC costume. Some of the original furnishings have been returned, while others are similar period pieces or copies. The servants' quarters are on the s side of the circular drive. Across the garden is a small **museum** illustrating the history of the house and the life of Robert E. Lee. From the portico be sure to take in the view E over Washington, which Lafayette claimed was the "finest view in the world."

Arlington National Cemetery ★
Arlington, Va. 22211 ☎ 629-0931. Map 4GHI&J2-3 🖾 ✗ by Tourmobile ➡ ◄ Open Apr-Sept 8am-7pm, Oct-Mar 8am-5pm. Metro: Arlington Cemetery.

A serene and dignified environment for a last resting place, the cemetery is approached by the Arlington Memorial Bridge with its dramatic gold statues at either end, and through the splendid gateway, built under President Franklin D. Roosevelt's Work Project Administration (WPA). The rolling, wooded slopes have row upon row of small, simple white gravestones interspersed occasionally with larger and more imposing monuments. Burial is now restricted to certain categories of people and their dependants: members of the armed forces who have served in a foreign war, Medal of Honor recipients, and important government or political figures.

The cemetery was formerly the estate of *Arlington House*, home of Robert E. Lee, which still dominates the area. The US Government took over the estate on the outbreak of the Civil War and in 1865 began using it as a national cemetery. It now honors the dead of both armies in the Civil War. A **Confederate Monument**, in bronze and granite, surmounted by a female figure facing s, stands on the w side of the cemetery near McPherson Dr. To the s of the house, a huge granite sarcophagus marks a vault containing 2,111 unknowns of the Civil War. Anonymous victims of more recent wars are commemorated by the **Unknown Soldier's Tomb**, a chastely carved marble block standing before the **Arlington Memorial Amphitheater**, watched over constantly by soldiers of the Third Infantry who, in a fine display of military drill, change guard every half-hour during the day in summer and every hour in winter.

The most-visited grave is probably that of **President John F. Kennedy**, which lies off Sheridan Dr. on the slope below Arlington House. Marked by an eternal flame, it is approached by a terrace with a curving wall inscribed with words from Kennedy's Inaugural Address. The modest grave of his brother, **Robert F. Kennedy**, is nearby. A little farther up toward the house is the table-like gravestone of **Major Pierre L'Enfant**, commanding a splendid view over the city that he planned.

Arthur M. Sackler Gallery
1050 Independence Ave. SW, DC 20560 ☎ 357-2700. Map 6G7 ⊡ ✗ Open 10am-5.30pm. Closed Christmas. Metro: Smithsonian.
The focus of this new museum, which opened in 1987, is the art of the Near and Far East. Dr Arthur M. Sackler is a New York psychiatrist and medical publisher who pledged his collection of 1,000 Asian and Near Eastern works to the Smithsonian and donated $4 million toward the construction of an underground museum to house the collection. The museum is part of the new Quadrangle complex behind the Smithsonian Castle, which also houses the National Museum of African Art. The Sackler Gallery complements the already strong Oriental collection of the neighboring *Freer Gallery*, and the two will work hand in glove, sharing the same curatorial and conservation staff, library and research facilities. There are major loan exhibitions as well as displays from the museum's own collection.

Arts Club of Washington
2017 I St. NW, DC 20006 ☎ 331-7282. Map 3E5 ⊡ ✿ Open Tues 1-5pm, Wed-Fri 2-5pm, Sat, Sun 1-5pm. Closed Mon, hols. Metro: Foggy Bottom, Farragut West.
This organization, whose aim is to support the arts in the Greater Washington area, occupies two adjoining historic houses. No. 2017 was built in 1802-5 and served for a time as the Executive Mansion under President James Monroe. No. 2015 next door was built around 1870. Apart from their interest as period houses, the buildings house a permanent collection of works by Washington artists as well as changing exhibitions of work by contemporary artists from Washington and elsewhere.

Arts and Industries Building
900 Jefferson Dr. SW, DC 20560 ☎ 357-2700 (central Smithsonian info.). Map 6G7 ⊡ ✗ ⇌ Open 10am-5.30pm. Closed Christmas. Metro: Smithsonian.
The second oldest of the Smithsonian buildings on the *Mall*, this quintessentially Victorian structure, with its turrets and polychromatic brickwork, was completed in 1881 to house objects given to the Smithsonian from the United States International Exposition, held in 1876 to mark the centenary of Independence. In 1980 it was extensively restored.

Its four wings, radiating out from a central rotunda, resplendent with fountain and potted plants, contain a startling selection of objects illustrating the wonders of 19thC inventiveness, brought from all over America and abroad. Pennsylvania is represented by objects as diverse as a railroad locomotive and a model of the Liberty Bell made out of sugar. There is another Liberty Bell in tobacco from North Carolina, a bale of cotton from Mississippi, optical instruments from Paris and silverware from England. The growing pride in American industrial might, felt in 1876, is reflected in the impressive array of steam-powered machinery from pumping

engines to printing presses. There are also some fine models
of ships, particularly the 45ft (16m) model of the naval cruiser
Antietam.

The museum has a well-stocked gift store and a **Discovery
Theater**, which holds performances of films, puppetry,
drama, dance, mime and singing (☎ 357-1500 for details ✸).

Blair-Lee House
*1651 Pennsylvania Ave. NW, DC 20560. Map 6F6. Not open
to the public. Metro: Farragut West.*
Francis Preston Blair, an influential newspaper editor and
member of President Andrew Jackson's "Kitchen Cabinet,"
purchased the yellow Georgian row house in 1836. The
brick-front home to its left dates from 1858 and was the
residence of Rear Admiral Samuel Phillips Lee, who later
served as US Senator from Maryland. The two buildings were
joined in 1943 to become the President's Guest House. Harry
S. Truman lived there from 1948 to 1952 during renovations to
the White House. Two Puerto Rican nationalists stormed the
entrance in 1950 in an attempt to assassinate the President.
One was killed, as was a guard. The second would-be killer
was captured and sentenced to life imprisonment.

B'nai B'rith Klutznick Museum
*1640 Rhode Island Ave. NW, DC 20036 ☎ 857-6583. Map
3E6 ▣ ✖ 🎨 ✖ by appt ✸ Open Sun-Fri 10am-5pm. Closed
Jewish and state holidays. Metro: Farragut North.*
This is the world headquarters of B'nai B'rith (Sons of the
Covenant), an international organization existing for the
purpose of "uniting Jews in their highest interests and those
of humanity." Judaica of all kinds is the theme of the
museum. Frequent temporary exhibitions are held on various
aspects of Jewish life and history, as well as the permanent
exhibition of over 400 objects: ancient Jewish pottery and
coins, ritual implements, regalia, silverware and much else.
The museum shop sells Jewish American craftwork. Behind
the museum is the **Harold and Sylvia Greenberg Sculpture
Garden**.

Bureau of Engraving and Printing
*14th and C St. SW, DC 20228 ☎ 447-9709/9976. Map 6G-H6
▣ 🎨 Open Mon-Fri 9am-2pm. Closed Sat, Sun, hols.
Metro: Smithsonian. Washington Mall Tourmobile.*
The Bureau of Engraving and Printing, the US Government
security printer, is the world's largest establishment of its
kind. It employs 3,500 people and operates 24hrs a day, using
the most up-to-date machinery. The average life of a dollar
bill is only 18 months, so the presses are kept busy
replenishing the supply. As well as banknotes, the bureau
also prints Treasury Bonds, postage stamps, White House
invitations, government certificates and other official
documents.

The self-guided tour of the building takes you along
glassed-in galleries overlooking rooms where stamps and
banknotes roll off huge presses and where bills are stacked
ready for circulation. "This stack contains $6,400,000 in $20
bills," a recorded voice tantalizingly announces. The tour
ends in an exhibit hall with a souvenir store. Free samples are
not available, but a small bag containing the shreddings from
$150 worth of bills can be bought. Coins are produced not

here but by the Mint, whose works are in Philadelphia, Denver and San Francisco.

Capital Children's Museum
800 3rd St. NE, DC 20002 ☎ 543-8600. Map 8F10 🖼
✗ *Mon-Fri 10am, 11.30am, 1pm ✹ ⬅ Open 10am-5pm. Closed major hols. Metro: Union Station.*
If your child is itching to learn how to operate a computer, write with a quill pen, run a printing press or make a radio program, this is the place where he or she can do all of these things and many more. By having fun, the children acquire much valuable knowledge about the modern world. The computer section is a good example. Each child sits in front of a screen with a computer keyboard and, under the guidance of instructors, can learn how to make pictures on the screen using different colors and shapes. There is also a talking computer. "My name is Wisecracker," it intones in an eerie, science-fiction voice, "come talk to me." It will then repeat whatever you type into it, even gibberish. There are also free craft activities and puppet shows on Fri-Sun for an extra fee.

Capitol ★
E end of Mall on Capitol Hill ☎ 224-3121. Map 7G9 🖼
🖼 *on 3rd floor ✗ ⬛ Open June-Labor Day 9am-8pm; rest of year 9am-4.30pm. Closed some major hols. Metro: Capitol South, Union Station.*
The Capitol, seat of the Congress, was appropriately made the center of L'Enfant's Washington plan, with all the streets numbered or lettered outward from it. Unlike the *White House*, it is unashamedly grand, standing on the hill that L'Enfant once described as "a pedestal waiting for superstructure," its vast white dome surmounted by a figure representing Liberty. Its grandeur does not intimidate but rather encourages the visitor to enter and admire the place where the supreme lawmaking body of the richest nation on earth meets, deliberates and decides. How many other legislative buildings in the world are so freely accessible? To view a session of the House of Representatives or the Senate you need a pass from your Congressman if you are a US citizen, or a passport or other identification if you are an overseas visitor (Congress is usually in session from Jan to Oct, with occasional recesses).

Emily was staring. "The Capitol," she said, with reverence.
Behind them Union Station, and its triumphal arches, behind them the central figures of Freedom and Imagination.
The Capitol faced east. The dome was a massive bubble swimming in a golden heat haze.
Faith Baldwin, *Washington, USA*

The Capitol evolved piecemeal over many years. It was begun in 1793 to a design by the amateur architect Dr William Thornton, one of a series of nine architects who shaped the building. By 1800 it was sufficiently far advanced for the House and Senate to move there from Philadelphia. The Supreme Court and the Library of Congress also used the building in the early days. In 1814 British forces set fire to the Capitol, and, although saved from total destruction by a heavy rainfall, it needed extensive rebuilding. By 1819 it was

SECOND FLOOR

South

East Front

Floor plan of the US Capitol, home of the Senate and House of Representatives since 1800. Visitors can tour part of the main floor, with its historic paintings and sculptures, and from the floor above there is access to the public galleries of the House and Senate chambers.

once again ready for occupation. Since then frequent modifications have been made. In the 1860s the old copper-covered wooden dome was replaced by the present cast-iron one, and in 1962 the E side was extended by 32½ft (10m) to provide more space.

The point of departure for tours is the huge **rotunda** beneath the dome. A white marble disc in the center of the floor marks the spot where many presidents have lain in state. Among the works of art in the rotunda are statues of American statesmen, and eight large paintings depicting scenes from American history. The four by John Trumbull of events from the Revolutionary period are particularly interesting, as the artist was present on each occasion. The center of the dome also has a remarkable painting, *The Glorification of the Spirit of George Washington* by the Italian artist Constantino Brumidi, an immigrant who worked for 25yrs on the Capitol's interior.

To the S of the rotunda is the **Statuary Hall**, now filled with statues commemorating worthy citizens of various states. This room, formerly the House chamber, has a remarkable acoustic property called a parabolic reflection, which enabled John Quincy Adams (later President) to eavesdrop on members of the Opposition. A brass disc marks the spot where Adams sat, and where he died. Stand here and listen as the guide speaks very quietly from across the room; you will be astonished at how clearly the voice carries.

Ascend to the next floor by one of the building's four grand staircases, and from this level, enter the visitors' galleries of both the Senate (in the N wing) and the House of Representatives (in the S wing). The **Senate chamber** seems surprisingly small, but there are only 100 Senators — two for each state, irrespective of size. It is restrained in decor except for the huge tasseled canopy over the chair of the Speaker

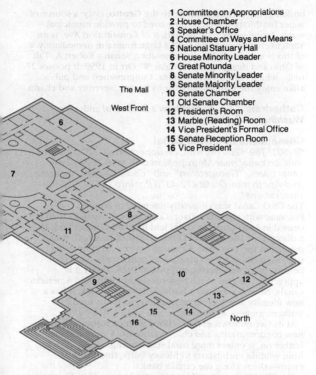

1 Committee on Appropriations
2 House Chamber
3 Speaker's Office
4 Committee on Ways and Means
5 National Statuary Hall
6 House Minority Leader
7 Great Rotunda
8 Senate Minority Leader
9 Senate Majority Leader
10 Senate Chamber
11 Old Senate Chamber
12 President's Room
13 Marble (Reading) Room
14 Vice President's Formal Office
15 Senate Reception Room
16 Vice President

The Mall

West Front

North

(who is always the US Vice-President). The much larger
House chamber has some interesting decorative features
including a frieze of medallions depicting great lawgivers of
history from Moses to Thomas Jefferson. It is here that the
President addresses the joint session of Congress. There is a
fixed number of 435 Representatives, and each represents a
given number of people rather than a state. The two houses
are equal in legislative power.

The Senate offices are in two buildings N of the Capitol: the
Russell Building, in use since 1909, and the **Dirksen
Building**, completed in 1958. These are connected to the
Capitol by a special subway train, which the public can use.
The Representatives have their offices in the **Cannon**,
Longworth and **Rayburn Buildings** to the S (dating from
1908, 1933 and 1965 respectively), connected to the Capitol
by pedestrian tunnels. A special book-conveyor tunnel links
the Capitol with the *Library of Congress*. If you visit the
Senate cafeteria, try a bowl of the bean soup that has become
a Capitol institution.

The Capitol is surrounded by a fine park, superbly laid out
by the landscape architect Frederick Law Olmsted in 1872. To
the W the land drops away in terraces to a pool overlooked by
the dramatic bronze monuments to General (and later
President) Ulysses S. Grant, showing a Civil War battle with
the intrepid Grant surveying the scene from his horse. Note
also, at the foot of the slope, just to the NW of the Capitol

building, the arched entrance to the **Grotto**, once a source of water for thirsty travelers, now used to provide municipal water. In the section of the park N of Constitution Ave. is an attractively terraced area with a large fountain; immediately W of this is a **monolith** commemorating Senator Robert A. Taft of Ohio and designed by Douglas W. Orr in 1959. It houses 27 bells, which chime every 15mins. Congressmen and public alike enjoy the Capitol park for its beauty, serenity and charm.

Cathedrals   See *St Matthew's Cathedral* and *Washington Cathedral.*

Chesapeake and Ohio Canal

☎ *(301) 789-4200 (for info. on upper canal), 229-3614 (for info. on canal near Metropolitan DC). Map 2E2-4. Two canal boats, "Georgetown" and "Canal Clipper," operate mid-Apr to mid-Oct ☎ 472-4376 (for info.), 229-2026 (for reservations).*

The C&O Canal was originally intended to connect the Potomac with the Ohio River. Construction began in 1828 but ceased in 1850 once the canal had reached Cumberland, Md., a distance of 184½ miles (277km). Most of its length runs parallel to the Potomac. Although never a great financial success, it did carry goods such as grain, timber and coal before commercial traffic stopped in 1924. Today it is appreciated as one of the best-preserved of the old American canals. Now designated a National Historical Park, it has a new identity as a recreational facility, its paths used by walkers, joggers and cyclists.

At its Georgetown end, it is lined with picturesque houses, new condominiums and chic restaurants. A short distance farther on, it enters more rural surroundings. Many people, from wildlife enthusiasts to history buffs, find much to engross them along the canal's banks.

The **Monocacy Aqueduct**, near Dickerson, is an impressive piece of engineering, as is the 3,117ft (950m) **Paw Paw Tunnel**, which takes the canal through a mountain. Locks, bridges, lock houses and other such remains from the canal's working heyday have been preserved.

The canal is ideal for an afternoon's excursion or a week-long hike, and there are "hiker-biker" overnight campsites roughly every 5 miles (8km), as well as three drive-in campgrounds. The **Great Falls Tavern** (☎ *(301) 299-3613; open 9am-5pm; closed hols*) houses a museum and a visitors' center. Other visitors' centers on the canal are located in Georgetown between Thomas Jefferson St. and 30th St. NW, and at the terminal in Cumberland, Md. These centers provide useful information about conducted walks and evening programs.

Chinatown
Map 7F8.
The continuing eastward redevelopment of Old Downtown, spurred by the opening of the new Convention Center, has gobbled at the edges of what was once a ten-square-block Chinese enclave. What remains is a short strip of H St. between 5th and 7th Sts., with a dwindling number of dingy side-street stores on its perimeter. An estimated 500 Chinese still live in the neighborhood, less than one percent of the total residing in the metropolitan area. Optimistic promoters

recently installed a grandiose gateway over H St., funded in part by the People's Republic of China. A million dollars' worth of fierce dragons and colorful tiles, it heralds the presence of a handful of restaurants purveying Hunan, Szechuan and Cantonese cookery. They are the principal reasons for a brief excursion.

Church of the Epiphany

1317 G St. NW, DC 20005 ☎ 347-2635. Map 6F7 ⬚ Open 10am-2pm. Sun services 7.45am, 8am, 11am. Organ recitals Tues 12.10pm. Metro: Metro Center.
A century ago this lovely Neo-Gothic Episcopal church was attended by Washington's upper crust. Today, as the *Old Downtown* area steadily revives, the church is once again coming into its own. It has a graceful, soothing interior, lit by rich stained-glass windows, and possesses a fine pipe-organ.

Columbia Historical Society *(Christian Heurich Memorial Mansion)*

1307 New Hampshire Ave. NW, DC 20036 ☎ 785-2068. Map 3D5 ⬚ ✗ by appt. Open Wed, Fri, Sat noon-4pm. Closed Mon, Tues, Thurs, Sun, hols. Metro: Dupont Circle.
Of all the great Washington houses open to the public, this is one of the most opulent. Since 1956 it has been the home of the Columbia Historical Society, founded in 1894 to record, teach and preserve the historical heritage of Washington, DC. The society maintains an extensive library of Washingtonia, publishes a periodical, Records of the Columbia Historical Society, and holds lectures. Appropriately, the house it occupies is itself a historic monument, which the society has renovated while keeping the decor and furnishings as near to the original as possible.

The house was built in the 1890s by Christian Heurich, a German immigrant who made a fortune as a brewer. His home combined advanced technological features, such as a poured concrete shell for protection against fire, with an almost regal lavishness of decoration, carried out by German-American builders and craftsmen. The three floors of rooms open to the public include the **Dining Room**, with its rich woodwork, and the **Blue Parlor** resplendent with elaborate plaster moldings, a delicately painted ceiling and original family furnishings. An added attraction is the charming garden entered from Sunderland Pl. and used as a park by local people.

Corcoran Gallery of Art ★

17th St. and New York Ave. NW, DC 20006 ☎ 638-3211. Map 6F6 ⬚ ✗ by appt ☎ 638-1070. Open Tues-Sun 10am-4.30pm, Thurs until 9pm. Closed Mon, some major hols. Metro: Farragut West.
The Corcoran, which is not part of the Smithsonian empire, is the city's most important private art museum and one of the major galleries of the country. Founded by the banker W. W. Corcoran in 1859, it was formerly housed in what is now the *Renwick Gallery* and later moved to its present building, an imposing edifice designed by Ernest Flagg in the palatial, classical style of the Beaux Arts school.

The collection divides into European and American sections. The former, enriched by the acquisition of the W. A. Clark collection in 1928, includes Renaissance works by Titian and others, 17thC Dutch and Flemish masters, British works of art by, among others, Gainsborough, Turner and Raeburn, and French paintings up to the Impressionists, including a particularly rich collection of Corots. There are also Greek and Egyptian figurines, Beauvais and Gobelins tapestries, majolica ware, stained glass from Soissons Cathedral, and an entire room of Louis XVI period, complete with Marie Antoinette's harpsichord, brought from the Hôtel de la Tremoille in Paris.

The American collection is one of the nation's finest and reveals the extraordinary richness and diversity of American art. To view these works is to catch a glimmer of the soul of America. The collection embraces the stiff, amateurish portraiture of early colonial days, the romanticized Western scenes of Albert Bierstadt, the strange visionary works of Elihu Vedder, the tranquil landscapes of the so-called Luminous School of 19thC artists. All the great names of American art are here: Winslow Homer, Mary Cassatt, John Singer Sargent. A surprising inclusion is Samuel F. B. Morse, inventor of the Morse code as well as being a talented painter. His *Old House of Representatives*, an atmospheric painting of the chamber lit by candlelight, hangs in the main hallway. Contemporary American artists are well represented: Louise Nevelson, Joseph Cornell, Jules Olitski, Helen Frankenthaler among others. Temporary exhibitions are also held here.

As well as a gallery, the Corcoran is the only accredited art school in Washington, offering both full-time courses and classes for anyone of any level. Evening recitals are given in its acoustically fine auditorium. The Corcoran undeniably lives up to the inscription over its entrance: "Dedicated to art."

Custis-Lee Mansion See *Arlington House*.

Daughters of the American Revolution (DAR)
1776 D St. NW, DC 20006 ☎ 628-1776. Map 6F6 🔲 🔲 for library ⚥ ✻ Open Mon-Fri 8.30am-4pm, Sun 1-5pm. Closed Sat. Tours Mon-Fri 10am-3pm, Sun 1-5pm. Metro: Farragut West, Farragut North.

The DAR is an organization of women whose direct ancestors helped in the struggle for American Independence. The headquarters cover an entire city block. The address and telephone number both contain the date 1776, the year of the Declaration of Independence. Three connecting buildings occupy the site: the **Administration Building**; the **Memorial Continental Hall**, an imposing Beaux Arts edifice built in the early 1900s; and the **Constitution Hall**, a 1920s Neoclassical building by John Russell Pope used for conferences and cultural events.

The museum has 33 period rooms, representing various states of the Union and furnished in different styles. Their contents reflect the craftsmanship and decorative arts of America before the Industrial Revolution. They include a Californian adobe parlor of 1860, a 1775 Massachusetts bedroom, and a kitchen from an Oklahoma farmhouse complete with an assortment of 19thC kitchenware. A popular series of rooms, especially with children, is the **New Hampshire attic** with its marvelous collection of toys, dolls and games.

The museum **gallery** contains permanent and changing exhibits from the museum's extensive decorative arts collection. There is also a superb genealogical **library** open to the public for a small fee.

Decatur House
748 Jackson Pl. NW, DC 20006 ☎ 673-4030. Map 3F6 ⬛ *Ӿ Open Tues-Fri 10am-2pm, Sat, Sun noon-4pm. Closed some major hols. Metro: Farragut West, Farragut North.*
Commodore Stephen Decatur (1779-1820), hero of the struggle against the Barbary pirates and of the War of 1812, is one of the most dashing figures in American naval history. He is also famous for his immortal and much misquoted toast: "Our country — in her intercourse with foreign nations, may she be always in the right, and always successful, right or wrong."

After coming to Washington, covered in glory, he commissioned the prominent architect Benjamin Henry Latrobe to design him an elegant, red-brick house in *Lafayette Square*, where he and his wife entertained lavishly. After Decatur's tragic death in a duel in 1820 Mrs Decatur moved to Georgetown, and subsequently the house enjoyed a succession of other distinguished tenants including diplomats and congressmen.

In 1871 it became the home of General Edward Fitzgerald Beale and his wife. They introduced Victorian features to the house, and later Beale's son and daughter-in-law lived there. Since 1956 it has been owned by the National Trust for Historic Preservation who maintain the building along with its furnishings and memorabilia of the Decatur and Beale eras. The Trust also has a fine bookstore and gift store nearby at 1600 H St., next to the *Truxtun-Decatur Naval Museum*.

Department of the Interior Museum
18th and C St. NW, DC 20240 ☎ 343-2743. Map 5F5 🖸 ▣ *Open Mon-Fri 8am-4pm. Closed Sat, Sun, hols. Metro: Farragut West.*
The agencies that come under the umbrella of this department and are represented in its museum include the National Park Service, the Bureau of Reclamation, the Geological Survey, the Bureau of Land Management and the Bureau of Indian Affairs. The exhibits range from stuffed animals, displays on endangered species and scarce, nonrenewable sources of power, documents and pictures illustrating the opening of the West, to mineral samples from different parts of the country. One of the most interesting sections deals with the Native Americans, with a diorama of a Navajo settlement, headdresses, bows and arrows, and other Indian artifacts.

In the same building there is a shop selling attractive but highly priced Indian craftwork — from textiles and basketwork to jewelry and pottery — and a National Park Service office, which provides useful leaflets about its facilities. The department also has a comprehensive library (*open Mon-Fri 7.45am-5pm*).

Dolls' House and Toy Museum
5236 44th St. NW, DC 20015 ☎ 244-0024 ⬛ 🌂 *Ӿ for 12 or more by appt. Open Tues-Sat 10am-5pm, Sun noon-5pm. Closed Mon, major hols. Metro: Friendship Heights.*
Flora Gill Jacobs, author of *A History of Dolls' Houses*, founded this entrancing museum in 1975, using her own

extensive collection, only part of which is on display at any one time. The remainder is used for special and seasonal exhibitions. The emphasis is on dollhouses, but many antique toys are also represented. Most of the objects are Victorian.

The museum provides not only nostalgic interest but also a fascinating glimpse in miniature into social and architectural history. There is a terrace of typical Baltimore row houses in bright red brick, a milliner's store complete with minute hats, a circus tent with clowns, acrobats and performing animals, and a family house where each room is perfect in every detail from the curtain tassels to a tiny pack of playing cards on a table. The museum also sells books, toys, dollhouses and related accessories.

Downtown   See *Old Downtown*.

Dumbarton Oaks ★
1703 32nd St. NW, DC 20007 ☎ 338-8278. Map 2C-D3 ▣ ▨ for garden ✗ by arrangement. Art collection open Tues-Sun 2-5pm. Closed Mon, hols. Rare book room open Sat, Sun 2-5pm. Gardens open Apr-Oct 2-6pm ▨ Nov-Mar 2-5pm. Closed hols. Bus: Georgetown routes.
This remarkable institution is the result of the vision of Ambassador and Mrs Robert Woods Bliss, who bought the house in 1920, remodeled it to contain their art collection and created around it a deliciously romantic garden. In 1944 the name of Dumbarton Oaks flashed briefly across the news headlines of the world when its Music Room was used as the setting for the conference that gave birth to the United Nations.

The museum, now a branch of Harvard University, has two main collections: one of Byzantine art, the other of pre-Columbian art. Each is linked with a research center and library. The **pre-Columbian collection** is housed in a modern pavilion, ingeniously designed by Philip Johnson, and consisting of a cluster of eight small circular rooms. Stand and talk near the center of any of the rooms and observe the curious reverberating sound effect. There are also other works of art that are not part of the main collections — for example, El Greco's *The Visitation*, which hangs in the Music Room. The room is still used for concerts, which are open to the public.

The house also has a landscape garden department, which runs a research program and a library. Although the Dumbarton Oaks libraries are restricted to scholars, the public can view displays in the rare book room.

Don't miss the **garden** itself, built on a dramatically terraced slope and enriched by trellises, pergolas, pools, gazebos and a profusion of statuary and ornament. This undoubtedly is one of the most memorable gardens in the USA.

Executive Office Building
17th St. and Pennsylvania Ave. NW, DC 20503. Map 6F6. Closed to public. Metro: Farragut West.
This landmark lies just to the w of the White House — a vast, ornate building designed by A. B. Mullet in French Second-Empire style and completed in 1888. Its incongruity with other federal buildings bothered Washingtonians for decades, and the building narrowly escaped demolition. Now, cleaned and restored, it houses White House staff and

various government agencies. The public are not allowed inside, but they can admire the exuberance of its facades, which provides a refreshing change from the Neoclassical mode so prevalent in Washington. It is especially appealing when illuminated at night.

Federal Bureau of Investigation *(FBI)* ★
J. Edgar Hoover Building, 10th St. and Pennsylvania Ave. NW, DC 20535 ☎ 324-3447. Map 6F7 ▣ ✠ Ⴗ compulsory, every 15-20mins. Open Mon-Fri 9am-4.15pm. Closed Sat, Sun, hols. Metro: Federal Triangle.

Since 1975 the national crime-fighting force of the USA has occupied a forbidding, buff-colored concrete building named after the formidable J. Edgar Hoover, who became head of the FBI in 1924 and ran it with an iron hand until he retired in 1972 at the age of 77. When the building was opened, a Washington Post writer remarked that it "would make a perfect stage set for a dramatization of George Orwell's *1984.*"

Despite its austere building, the FBI does an excellent job in projecting to visitors its image of "Fidelity, Bravery, Integrity." Friendly, uniformed young guides usher you through a startling series of exhibits, such as an arsenal of criminal weapons, a rogues' gallery of famous villains, including Al Capone and John Dillinger, and a current list of the ten most wanted fugitives with their photographs (one visitor recognized his next-door neighbor). Some frightening statistics are given: a murder in the USA every 23mins, a rape every 6mins, a burglary every 8 seconds. The reassurance offered is that wherever you are in the country an FBI agent can be on the spot within an hour.

The bureau deals with a variety of offenses including interstate flight, espionage, obscene telephone calls and certain types of fraud. It will also help local police forces investigate such crimes as kidnapping, rape and murder. Its resources for this include highly sophisticated laboratories (seen on the tour) where anything from blood to paint samples can be analyzed.

The tour ends in the firing range, with an impressive display of sharp-shooting by an FBI agent. The FBI tour is one of the most popular in the city, and no doubt helps to recruit many future agents.

Folger Shakespeare Library
201 E Capitol St. SE, DC 20003 ☎ 544-7077 (library), 546-4000 (theater box office). Map 8G10 ▣ Ⴗ Open mid-Apr to Labor Day 10am-4pm. Rest of year closed Sun. Closed hols. Metro: Capitol South.

Like so many other great American institutions of learning and culture, this one is the creation of a businessman with a dream: the late Henry Clay Folger, oil tycoon and Shakespearean scholar.

Its vast library of Shakespearean and Renaissance works is open to scholars only, but there is an **exhibition gallery** in the style of an Elizabethan great hall where many of Folger's treasures are displayed in rotation — books, manuscripts, portraits and relics.

There is also a **theater**, beautifully built in the manner of a playhouse of Shakespeare's time, where a resident company performs plays by the Bard as well as some contemporary dramatists. The library is also a center for poetry readings, concerts and lectures, and houses a shop which sells everything from busts of Shakespeare to books on the Renaissance. Note the simple elegance of the 1930s exterior, with its series of reliefs of scenes from the plays.

Ford's Theatre ★
511 10th St. NW, DC 20004 ☎ 426-6924. Map 6F7 ▣ ⚐ ♣ Museum open 9am-5pm. Closed Christmas and during rehearsals and performances, Sept-June. Metro: Gallery Place, Metro Center.

This is the place where President Abraham Lincoln was assassinated on the night of April 14, 1865 while he sat watching the comedy, *Our American Cousin*. As the house exploded into laughter at the words "sockdologizing old mantrap," another explosion was heard from the box to the right of the stage, where Lincoln sat. John Wilkes Booth, noted actor and Confederate fanatic, had entered the box and shot Lincoln in the head. Booth jumped from the box, breaking a leg, and left through a back door, escaping on horseback. Some days later the cavalry caught up with him, and he was shot while attempting to resist arrest.

The attractive theater is now owned by the National Park Service. Restored in the 1960s to its original appearance, it once again functions as a theater as well as a museum. During the day visitors can view the auditorium and the fateful box and hear a short lecture on the assassination. In the basement are two exhibitions. One, focusing on Lincoln's life and career, has memorabilia, documents and a taped commentary. The other, relating to Booth and the other conspirators, includes the murder weapon, a small Derringer pistol. (See also *Petersen House*.)

Fort Leslie J. McNair
4th and P St. SW, DC 20319 ☎ 693-8214. Map 7J8. Not open to public.

Founded in 1791, this is the oldest functioning military post in America. It now houses the prestigious National War College, the Industrial College of the Armed Forces, the Inter-American Defense College and the headquarters of the US Army Military District of Washington. On a peninsula between the Washington Channel and the Anacostia River, it contains some impressive buildings, notably the War College — a somewhat forbidding red-brick structure with a vast portico, incongruously overlooking a little golf course for military personnel. Although the public cannot enter the buildings, the fort is worth a quick drive around if you happen to be in the area.

Franciscan Monastery
1400 Quincy St. NE, DC 20017 ☎ 526-6800 ▣ ⚐ Church and gardens open 8.30am-5pm. Tours 9am-4pm approx. every 45mins. Metrorail to Brookland station; Metrobus to monastery gates.

Also referred to as Mount St Sepulcher or the "Holy Land of America," this place has more than a touch of Hollywood kitsch about it — which is not to denigrate the spirit of reverence in which it is visited by Catholics and non-Catholics alike. The monastery's Byzantine-style **church**, consecrated in 1899, contains reproductions and impressions of a number

of Holy Land shrines and sacred places, such as the Holy
Sepulcher, the Stone of Anointing, the Grotto of the
Annunciation and the Grotto of the Nativity. Visitors can also
walk through a small-scale version of the Roman Catacombs.
Outside in the attractive grounds are more re-creations of
shrines: the Grotto of Gethsemane, the Tomb of the Blessed
Virgin and the Grotto of Lourdes.

Frederick Douglass House *(Cedar Hill)*
*1411 W St. SE, DC 20020 ☎ 426-5960 (house), 426-5961
(group tour reservations). Map 8J11 ⊡ ✗ Open Apr-Labor
Day 9am-5pm; rest of year 9am-4pm. Closed Christmas,
New Year's Day. Tourmobile.*

Frederick Douglass (1817-95) was the leading spokesman for
American blacks in their struggle for freedom and justice
during the 19thC. He lectured and wrote books about his own
early life under slavery, campaigned tirelessly for abolition,
helped recruit blacks for the Union army during the Civil War
and finally settled down to a distinguished old age in
Washington. He lived first in A St. (see *National Museum of
African Art*), then bought Cedar Hill, this elegant white
house on a height overlooking the Anacostia River. All the
furnishings, except for curtains and wallpaper, are original.
Douglass' library and other belongings are still *in situ*, and
the whole house is redolent of the spirit of a very remarkable
man. On arrival you are directed to the **Visitors' Center** at
the foot of the hill where a film is shown about Douglass' life,
and books about black liberation, including Douglass' own,
are on sale.

Freer Gallery of Art
*1200 Jefferson Dr. SW, DC 20560 ☎ 357-2104. Map 6G7 ⊡
✗ Open 10am-5.30pm. Closed Christmas. Metro:
Smithsonian.*

Closed for renovation until 1992, a new exhibition gallery will
then connect with the adjacent *Arthur M. Sackler Gallery*.
The two museums share a mission to promote awareness of
Asian art. This one was founded by the refined railroad-car
manufacturer, Charles Lang Freer, who in 1906 donated his
collection to the nation. The building, opened in 1923, is a
low, gray structure in the style of a Florentine palace,
surrounding a tranquil little courtyard.

Georgetown
Map 2C, D&E2-4.

Georgetown is one of those urban villages, like Montmartre in
Paris, that are almost as famous as the cities they belong to;
and in fact Georgetown predates Washington. It was founded
in 1751 and named after George II of England. In common
with its Paris counterpart, it is elegant and gracious in parts,
while fraying to brash commercialism in others.

  The best way to approach Georgetown is over the P St.
Bridge into the prettiest part of the district, an area of
tree-lined, brick-paved streets with rows of neat houses that
have more than an echo of Georgian London. Solidly
residential, save for the occasional recherché little shop, these
hushed streets seem to wait perpetually for the twilight hour
when congressmen, lawyers, heiresses and ex-ambassadors
gather in softly lit rooms to take pre-dinner cocktails and talk
the gossip of power. No. 1607 28th St. was once the home of

Senator Edward Kennedy. His brother John lived at 3307 N St., farther up to the W, before he became President.

Walk uphill to the N and you will pass many large, gracious mansions. Most of these are private homes, but an exception is **Dumbarton House** (*2715 Q St.* ☎ *337-2288* 🔲 *but donations welcomed; open Mon-Sat 9am-12.30pm; closed Aug, Christmas-New Year, Sun, hols*), not to be confused with nearby *Dumbarton Oaks*. A fine early Federal house of about 1799, it is now headquarters of the Colonial Dames of America, who preserve it as a museum with 18th and 19thC furnishings, domestic objects and memorabilia.

Farther uphill, with its entrance in R St., is **Oak Hill Cemetery**, a serene place with a romantic atmosphere reminiscent of Père Lachaise in Paris. Next to the cemetery is the quiet oasis of **Montrose Park**, on the W side of which is Lover's Lane, leading down to the even more secluded **Dumbarton Oaks Park**. Dumbarton Oaks estate, with its museum and glorious gardens, is immediately to the W of Montrose Park.

Her imagination in those early days fastened itself on certain of these Georgetown dwellings. As the first dying leaves of October swirled on the rusty brick sidewalks and streets and the lamplights flickered in the dusk, she walked down the hill from Rock Creek Park toward her own apartment, admiring those mansions and quaint old town-houses and the clapboards with coach lamps and gabled roofs and dormers and brightly colored doors which to her seemed touched, ever so fragilely, with age and influence.

Willie Morris, *The Last of the Southern Girls*

In the opposite direction is the southern part of Georgetown and the environs of the *Chesapeake and Ohio Canal*. One of the most interesting historical buildings in this area is **Old Stone House** (*3051 M St. NW* ☎ *426-6851* 🔲 *𝕶 open Wed-Sun 9.30am-5pm; closed some major hols*). Now supervised by the National Park Service, it is believed to be the only surviving pre-Revolutionary building in DC. Once a cabinetmaker's home and workshop, it has five rooms furnished in typical 18thC manner and a spacious garden at the back. The guided tours are given by docents (trained guides) in period costume.

On leaving this cozy haven you enter the commercialized environs of M St., a thoroughfare which, together with the intersecting Wisconsin Ave., represents the bustling, pleasure-seeking side of Georgetown. These streets are lined with boutiques, bars, discos, cafés and restaurants with French names. At 3222 M St., backing onto the canal, is **Georgetown Park**, which is not a park but a multilevel modern development with shops and restaurants surrounding a central skylit atrium. Its prolonged construction, involving the demolition of several elderly buildings, aroused much controversy, but there is no denying that it is a stylish and lively place.

W of Wisconsin Ave. are more quiet, residential streets, and on the western fringe of the district is the Jesuit-run **Georgetown University**, the oldest Catholic university in the USA and a prestigious place of learning. The main building, **Healy**, with its soaring Victorian Gothic spires, is one of the landmarks of western Washington.

Hillwood ★

4155 Linnean Ave. NW, DC 20008 ☎ 686-0410 📷 *📶*
✗ compulsory ▣ ➤ ◁ Tours at 9am, 10.30am, noon,
1.30pm (reservations required). Closed Tues, Sun, hols.
Children under 12 not admitted. Metro: Van Ness, then
walk one mile (1.6km).

Hillwood is a dazzling museum that was once the home of a
dazzling woman. Marjorie Merriweather Post's life was the
stuff of which Hollywood films are made. Daughter of Charles
William Post, founder of the Postum Cereal Company, she
inherited a fortune, beauty and a taste for high living and
high art. One of her four husbands, Joseph E. Davies, was
Ambassador to the Soviet Union from 1937 to 1938. During
their stay in Moscow she started to buy Russian *objets d'art*
and thus laid the foundation for her great collection, which
focused mainly on the art of Imperial Russia and that of 18thC
France. She acquired Hillwood in 1955 and enlarged it so that
her collection could be installed there. After her death in 1973
the house became a museum, as she had intended.

Tours of the house, lasting about 2hrs, are limited to 25
people at a time, and there is often a waiting list, so reserve
well in advance. The tour begins at the Visitors' Center, where
a film is shown about the collection and its creator, then
proceeds through the house itself. The rooms on show
include the **Pavillon** where Marjorie Post used to hold square
dances and show movies to her dinner guests; the **French
Drawing Room**, in Louis XVI style, with Beauvais tapestries,
a chair from the household of Marie Antoinette and a
charming portrait of the Empress Eugénie by Winterhalter; the
Porcelain Room, containing dinner services used by
Catherine the Great; and the **Icon Room**, which has a
staggering display of icons, chalices, Fabergé jeweled Easter
eggs and other treasures. The more domestic rooms are still
redolent of the privileged life that was lived here. The
collection contains a number of portraits of Marjorie Post
herself, a striking woman even in old age.

The museum has three annexes in the grounds. One is a
copy of a Russian dacha containing more Russian works of
art. The second houses the paintings, sculptures and
furnishings collected at the turn of the century by C. W. Post.
The third, added in 1983, contains American Indian artifacts
formerly exhibited by Marjorie Post at Topridge, her camp in
the Adirondacks. There is also a gift shop and a greenhouse
where plants can be bought.

The 25 acres (10ha) of beautifully landscaped grounds are a
delight. There is a French formal parterre, a rose garden, a
Japanese garden, a pet cemetery and many meandering paths
and secluded corners. The gardens alone can be seen for a
reduced fee (*open 11am-3pm; closed Tues, Sun, hols*).

Hirshhorn Museum and Sculpture Garden ★

Independence Ave. and 8th St. SW, DC 20560 ☎ 357-2700.
Map 7G8 📷 *📶 with flash and tripod ✗ ▣ summer only.*
Open 10am-5.30pm; extended summer hours announced
annually. Tours of permanent collection Mon-Sat 10.30am,
noon and 1.30pm, Sun 12.30, 1.30, 2.30 and 3.30pm.
Closed Christmas. Metro: L'Enfant Plaza.

There are few more exciting places in the world than this in
which to look at modern art. The collection, one of the largest
ever assembled by a private individual, was a gift to the US

Government from the late Joseph Hirshhorn, a Latvian immigrant who made a fortune in uranium. A ravenous and independent-minded collector, he ignored fashion and stuck to gut reaction as his criterion. The result is a collection of rare breadth and impact.

The building housing the collection, opened to the public in 1974 under the umbrella of the Smithsonian Institution, is a daring piece of work: a great concrete drum on four massive legs. Some said it spoiled the *Mall*, but as the Smithsonian's Secretary S. Dillon Ripley said, "If it were not controversial in almost every way it would hardly qualify as a place to house contemporary art. For it must somehow be symbolic of the material it is designed to encase."

A useful orientation film, 12mins in length, is shown continuously in a room on the lower level. Only about 900 out of the many thousands of works in the collection can be shown at any one time. These are displayed in the galleries on the second and third floors — paintings in the artificially-lit outer circle, sculptures in the inner circle looking onto the courtyard. The emphasis is on American and contemporary art. There are works by Milton Avery, Stuart Davis, Robert Henri, Edward Hopper, Sol Le Witt, Richard Estes, Frank Stella and Kenneth Nolan, among others. Many are by immigrant artists such as Josef Albers, Willem de Kooning and Max Weber. But European artists are not under-represented. They include Balthus, Francis Bacon, Jean Dubuffet, Georg Grosz, René Magritte and Joan Miró.

The outside of the building is windowless, save for a 70ft (21m) balcony and window commanding a superb view to the N over the Mall. On the museum's plaza are some monumental works of sculpture, including a huge, brightly colored, angular metal creation by Mark di Sivero entitled *Isis*, 42ft (13m) high and weighing 30 tons. The plaza also has an outdoor café, which is open in the summer.

Other less gigantic works of sculpture, many of them figurative bronzes, are displayed in the delightful sunken **Sculpture Garden**, opposite the museum on the other side of Jefferson Dr. This quiet oasis, with its lawns, pool and greenery, is a marvelous environment in which to contemplate such works as Rodin's *Burghers of Calais*, Matisse's series of *Backs* and a number of Henry Moore's *Reclining Figures*.

Joseph Hirshhorn's gut reactions have served us well, and this important collection continues to expand.

House of the Temple
1733 16th St. NW, DC 20009 ☎ 232-3579. Map 3D6☒
✗ compulsory. Open Mon-Fri 8am-3pm. Closed Sat, Sun, hols. Metro: Dupont Circle.
The richly symbolic world of freemasonry is powerfully exemplified in this building, headquarters of the Supreme Council of the 33rd Degree of the Scottish Rite of Freemasonry for the Southern Jurisdiction of the United States (to abbreviate an even longer title). The building was designed by the brilliant Neoclassical revivalist John Russell Pope and is based on the Mausoleum at Helicarnassus in Asia Minor, one of the Seven Wonders of the ancient world, and thus complements the **George Washington Masonic Memorial**, which is inspired by another of the Seven Wonders, the Pharos Lighthouse. Pope's building is the more

distinguished of the two (in fact he received a medal for it): a great square stone structure, surrounded by 33 Ionic columns and rising to a pyramidal roof. The imposing bronze door is approached by a long flight of steps guarded by two sphinxes representing Wisdom and Power.

The interior is equally impressive, especially the main **Temple Room**, a soaring chamber decorated with immense lavishness; the windows, for example, are glazed not with glass but with alabaster. There is a series of museum rooms containing masonic memorabilia, and a superb library of books on masonry and related subjects. More unexpected is one of the world's greatest collections of books on and by the Scottish poet (and freemason) Robert Burns.

Islamic Center
2551 Massachusetts Ave. NW, DC 20008 ☎ *332-8343. Map 2C4* ▢ ✗ *Open 10am-5pm. Closed Fri to non-Muslims. Metro: Dupont Circle.*

Amid the discreet opulence of Massachusetts Ave. with its many embassies, there stands a corner of the Middle East, marked by a slender minaret. This is the Islamic Center, comprising a mosque, library, study center and bookstore, which was built between 1949 and 1953 on the initiative of the ambassadors from leading Muslim nations. The construction was overseen by the Egyptian Ministry of Works, and the designer was an Italian expert on Islamic architecture, Mario Rossi, who himself became a Muslim late in life. Every Muslim country contributed money and objects.

In the magnificent **mosque room** itself there are carpets from Iran, tiles from Turkey, and a superb brass chandelier from Egypt. When entering the mosque, visitors must remove their shoes, and women must dress so as to expose only their hands and faces. The staff of the center are friendly and always pleased to inform visitors about their religion.

Iwo Jima Statue   See *Marine Corps War Memorial.*

Jefferson Memorial ★
Tidal Basin, W Potomac Park ☎ *426-6821. Map 6H6* ▢ *Closed Christmas. Tourmobile.*

This attractive monument was a cause célèbre at the time it was built. When in the 1930s it was decided to erect a memorial to America's third president, the site chosen was a point on the Tidal Basin directly s of the White House, forming the lower point of a cross whose other points were marked by the Lincoln Memorial, the White House and the Capitol. The architect was John Russell Pope, designer of the w wing of the *National Gallery of Art* and of the masonic *House of the Temple*. His elegant design for a shallow-domed Neoclassical rotunda immediately aroused opposition. The Commission of Fine Arts condemned both site and design, modernist architect Frank Lloyd Wright called it an "arrogant insult to the memory of Thomas Jefferson," and a group of female conservationists threatened to chain themselves to the cherry trees that stood in the way of construction. But the project had the strong support of President Roosevelt, who admired Pope's building and wanted it in exactly that spot. If a tree was in the way, he said, "we will move the tree and the lady and the chains and transplant them to some other place." And so the building went ahead, although Pope did not live to see its completion in 1943.

The monument is a delight, with its ring of Ionic columns and its airy interior dominated by Rudolph Evans' vast bronze statue of Jefferson, that Renaissance man who, among other things, was architect, statesman, inventor and botanist. Around the inner frieze are his words: "I have sworn upon the altar of God eternal hostility against every form of tyranny over the mind of man."

Works on Jefferson are available at a small bookstall in the basement, along with postcards and memorabilia. On summer evenings, regular military band concerts are given on the steps of the monument. It is a most serene place.

Kenilworth Aquatic Garden

Kenilworth Ave. and Douglass St. NE, DC 20019
☎ *426-6905* ✆ *Open 7am-sunset. Metro: Deanwood.*
Located on the edge of the Anacostia River opposite the National Arboretum, this remarkable nature reserve consists of a series of ponds divided by paths. Water lilies, water hyacinths, lotuses and a variety of other aquatic and waterside plants grow here in abundance, producing glorious blooms in summer. Best go in the early morning, as many of the tropical flowers close during the day. The wildlife includes fish, turtles, frogs, muskrats, opossums and racoons.

Kennedy Center for the Performing Arts

New Hampshire Ave. and Rock Creek Parkway, DC 20566
☎ *254-3600, restaurants* ☎ *833-8870. Map 5F4* ✆ ▨ *for performances* ✗ *start from Motor Lobby A (one floor down) daily 10am-1pm* ▣ ═ ▱ *Open 10am-11pm. Box office open Mon-Sat 10am-9pm, Sun, hols noon-9pm. Metro: Foggy Bottom.*
The most surprising thing about this great cultural complex overlooking the Potomac is that it was not built many years earlier. Until it was opened in 1971, Washington had no major center for the performing arts and was regarded as something of a backwater when it came to music, opera and drama — an extraordinary state of affairs for a great world capital. To remedy the situation, a scheme for a national cultural center was initiated under Eisenhower in 1958 and received active support from John F. Kennedy. But, initially lacking congressional funding, the project progressed painfully slowly, until Kennedy's assassination in 1963 and the decision to turn the center into a memorial to him finally spurred Congress into voting the money to finish it.

The building was designed by the prominent architect Edward Durrell Stone and built on a grand scale. Two vast transverse halls connect with an even vaster **Grand Foyer** opening onto the river terrace and with access to the three main auditoriums: the **Eisenhower Theater**, the **Opera House** and the **Concert Hall**. The **American Film Institute Theater** is on the ground floor, and the top floor has a 500-seat auditorium called the **Terrace Theater** and a library of the performing arts.

Two companies, the National Symphony Orchestra and the Washington Opera, are based here. But the center is also host to many great companies and orchestras from other parts of the country and abroad. Materials, decorations and fittings were donated by various countries: marble for the walls from

Italy, chandeliers from Sweden and Austria, mirrors from
Belgium, curtains from Japan, tapestries from France. The
overall design of the building is a huge rectangle in plain
white marble, surrounded on all sides by an immensely broad
colonnade of slender metal pillars. It has the austere
monumentality of a design by Albert Speer, but with a
lightness of touch that saves it from being forbidding. From
the roof terrace, there is a stunning view over the city and
across the Potomac.

Some still scoff at the center and its design. Its furnishings
and decorations undoubtedly do have a touch of
department-store gaudiness; and the great rough-cast bronze
head of Kennedy that dominates the Grand Foyer is not to
everyone's taste. But these are minor quibbles. The Kennedy
Center is a triumph, not least in the way that it has brought
Washington into the major league of world cities in the fields
of music, opera and drama.

Lady Bird Johnson Park and Lyndon Baines Johnson Memorial Grove

George Washington Memorial Parkway. Map 4&5G,H,I 3-5
☒ ⬥ *Open 8am-sunset.*
Sited on a long, narrow island running parallel to the shore of
the Potomac near Arlington Cemetery, this park was
dedicated to Mrs Johnson, a lover of the countryside, in 1968.
Despite the noisy George Washington Memorial Parkway that
runs through the island, this is a refreshing place which
blazes every year with daffodils and flowering dogwood.

At the southern end of the park is a memorial grove named
after Lyndon Baines Johnson. In the center is a monument to
LBJ in the form of a pink granite monolith, large and
rough-hewn like the man himself.

Lafayette Square

Map 3F6. Metro: McPherson Square, Farragut West.
With the White House on its southern side, this square or
park is one of the focal points of Washington. The equestrian
statue in the center of the park is not of Lafayette but of
Andrew Jackson, hero of the War of 1812 and later the first
"log-cabin" president. Lafayette himself is portrayed in one of
four statues, at the corners of the square, of foreigners who
fought in the American Revolution. The others are Comte de
Rochambeau, another Frenchman; Baron von Steuben, a
Prussian; and Koscinszko, a Pole. The park is a pleasant, leafy
oasis in the busy heart of the city where office workers picnic
and chess games are played.

The square was once the center of high social life in
Washington, but is no longer residential, and only its western
side retains its facade more or less intact, thanks to President
Kennedy who prevented its demolition. The *Decatur House*,
at the NW corner, is open to the public. Its architect, Benjamin
Latrobe, also designed **St John's Episcopal Church** on the N
side, which was completed in 1816 and is known as the
"Church of the Presidents." Pew 54 has been reserved for
worshipers from the White House since President Madison
started the tradition. With its crisp, Classical design, delicate
wooden bell tower and serene white interior, St John's is one
of the most pleasing churches in the city.

Another building worth noticing, although not open to the
public, is **Dolley Madison House** at the corner of Madison

Pl. and H St. The widow of the President lived here from 1837 to 1849, a tireless socialite to the last.

Library of Congress ★
10 1st St., DC 20540 ☎ 287-5000. Map 8G10 ⬚ 🌜 ➡ in Madison Building. Open (main reading room) Mon-Tues, Thurs-Sat 9am-5.30pm, Wed 9am-9pm; (exhibit halls) Mon-Fri 8.30am-9.30pm, Sat 8.30am-5pm, Sun 1-5pm (Madison). Closed Sun (Jefferson), Christmas, New Year's Day. Tours Mon-Fri 9am-4pm every hr on the hr. Metro: Capitol South.

This wonderfully frothy building stands just to the E of the US Capitol. A foretaste of the building itself is the superb **Fountain of the Court of Neptune**, which faces onto 1st St. below the entrance and is reminiscent of the Trevi Fountain in Rome. But the fountain is overshadowed by the amazing **foyer**, a huge hall with a great double marble staircase lit by a stained-glass skylight high above. There is a profusion of stone cherubs, garlands of fruit, bronze figures holding torches, balustrades, Corinthian columns, a floor inlaid with the signs of the zodiac, and acres of beautifully painted frescoes. The richness is breathtaking. But a closer examination of the frescoes will reveal that one series shows the colophons of the great printers of the past, and at the back of the hall a pair of glass display cases contain a Gutenberg Bible and a contemporary handwritten Mainz Bible. This is indeed a library, probably the greatest library in the world, and, more than that, one of the most civilized institutions of learning ever created.

They crossed the green park to the new Library of Congress recently opened, glittering with mosaic, gorgeous with Pompeian red...hour after hour passed, and still they had not seen it all, the endless corridors, the wide, shallow-stepped staircases leading on and on to new wonders.

Frances Parkinson Keyes, *Queen Anne's Lace*

The library was built when the collection of books became too large for the Capitol. It was designed by two mid-European architects, Smithmeyer and Pelz, who produced a richly eclectic mixture of styles. Much of the credit for the success of the main building, the **Thomas Jefferson**, goes to the army engineers who completed the job, which they did with military thoroughness. One officer, for example, was appointed to co-ordinate the color scheme, and the result is certainly pleasing. The building was finished in 1897, 24yrs after the plans were originally chosen.

Even more impressive than the foyer is the **main reading room** with its great soaring dome. The cupola is painted with a fresco of figures representing the nations and cultures that have most advanced the cause of learning. The figure for Germany is a portrait of General Casey, the engineer who supervised the construction of the building (and also, incidentally, that of the *Washington Monument*).

The conducted tour starts with an introductory slide-and-sound presentation and takes in the most imposing parts of the building. Some of the less prominent areas are also worth seeing: for example, the **Hispanic Division** with its striking 1940s' murals by the Brazilian artist Candido Portinari.

The Library of Congress has two more recent buildings that

were necessitated by the continued growth of its collection. The **John Adams Building** to the E, dating from the 1930s, is a complete contrast, but a fine specimen of its time, with rich Art Deco ornamentation. The **James Madison Memorial Building** to the S, completed in 1980, is the largest library building in the world, although its architecture is less memorable than that of the other two buildings. The severity of the interior is broken only by the **James Madison Memorial Hall**, which contains a statue and exhibits. In all three of the buildings, manuscripts, rare books, prints, drawings and maps are exhibited in the hallways and on the walls of many of the corridors.

The library was originally only for the Congress but has long since been open to the public. Anyone above school age pursuing serious research may use its vast facilities. It contains not only 20 million books and pamphlets and over 35 million manuscripts, but also nearly 4 million maps and atlases, 10 million prints and photographs, and copies of 1,200 different newspapers. Its **music department** has a vast number of scores and a fine collection of musical instruments. The **Motion Picture, Broadcasting and Recorded Sound Division** has, among other things, more than 250,000 reels of motion pictures, which researchers can arrange to view. An outpost of the Performing Arts Library is situated on the roof terrace of the *Kennedy Center*.

In the library's **Coolidge auditorium** and the adjacent **Whittall Pavilion**, frequent concerts, poetry readings, lectures and symposia are held. Once a month, from May to Oct, folk music and dancing groups from various traditions perform on the plaza in front of the Jefferson Building.

Lillian and Albert Small Jewish Museum

701 3rd St. NW, DC 20001 ☎ *881-0100* 🖾 ✗ *compulsory. Open Sun 11am-3pm, other days by appt. Closed Aug, Jewish hols. Metro: Judiciary Square.*

The building housing this museum is the original Adas Israel Synagogue, the first synagogue in Washington, built in the 1870s and originally at 6th and G St. NW. After the congregation moved away, the building became a Christian church, then a grocery store. Saved from demolition in the late 1960s, it was towed in a precarious condition to its present site and lovingly restored. Apart from a small permanent exhibition on the building itself, the museum mounts temporary exhibitions focusing on the life and history of Washington's Jewish community.

Lincoln Memorial ★

W end of Mall ☎ *426-6895. Map 5* 🖾 ✗ *of crypt. Open 8am-midnight. Closed Christmas. Metro: Foggy Bottom, Arlington Cemetery.*

Abraham Lincoln, 16th President of the United States and savior of the Union in the Civil War, has acquired a uniquely cherished place in the memory of the American people, and his memorial has become the most prestigious of the city's monuments. It is significant that it appears on both the penny and the $5 bill. It looks so congruous where it stands at the W end of the Mall that it is surprising to learn of the controversy surrounding its planning.

A commission to plan the monument was set up two years after Lincoln's death in 1865, but it was many years before any agreement was reached on the design or position of the memorial. At that time the present site was an unattractive marsh at the edge of the Potomac, and Joseph ("Uncle Joe") Cannon, Speaker of the House of Representatives, declared that he would "never let a monument to Abraham Lincoln be erected in that God-damned swamp." But the swamp was drained and became a worthy setting for the design by Henry Bacon that was finally chosen, a Parthenon-like structure surrounded by 36 Doric columns representing the 36 states that existed at the time of Lincoln's death. The design employs the same sleight-of-hand technique used by the ancient Greeks, whereby the walls and columns tilt slightly inward, the rows of columns bend outward and each one bulges a little around the waist. Without these tricks, the building would appear top-heavy and the rows of columns concave. The monument was completed in 1922.

Dramatically mirrored in the reflecting pool, it now forms a key element in the superb parkscape of the *Mall*. The seated statue of Lincoln inside, 19ft (6m) high, was carved out of white marble by Daniel Chester French, who has captured powerfully the massive yet accessible personality of the man. On the wall to the left is the Gettysburg Address, to the right is Lincoln's Second Inaugural Address, while behind the statue are the words: "In this temple as in the hearts of the people for whom he saved the Union the memory of Abraham Lincoln is enshrined forever."

The word "temple" is significant, for that is what this monument is. There was a time when visitors had to wear ties and speak in whispers in the presence of the statue. Now the atmosphere is less formal, but the mystique of the place is as powerful as ever. An intriguing sidelight is revealed while standing between the third and fourth column to the left of the statue. The hair on the back of Lincoln's head appears to form the profile of Robert E. Lee, commanding general of the rebel army of the Confederacy.

At certain times of the year there are conducted tours of the **crypt** below the monument, where the seepage of water from above has created curious formations of stalactites and stalagmites. Reservations can be made in advance by telephone, but these tours are so popular that there is often a waiting list of two months or more.

Malcolm X Park See *Meridian Hill Park*.

The Mall ★
Maps 6&7G. Metro: Smithsonian.
The Mall today is one of the finest town parkscapes in the world, but the effect was achieved with much toil and over a period of many years. Pierre L'Enfant saw its possibilities when he planned it in 1791, but the Mall remained more or less a visual mess until the early 1900s when Senator James McMillan, chairman of the Senate District Committee, launched a plan to landscape the Mall in a way that incorporated many of L'Enfant's original proposals. Even then it took a long time to evolve to its present state.

Gradually the clutter disappeared. A railroad was removed, a canal along the N side was filled in (although a former lock-keeper's cottage still remains) and a number of unsightly shacks were demolished. The *Washington Monument* was finished in 1888, the *Lincoln Memorial* and the reflecting pool were added in the 1920s and the *Jefferson Memorial* in 1943. In the 1960s and 1970s further improvements were made. The ugly temporary office buildings from the two world wars were removed, as well as the parking lots. In their place walkways and lawns were added. In 1976 **Constitution Gardens** were opened, with a lake and 50 acres (20ha) of tree-shaded parkland. The gardens contain a memorial to the veterans of the Vietnam War.

Today the Mall forms a splendid, green triumphal way extending for some 2 miles (3.5km) from the *Capitol* in the E past the great buildings of the Smithsonian on either side, past the Washington Monument and on down to the Lincoln Memorial and the Watergate Steps by the Potomac. The W end of the Mall is known as **West Potomac Park**. There are playing fields here, where you can watch polo, rugby, soccer and other sports (see *Sports and activities*).

One of the most beautiful features of the Mall is the **Tidal Basin**, overlooked by the Jefferson Memorial and surrounded by cherry trees given to Washington by Japan in 1912, which make a dazzling array when in blossom. The occasion is celebrated by the Cherry Blossom Festival. Another splash of color is provided by the "floral libraries" to the E of the Tidal Basin, a series of flowerbeds planted with a variety of species. The Mall is the scene of many other public events besides: Washington's birthday celebration, the Festival of American Folk Life, concerts and theatrical performances (see *Calendar of events* in *Planning and walks*).

The Mall is much more than just a park: it is an arena, a forum, an outdoor room of vast proportions. To obtain the most dramatic vantage point, stand on the steps of the Lincoln Memorial and look past the Washington Monument toward the Capitol. Here the spirit of L'Enfant's vision is triumphantly realized.

Marine Corps War Memorial
Fort Myer Dr., Arlington, Va. Map 4G2 🗺 ➡ *Metro: Rosslyn, Arlington Cemetery.*

In a commanding position just N of Arlington National Cemetery, this striking sculpture honors the men of the US Marine Corps who have died for their country since 1775. It illustrates one of the most glorious moments in the history of the Marines: the capture of the Pacific island of Iwo Jima from the Japanese in 1945. The work is based on the famous photograph by Joe Rosenthal showing six men raising the US flag on the island. It was designed by Horace W. Peaslee and sculpted by Felix de Weldon, who took nine years to complete the job. Four times life-size, it is the largest sculpture ever cast in bronze. (There is a performance by the Marine Drum and Bugle Corps and Silent Drill Platoon mid-May to Labor Day every Tues at 7.30pm.)

A stone's throw to the S of the monument is the **Netherlands Carillon**, a tower with 49 bells presented to the US by the Netherlands in thanks for American aid in World War II. Free concerts are given there Apr-Sept Sat, hols (☎ *426-6700 for details*).

Meridian Hill Park
16th and Euclid St. NW, DC. Map 3B-C6.

About 1½ miles (2.5km) up 16th St. from the White House is an area that might have been one of the most fashionable in the city. That was the hope of a rich senator's widow named Mrs John B. Henderson who lived here in a now demolished mansion in the early part of this century. Her dream was not realized, but the 12-acre (5ha) park built by the Government as a result of her agitation still remains. It is part French, part Italian in character, with a water cascade, a pond, terraces with balustrades, formal promenades and statues of Dante, Joan of Arc and President James Buchanan.

The park has become somewhat faded and melancholy, and in recent years it has been a haunt of vagabonds and drug addicts. But there are hopes that it will regain its former charm and beauty. The DC Government has tried, with limited success, to rename it Malcolm X Park, but the old name is more appropriately romantic.

Mormon Temple

9900 Stoneybrook Dr., Kensington, Md. 20795 ☎ *587-0144* ◻ ➤ *Temple closed to non-Mormons. Visitors' Center open 10am-9.30pm.*

Approached along the Capital Beltway, this building gives a first impression of a science-fiction illustrator's creation: a soaring white edifice with six needle-sharp spires made of a gold and steel alloy, one of them surmounted by an 18ft-high (5.5m) figure of the Angel Moroni covered in gold leaf. In the sunlight, spires and angel gleam dazzlingly. The temple, completed in 1971, is built of Alabama marble. Even the windows are marble planed to a thickness of ⅝in (16mm), so that they are translucent. Around the building, 57 acres (23ha) of grounds have won awards for their landscaping.

In the Mormon faith, or the Church of Jesus Christ of Latter-Day Saints, a temple, as distinct from a church, exists for marriage (for eternity) and for the baptism of ancestors by proxy. Only Mormons in good standing may enter the temple. Others, however, are given a cordial welcome at the **Visitors' Center**, where they are given a short talk on Mormon beliefs, then shown a series of dramatic life-size tableaux featuring the prophets Isaiah and Mormon, Christ and his Disciples, and Joseph Smith, the founder of the Church. Then, in a film, Mormons in different walks of life explain their beliefs.

National Air and Space Museum ★

6 Independence Ave. SW, DC 20560 ☎ *357-2700. Map 7G8* ◻ ▣ *for Langley Theater and Planetarium* ☀ *except with special permission* ✗ *free highlight tours and for groups by arrangement* ▣ ✳ ➤ *Open 10am-5.30pm, extended summer hrs announced annually. Closed Christmas. Metro: L'Enfant Plaza.*

It would be hard to imagine a more compelling testament to man's age-old dream of flight than this dazzling museum with its unique array of flying machines, spacecraft and exhibits relating to all aspects of air and space travel and technology. The museum is housed in a crisp white building on the Mall, opened in 1976, with 23 galleries, each devoted to a single subject or theme. All the aircraft are genuine, and most of the spacecraft, although occasionally a replica has been used where the craft was not brought back to earth.

From the Mall side, the first gallery is **Milestones of Flight**, containing such epoch-making craft as the Wright brothers' 1903 Flyer, Lindbergh's *Spirit of St Louis* and the Apollo 11 Command Module, all of which look impossibly fragile to have survived their legendary journeys. Room has recently been made for the Voyager, the lightweight plane that flew around the globe in 1986 without refueling. Galleries to the w contain other historic airplanes of various periods: gliders, passenger airliners, cargo carriers and helicopters. Turn left from the Mall entrance into the **Space Hall**, with examples of space boosters, guided missiles and manned spacecraft. Exhibits here include the Skylab Orbital workshop, America's first space station, which visitors can walk through. Other displays on this floor include **Looking at Earth, Flight Testing, Stars** and **Lunar Exploration Vehicles**. Also on the ground floor is the **Langley Theater**, which shows four aviation- and space-related films daily. The films were produced using a large-format projection system and are shown on a screen the height of a five-story building. So convincing is the illusion of reality in such films as *To Fly* that you will literally want to hold on to your seat as you hurtle over a clifftop or swoop just above the surface of a river as it plunges into a waterfall. The Langley Theater is also used for free evening lectures.

Also well worth the small entrance charge is the **Albert Einstein Planetarium** on the second floor, one of the most advanced planetariums in the world, which creates startling images of the sun, moon, planets and stars by the use of a Zeiss model VI projector. After visiting the Planetarium, you can continue your imaginary space journey by going to the **Exploring the Planets** gallery, where the moving surface of Mars is visible through a porthole. If you want to go back to the early days of flight, visit the **Balloons and Airships** gallery, where the exhibits include the original Zeppelin, a model of the ill-fated Hindenburg and a model of the Montgolfier balloon. The third floor of the building houses a library, offices and a restaurant. Two new restaurants have been added in a glass annex E of the main structure.

If, having seen the museum, you are still eager to see more aircraft and spacecraft, take a trip out to the **Paul E. Garber Facility** (*3904 Old Silver Hill Rd., Suitland, Md.* ☎ *357-1400* 🏧 *К̶ Mon-Fri 10am, Sat, Sun 10am, 1pm, reservations must be made 2wks in advance*). The facility is the storage, restoration and preservation center of the museum, where you can see 90 aircraft as well as many spacecraft, engines, propellers and other flight-related objects. Take a look also at the restoration workshop. Note, however, that this is a "no-frills" museum with no heating or air conditioning — it is strictly for the keenest air-and-space buffs.

National Aquarium

Department of Commerce Building, 14th St. and Constitution Ave., DC 20230 ☎ *337-2826. Map 6F6-7* 🏧 🖵 *Open 9am-5pm. Closed Christmas. Shark feedings: Mon, Wed, Sat 2pm; piranha feedings: Tues, Thurs, Sun 2pm. Metro: Federal Triangle.*

This is a strange place in which to find an aquarium: tucked away in the basement of the Department of Commerce, one of the sober government buildings in the Federal Triangle. It is in fact the oldest aquarium in the country, dating from 1873, though it has only been at its present location since 1932. Originally run by the US Fish and Wildlife Service, it is now operated by a private nonprofit group, the National Aquarium Society.

It has about 1,000 specimens representing 225 different species, half freshwater and half saltwater. There is plenty to marvel at: the archer fish (*Toxotes jaculator*), for instance, which shoots small jets of water to dislodge insects from overhanging vegetation, or the blue damselfish, a tiny, darting sapphire, as well as turtles, sharks, horseshoe crabs, eels and many other creatures of the deep. There are also recordings of the sounds made by marine animals.

On your way out stop in the lobby to catch a glimpse of a typical Federal Triangle interior with its Neoclassical expanse of marble. And observe the meter that continually records the growth of the US population — every 16 seconds it clocks up another American.

National Arboretum
24th and R St. NE, DC 20002 ☎ *475-4815, 475-4857 (tour reservations for 10 or more)* 🖭 ✗ *Open Mon-Fri 8am-5pm, Sat, Sun, hols 10am-5pm. Closed Christmas. Metrobus to Stadium-Armory Station.*

An idyllic Arcadia incongruous among the bleak surroundings of E Washington, this park boasts a herb garden, *bonsai* collection, aquatic gardens, lakes, a nature trail and over 400 acres (162ha) of hilly countryside containing many varieties of trees, shrubs, and flowering plants. The arboretum is particularly proud of its azaleas, a glorious panoply in springtime. You can drive around, and there is a designated picnic area. A visit to this park is well worth the journey to the eastern fringes of the city, but is awkward without a car.

National Archives and Records Service
Constitution Ave. and 8th St. NW, DC 20408 ☎ *523-3000. Map 7G8* 🖭 ✗ *by arrangement. Exhibition hall open Apr-Labor Day 10am-9pm, Sept-Mar 10am-5.30pm. Closed Christmas. Research rooms open Mon-Fri 9am-10pm, Sat 9am-5pm. Closed Sun, major hols. Metro: Federal Triangle.*

"We hold these Truths to be self-evident, that all Men are created equal, that they are endowed by the Creator with certain unalienable Rights, that among these are Life, Liberty and the Pursuit of Happiness...." These words, which most American schoolchildren learn by heart, are part of the Declaration of Independence of 1776, written principally by Thomas Jefferson. The Declaration of Independence, the Constitution and the Bill of Rights are known together as the Charters of Freedom, and the original documents are the most treasured possessions of the National Archives. They are displayed in a great domed, semicircular temple in which the public files reverently past a kind of altar where the charters are kept in helium-filled bronze cases that descend at night or, in states of emergency, into a bomb- and fire-proof vault. A new gallery staging temporary exhibits from the permanent collection circles around in back of the "shrine," as the guards call it, passing through the gift store. Also on display is one of 16 known copies of the Magna Carta, forerunner of the US Constitution. This one is King John's 1297 version, on indefinite loan from a prominent Texan. Facsimiles of the charters, as well as pictures, books and postcards, can be bought at the sales desk.

The Charters of Freedom are only a tiny part of the vast collection of US government records housed in the archives, from Acts of Congress to applications for federal jobs. A selection of some of the more interesting documents is displayed in the corridors of the building, but access to the main files is reserved for serious researchers. But the public can hear the Watergate tapes: portions are played Mon-Fri from 10.15am. From the Pennsylvania Ave. entrance you will be directed to the appropriate room. Don't overlook the building itself. Designed by John Russell Pope, it is an imposing Classical-style edifice approached by immense flights of steps.

National Building Museum   See *Old Pension Building.*

National Gallery of Art ★
Constitution Ave. NW, between 4th and 6th St., DC 20565 ☎ 737-4215. Map 7G8 ⬛ ✸ *for temporary exhibitions only* ✗ ⬛ *Open Mon-Sat 10am-5pm, Sun noon-9pm. Closed Christmas, New Year's Day. Metro: Archives.*

This is a relative newcomer to the major league of art galleries, yet it is now ranked among the top dozen in the world. In paintings it outstrips most other galleries in North and South America, especially in the field of European Old Masters and Impressionists. The gallery owes its existence to the financier and statesman Andrew W. Mellon, who formed the nucleus of the collection, partly by buying from the Soviet government in the 1930s when it was selling art treasures to pay for tractors and other necessities. Mellon bequeathed the collection to the nation and provided funds for the construction of the West Building. The daily running of the gallery is now funded by the Federal Government, but the acquisition of works of art is financed privately.

West Building
It is hard to believe that the massively Neoclassical West Building, designed by the indefatigable John Russell Pope (*National Archives, Jefferson Memorial, House of the Temple*) was opened as recently as 1941. Unlike the Louvre and many other great galleries, it was purpose-built as a museum. It houses works of art from the 10thC up to the mid-20thC.

Tours of the West Building start in the great rotunda, which has a fountain to Mercury in the center and is encircled by massive pillars of green Tuscan marble. The works, divided by nationality and subdivided by time period, are arranged in the following ten groups.

Florentine and Central Italian art   The range extends from the highly stylized paintings of the Byzantine period, with their deliberately stiff figures and lack of perspective, to the more naturalistic paintings of the Renaissance, when art had begun to free itself from religious constraints. The star item is the gallery's single Leonardo da Vinci, a painting of about 1474 portraying the young Florentine noblewoman Ginevra de' Benci, so accurate in its detail that even the subspecies of tree in the background is identifiable: a kind of juniper, which is a pun on the subject's name. Its acquisition in 1967 helped to make this one of the most comprehensive collections of Italian medieval and Renaissance paintings in the world. Also remarkable is the ceremonial shield with Andrea del Castagno's painting *The Youthful David* from about 1450, very rare of its kind.

Venetian and North Italian art   The lavish art in this collection reflects the prosperity of the great maritime city of

Venice in its heyday. Typical of this period is Giovanni Bellini's elaborate *Feast of the Gods*, reworked by his pupil Titian. Other Titians, such as the arresting portrait of *Doge Andrea Gritti*, fill an entire room. Giorgione's peaceful *Adoration of the Shepherds* and Jacopo Sansovino's enchanting bronze figure of *Venus Anadymone* are also noteworthy.

Italian art of the 17th-18thC Visual drama and complexity of technique were the hallmarks of the Baroque era. One of the best examples is *The Lute Player*, painted by Orazio Gentileschi in about 1610, a masterly composition of abruptly contrasting light and shadow. By the 18thC view-painting had come into vogue to satisfy the demands of travelers who took the Grand Tour of Europe. Giovanni Paolo Panini's interiors of the Pantheon and of St Peter's, Rome, are distinguished examples of this genre. There are also some Canalettos, including a typical example, *Venice, the Quay of the Piazzetta*.

Spanish art During the 15th and 16thC Spanish art was dominated by foreign immigrants such as El Greco, represented here by *Laocoön, Saint Martin and the Beggar* and a cadaverous *St Jerome*. But from the 17thC Spain produced its own great artists: Zurbarán, Murillo, Velázquez and Goya. All are included here. Note Velázquez' penetrating study for a portrait of Pope Innocent X — "All too true," said the Pontiff when he saw the finished work. Goya has a room to himself, whose highlights are his famous portrait of the beautiful *Señora Sebasa Garcia* and one of his paintings of the Duke of Wellington.

Flemish, German and Dutch art This is a particularly rich and extensive part of the collection. Here are encountered the austere, meticulous works of such early Flemish painters as Van Eyck and Rogier van der Weyden. Among the German works is a small *Crucifixion* by Matthias Grünewald, the only one of his paintings in the USA. This section also includes a great galaxy of Dutch artists of the 17thC. Among many fine Rembrandts, note particularly the *Self-Portrait* with its troubled expression, painted when the artist was 53, after his fortunes had begun to decline. Rubens is here too: see, for example, his huge and dramatic *Daniel in the Lion's Den*. So too are Van Dyck, Vermeer and other painters of the Dutch golden age. Look closely at the *Vase of Flowers* by Jan de Heem. Not only does it show an impossibility, since in nature none of the flowers depicted bloom concurrently, but it is full of symbolism: a butterfly at the top to indicate the spiritual life; moths, snails and faded flowers at the bottom to stand for worldly decay.

French art of the 17th, 18th and early 19thC The age of Louis XIII and XIV produced an art that looked toward Classical and Renaissance models for inspiration. The masters of this era include Claude Lorrain (*Landscape with Merchants* and *The Judgment of Paris*) and Nicolas Poussin, with his serene colors and geometric harmony (*Holy Family on the Steps* is a fine example). In the late 17th and early 18thC French art became more light-hearted, developing into the delicate, sensual style known as Rococo. The tone was set by Antoine Watteau whose work is here exemplified by his *Italian Comedians* and by *Ceres*, an oval panel with the four summer months of June, July, August and September symbolized astrologically by a pair of twins, a crayfish, a lion and the goddess Ceres herself representing Virgo. Paintings by Boucher (*Allegory of Painting*) and Fragonard (*A Young Girl Reading*) illustrate how this style was continued until well into the 18thC. Gradually, however, it gave way to the more severe, earnest Neoclassical style. This section ends with the great Neoclassical masters, notably Ingres (*Portrait of Madame Moitessier*) and David (*Napoleon in His Study*).

British art   Portraiture was one of the great fortes of British art in the 18thC, and this collection contains some choice examples. The two supreme masters of the "Grand Manner," Gainsborough and Reynolds, are here. So are Romney, Hoppner, Raeburn and Lawrence. There are works by both of the great early-19thC English landscape artists, Constable and Turner. Typical of Turner's genius is his *Keelmen Heaving Coals by Moonlight*, where the port of Newcastle is transformed into a glowing, dreamlike vision.

American art   Portraiture, much influenced by English models, dominated American art in the 18th and early 19thC. Benjamin West, one of the greatest American painters of this era, lived and worked in London, where he significantly influenced visiting compatriot artists. His masterly *Self-Portrait* hangs here, together with other great portraitists such as Charles Wilson Peale and Edward Savage. Pride of place, however, goes to Gilbert Stuart, unofficial "court portraitist" of the young republic. The gallery possesses 41 Stuarts, including his famous set of the first five presidents. A total contrast is the large amount of naive or primitive art by untrained 19thC painters, much of it charming and fresh.

The late 19th and early 20thC saw a notable flourishing of American art. The spirit of rural America at this time is vividly captured in the work of Winslow Homer. In his sea painting *Breezing Up* you can almost feel the wind and the spray. One of the greatest American artists of all time, James McNeill Whistler, also has many paintings here, ranging from his exquisite portrait, *L'Andalouse, Mother-of-Pearl and Silver*, to his typically hazy view of the Thames, *Chelsea Wharf, Grey and Silver*.

French art of the 19thC   Think of this period and you think automatically of the Impressionists, who are here in full force: Renoir, Cézanne, Monet, Pissarro, Seurat — a feast of liberated light and color. Note the curiously untypical Van Gogh, *Flowerbeds In Holland* (c.1883), a tranquil little scene quite unlike the feverish paintings of later years. The Post-Impressionists, such as Gauguin, are here too, as are the Symbolists: see Puvis de Chavannes' matching pair *Le Travail* and *Le Repos*. These artists pave the way for the full impact of 20thC art housed in the East Building of the gallery.

Lower-level galleries

A new set of galleries has recently opened on the lower floor. There is a print gallery devoted to rotating exhibitions from the National's rich collection of prints and graphics. Another has exhibits of Chinese porcelain and small bronzes; yet another contains French furniture. Before leaving the West Building it is also worth taking a look at the large and well-stocked shop on the ground floor, which sells books, cards and reproductions.

East Building

The East Building can be approached via an underground tunnel, which halfway along opens out into a spacious restaurant, verdant with indoor plants and with a huge window looking dramatically onto a falling wall of water. The passage continues with a moving sidewalk to the East Building. Alternatively, approaching from the outside, you will cross a plaza with a fountain and pass a great bronze sculpture by Henry Moore, *Knife Edge Mirror Two Piece.*

The East Building, designed by I. M. Pei and opened in 1978, looks like an iceberg with edges so sharp you could almost cut your fingers on them. Inside, the iceberg impression continues, as if the ice had been hollowed out to create an immense space bathed in pale light. The Central Court is dominated by a vast Alexander Calder mobile in red, blue and black, while around the courtyard are other impressive works such as Joan Miró's tapestry *Woman*; Anthony Caro's steel *Ledge Piece* looms over the entrance to the s part of the building housing the library, the Center for Advanced Study in the Visual Arts, the graphics collection and the administrative offices.

From the Central Court, there are stairs, escalators and bridges, which lead up, down and across to the various exhibition areas and provide a constantly changing spectacle of the building and its contents. Few works of art are permanently on view, and the building is primarily used for temporary exhibitions, either on loan or from the gallery's own collection. The emphasis is by no means entirely on contemporary art, and the temporary shows include work from many periods.

Free lectures (*Sun afternoons*) and film shows are held in the Auditorium, and these are often linked to exhibitions. These are among the best free events in the city. The museum will supply a program upon request.

A word of advice: do not try to see all of the National Gallery in one visit, especially if you want to include both buildings. One of the richest collections in the world, it merits two or even three visits.

National Geographic Society Explorers Hall

17th and M St. NW, DC 20036 ☎ *857-7000. Map 3E6* 🔲 ✻ *Open Mon-Sat 9am-5pm, Sun 10am-5pm. Closed Christmas. Metro: Farragut North, Dupont Circle.*

The National Geographic Society, through its monthly magazine and other publications, effectively conveys the exciting and unique character of our planet earth. It does the same here in the Explorers Hall in its headquarters. The introductory video presentation about man's earliest ancestors is followed by a tour through simulated Neanderthal and Cro-Magnon caves, emerging by a pool over which is suspended a vast globe. Nearby stands a giant basalt head from Mexico. Mementoes of exploration include the binoculars carried by Admiral Byrd on his polar flights in 1926 and 1929, under the sponsorship of the society. Other displays include a specimen of the giant Goliath frog from Cameroun, a film of underwater exploration, a working model of the solar system and many beautiful photographs of the natural and animal world.

A new interactive science center called "Geographica" incorporates an amphitheater simulating a space station, a planetarium, and touch screens chronicling undersea exploration. The displays employ computers and high-tech electronics to mount their dazzling images, which include live feeds from a weather satellite and the formation of a nearly-real tornado. Additional exhibits are planned.

Related temporary exhibitions are also held here, and there is a stall selling the society's publications. This is a great place to take children, and an eye-opener for adults too.

National Museum of African Art
950 Independence Ave. SW, DC 20560 ☎ *357-2700. Map 6G7* ▣ ⚹ *for certain exhibitions* 𝕂 ✱ *Open 10am-5pm. Metro: Smithsonian.*

Finding its old premises on Capitol Hill too cramped, this museum has moved to largely underground quarters in the new Quadrangle complex behind the Smithsonian Castle. The only museum in the USA devoted to the visual arts of sub-Saharan Africa, it has a collection of about 6,000 objects ranging from Benin bronze figures to vibrant woven textiles. Apart from a small number of objects on permanent display, the museum is devoted to temporary exhibitions, either of a thematic nature or dealing with particular regions or ethnic groups. The entrance to the museum is a striking pavilion with six shallow domes.

National Museum of American Art
8th and G St. NW, DC 20560 ☎ *357-2700. Map 7F8* ▣ 𝕂 ▱ *Open 10am-5.30pm. Closed Christmas. Metro: Gallery Place.*

There are some 32,000 works in this collection, illustrating the development of American painting, sculpture and graphic art from the 18thC to the present day. A large and representative selection is on permanent display, and temporary exhibitions are also held. The museum is strong on the 19th and early 20thC. Take a look at the works by Winslow Homer: limpid paintings bathed in a golden glow of fresh innocence that characterized the American world view during his creative life. Albert Bierstadt, though originally German, is American in another way, poignantly evoking the wild expanses of the West. Less typical are the works of Albert P. Ryder: eerie, dream-like scenes reminiscent of the French Symbolists.

Other great names of the period in this collection include George Catlin, Elihu Vedder, Thomas Moran, Frederic Church, Thomas Cole, James Whistler, Mary Cassatt and the sculptor Hiram Powers. The modern period is also well represented by such artists as Franz Kline, Willem de Kooning, Robert Rauschenberg, Stuart Davis and Edward Hopper. Particularly striking is James Hampton's visionary creation, *The Throne of the Third Heaven of the Nations' Millennium General Assembly*, consisting of 177 objects sheathed in glittering aluminum and gold foil (seen in the first-floor lobby).

The museum shop on the first floor sells books, catalogs, posters and reproductions. The museum organizes periodic concerts, symposia, lectures and other public programs.

The building, which it shares with the *National Portrait Gallery*, is the Old Patent Office, a massive 19thC Greek revival structure. The two museums share a fine library and a good cafeteria, which in summer spills out onto the attractive inner courtyard. A branch of the museum is the smaller *Renwick Gallery* near the White House. It also administers the **Barney Studio House**, built in 1902 on Sheridan Circle as artist Alice Pike Barney's home, studio and salon (*open for guided tours by appt* ☎ *357-3111*). See also *Walk 2* in *Planning and walks*.

77

National Museum of American History

Constitution Ave. and 13th St. NW, DC 20565 ☎ *357-2700.*
Map 6G7 ▣ *X* ▆ ✳ *Open 10am-5.30pm. Closed Christmas.*
Metro: Federal Triangle.

This museum will save archeologists of the future a great deal
of work when they come to study the civilization known as
the United States of America. It is as though someone had cut
a trench through the whole of the country's history and from
it had taken objects that reflect and have shaped the changing
patterns of life. In this immense collection, housed in an
austerely elegant 1960s building on the *Mall*, you can learn
how Americans of different eras worked, played, tilled the
soil, traveled, dressed, shopped, communicated, entertained
themselves and coped with the technical problems that
confronted them. Originally known as the National Museum
of History and Technology, the collection is very strong on
technological matters, and the scope of it extends beyond
America, as in the displays of Roman, Venetian and Islamic
glass on the third floor.

The first-floor lobby, entered from Constitution Ave., is
dominated by a Foucault pendulum, a 240lb (108kg) brass
bob suspended on a 70ft (21m) wire, which demonstrates the
rotation of the earth. The lobby area has a bookstore, an
auditorium and a complete country post office-cum-general
store, where you can buy stamps, including special issues,
and post a letter that will receive a "Smithsonian Station"
postmark. On the same floor the electricity section has
Edison's lightbulb; the motor vehicle room has the famous
Model T Ford; and the railroad collection has a majestic 1926
Pacific-type locomotive. Other displays include physical
sciences, medicine, folk art, typewriters, clocks and farm
machinery.

On the second floor, which can be entered from the Mall,
there is a souvenir shop and a lobby dominated by the
original Star Spangled Banner. Concealed by a curtain, the
much-restored flag is revealed briefly every hour on the
half-hour. The galleries on this floor contain a more intimate
kaleidoscope of American life: for example, a collection of
First Ladies' gowns, a display of the life of George
Washington, a remarkable set of original interiors from
different periods, and a permanent exhibition, *After the
Revolution: Everyday Life in America, 1780-1800,* which
illustrates the lives of three actual families.

The third floor has even more riches, among them displays
of firearms, military history, photography, news reporting,
money and medals, philately and musical instruments. There
is an auditorium where the instruments are played (*Mon-Fri
11am*). Other free demonstrations are given of spinning and
weaving, printing and typefounding, and operating machine
tools. In addition to the permanent displays, temporary
exhibitions also cover aspects of American life and history.

National Museum of Natural History

10th St. and Constitution Ave. NW, DC 20565 ☎ *357-2700,
357-2627 (guided tours). Map 6G7* ▣ *X Wed, Thurs, Sat,
Sun at 1.30pm or by arrangement* ▆ ➤ *Open 10am-
5.30pm. Highlight tours at 10.30am, 1.30pm. Closed
Christmas. Metro: Smithsonian.*

The great stuffed African bush elephant that stands in the
huge central rotunda of this museum seems calculated, like

the museum itself, to inspire the visitor with awe at the onward march of evolution, the vast multiplicity of life on our planet, and the complex phenomenon of man himself. There is plenty to marvel at here — first of all, the scope of the collection. The natural history part of the museum traces back to the earliest signs of life in the form of fossil ammonites 160 million years old. There are skeletons and models of prehistoric monsters and stuffed specimens of more recent origin: mammals, birds, sea life and reptiles. A special section is devoted to bones, and another to the "Dynamics of Evolution." By way of a change, the **Insect Zoo** houses live specimens.

Moving on to inorganic material, there are sections on the earth, moon and meteorites, minerals and gems. The dazzling display of gems always draws a crowd; its primary attraction is the famous **Hope Diamond**, the largest blue diamond in the world. Other startling exhibits include the world's biggest star ruby and a topaz the size of a goose egg.

This museum also doubles as the **Museum of Man**, housing a vast range of anthropological material from many different periods and cultures: Stone Age North American axe heads, Inca artifacts, ancient Egyptian coffins. There are also life-size dioramas; the one in which a South American Indian on a pony chases an ostrich across the grasslands is particularly effective.

The museum's special facilities include a **Naturalist Center** (*open Mon-Sat 10.30am-4pm, Sun noon-5pm*) for the use of amateur researchers, with books, scientific instruments and specimens that can be handled and examined. There is a **Discovery Room** (☎ *357-2747 for group reservations; open Mon-Thurs noon-2.30pm, Fri-Sun 10.30am-3.30pm*), where children can handle a variety of objects from the world of nature. Youngsters also enjoy climbing on Uncle Beazley, a life-size model of a triceratops dinosaur outside the Mall entrance.

The museum's café is rather expensive for indifferent food. Next door, an excellent shop sells books and museum-related objects. On the ground floor there is an auditorium for lectures and an area for temporary exhibitions. The whole makes a fascinating outing.

National Museum of Women in the Arts

1250 New York Ave. NW, DC 20005 ☎ 783-5000. Map 6F7 🔲 𝘬 *Open Tues-Sat 10am-5pm, Sun noon-5pm. Closed Mon, hols. Metro: Metro Center.*

Newest of the cultural institutions within the rejuvenated Old Downtown district, this one helps right a wrong, as well. The role of women in the evolution of the arts has long been neglected and often dismissed. The works on display in this early turn-of-the-century Renaissance Revival building make clear the rich diversity of their contribution.

Wilhelmina Holladay founded the museum and, with her husband, assembled the permanent collection that is now at its heart. Painters and sculptors from a score of nations are represented, with works from the 16thC to the present. They include Georgia O'Keefe, Helen Frankenthaler, Kathe Kollwitz and Mary Cassatt, among the few women artists of the last 100yrs to enjoy widespread recognition. Temporary exhibitions are frequently mounted, and the research center is a trove of information on the subject.

National Portrait Gallery
8th and F St. NW, DC 20560 ☎ 357-1300. Map 7F8 ▣ ✗ ▣
Open 10am-5.30pm. Closed Christmas. Metro: Gallery
Place.

This gallery shares the splendid Old Patent Office building
with the *National Museum of American Art*. Its collection
consists of paintings, prints, drawings, photographs and
sculptures of "men and women who have made significant
contributions to the history, development and culture of the
people of the United States." The presidents have a hall to
themselves, with an anteroom devoted solely to George
Washington. Most of the presidential portraits are predictably
reverential, except for the most recent ones — Nixon, Ford,
Carter and Reagan — which are sharply penetrating. One
second-floor room is devoted to rotating exhibitions of *Time*
magazine covers, based upon such themes as sports heroes,
movie stars or presidents.

Altogether the National Portrait Gallery has some 4,500
portraits in its collection. There is a museum shop on the first
floor, and the gallery shares a library and cafeteria with the
National Museum of American Art.

National Rifle Association of America
1600 Rhode Island Ave. NW, DC 20005 ☎ 828-6000. Map
3E6 ▣ Open 10am-4pm. Closed hols. Metro: Farragut
North, Dupont Circle.

With some 2½ million members, the NRA is one of the largest
voluntary organizations in the USA. It defends fanatically the
right of all Americans "to keep and bear arms" and employs
five full-time lobbyists to ensure that no law obstructs this
objective. The **Museum of Firearms** covers a remarkable
range, including old flintlock pieces, duelling pistols, Civil
War guns, sporting and competition rifles and
commemorative firearms. Many of them are superb works of
craftsmanship, however deadly. Fascinating, but chilling.

National Shrine of the Immaculate Conception
Michigan Ave. and 4th St. NE, DC 20017 ☎ 526-8300 ▣ ✗
Open Apr-Oct 7am-7pm, Nov-Mar 7am-6pm. Metro:
Brookland.

A glimpse of this building from the train is reminiscent of the
view of the Sacré Coeur on leaving the Gare du Nord in Paris.
There is the same dominating, hilltop position and the same
echo of Byzantine splendor. Located next to Catholic
University, the church was begun in 1914 and built in two
stages: first the enormous crypt, completed in 1926; then the
upper church, consecrated in 1959. Despite its imposing size,
this is not a cathedral, nor does it serve a parish. It is
primarily a shrine to the Virgin Mary in her capacity as
Patroness of the USA, and it is filled with Marian imagery.

Descriptions of the church abound in superlatives. It is the
biggest Catholic church in the Western hemisphere and
possesses one of the largest church organs in the world
(☎ *for details of recitals*). Its many splendid mosaics include
the world's largest one of Christ (67ft/20.5m high), and others
reproducing such works as Murillo's *Immaculate Conception*
and Titian's *Assumption*. The whole interior, with its
magnificent soaring central dome, colored marble pillars and
domed baldachin over the altar, combines richness, serenity
and dignity.

National Zoological Park

*3001 Connecticut Ave. NW, DC 20008 ☎ 673-4717. Map
2&3A-B4-5 ▣ ✗ by arrangement (☎ 673-4955) ▣ ✱ ☎
Open May to mid-Sept, grounds 8am-8pm, buildings
9am-6.30pm; mid-Sept to Apr, grounds 8am-6pm,
buildings 9am-4.30pm. Metro: Woodley Park-Zoo.*

Before the zoo was established in 1889 the Smithsonian
Institution had only rudimentary facilities for gifts of live
animals. Early records indicate that animals presented to the
Smithsonian were sent to the Philadelphia Zoo and to the US
Insane Asylum (now St Elizabeth's Hospital), where they
were used as a harmless diversion for patients.

By the late 1880s animals donated to the Smithsonian
formed a menagerie in the shadow of the Smithsonian Castle.
Finally in 1889 a proper home for the animals was created
when 163 acres (66ha) of then-suburban NW Washington
were set aside for a National Zoological Park, to be run as
part of the Smithsonian.

Conservation and preservation of endangered animals has
been a central concept throughout the zoo's history. The
threatened extinction of the American bison and the
diminishing number of other native North American species
helped focus public interest and support for the founding of
the zoo. Today the historic commitment to the preservation of
endangered species persists.

The zoo is one of the finest in the world. Many of the
exhibits have been skillfully laid out to resemble different
types of habitat. Polar bears, for example, can be seen
basking on simulated icebergs or watched through
underwater windows as they swim in their pool. Some of the
animals here, such as the rare Bongo antelope of central and
western Africa, and the endangered Indian rhinoceros, are
virtually impossible to see in the wild. Always popular are the
two giant pandas, Ling-Ling and her male companion
Hsing-Hsing, presented by the People's Republic of China in
1972. These are most active at feeding times: around 11am
and 3pm. All the creatures that traditionally belong to zoos
can also be found here: lions, tigers, giraffes, monkeys, exotic
birds and many more.

The zoo is continually being modernized and restructured,
but the old **Reptile House** remains, its exterior reminiscent of
a Byzantine cathedral. It contains a **Herplab** (*open Tues-Sun
noon-3pm, winter Fri-Sun*), where children can explore the
world of herpetology (the study of reptiles and amphibians).
They will also enjoy the **Zoolab** (*same opening times as
Herplab*) in the **Education Building**, where they can draw,
read, or handle skulls, eggs, crocodile skins and other animal
materials. Films about animals and the workings of the zoo
are shown in the Education Building on weekends and all
week in the summer. The building contains a bookstore and
gift store.

The zoo is mapped with a color-coded system of six
different trails, named after types of animal. The zebra trail,
for example, color-coded black, takes you past hoofed
mammals as well as kangaroos and pandas. By following all
six trails you will see the entire collection.

Navy Yard

*9th and M St. SE, DC 20024 ☎ 433-4882. Map 8 I10-11 ▣
✗ available for groups ▣ ✱ ☎ US Navy Memorial*

Museum open Mon-Fri 9am-4pm, Sat, Sun, most hols 10am-5pm. Closed major hols. US Marine Corps Museum open Mon-Sat 10am-4pm. Closed Sun, Christmas. Metro: Eastern Market, then a moderate walk.

This yard, the oldest naval facility in the country, was opened in 1799. It no longer functions as a gun factory, which it did for a century, but is worth a visit, especially for children with nautical leanings. They can explore the dock area along the Anacostia River and climb on the old guns and other military objects exhibited in the grounds. There are two museums and an art gallery in the yard as well as the destroyer *John Barry*, which can be toured.

The **US Navy Memorial Museum**, in Building 76, illustrates the history of the Navy from 1775 to the present. There are dioramas of battles, model ships, displays of weaponry and technology, flags and uniforms. Children can sit behind guns and train them on imaginary targets, or enter a submarine room and operate a periscope. Nearby is the **Navy Art Gallery**, which contains naval art.

The **US Marine Corps Museum**, in Building 58, is smaller but also interesting, explaining the history of the Corps with similar exhibits of weapons, uniforms, portraits, flags and memorabilia. A series of dioramas re-creates great actions by the Corps.

A popular event at the Navy Yard during the summer is the public presentation (*June-Aug Wed 8.45pm*), which consists of a band concert and a historical review of the Navy with slides and films on a wide screen. Advance reservations must be made (☎ *433-2678*).

The nearby Marine Corp Barracks (*8th and I St. SE*), the nation's oldest marine post, offers a spectacular sunset parade with marching band and precision drill teams (*mid-May to mid-Sept Fri 8.20pm*). Reservations must be made at least three weeks in advance (☎ *433-4073*).

The Octagon

1799 New York Ave. NW, DC 20006 ☎ 638-3105. Map 6F6 ▣ ✗ Open Tues-Fri 10am-4pm, Sat, Sun 1-4pm. Closed Mon, major hols. Metro: Farragut West.

This is a house with a curious shape and a colorful history. Built between 1797 and 1800, it was designed by Dr William Thornton, first architect of the Capitol. His design copes ingeniously with the awkward corner site, but it is really a heptagon rather than an octagon, unless the bow at the front qualifies as an extra side.

The house was occupied by President Madison while the White House was under repair after being set on fire by the British in the War of 1812. It was here, in what is now called the **Treaty Room**, that Madison signed the Treaty of Ghent which ended the war. The dispatch box that contained it remains, as well as the table on which the signing is believed to have been done.

Owned by the American Institute of Architects, the house has been well restored and furnished in the Federal style. Portraits include one of John Tayloe, the original owner, as well as those of Dolley Madison and Dr and Mrs Thornton. There is an interesting basement kitchen, complete with early-19thC implements, and on the second floor are galleries for changing exhibitions relating to architecture. The new AIA headquarters next door also holds occasional exhibitions.

Old Downtown
Maps 6&7F.

The word "downtown" once suggested a magic and glamor that inspired songwriters. That was before an epidemic of inner city decay affected most of the northeastern USA. In many cities deteriorating conditions were further aggravated by the riots that swept the country in 1968. After years of blight the tide has turned and many inner cities, including Washington, are undergoing urban revival.

Symbolic of this renaissance is the **Willard Hotel** at the w end of Pennsylvania Ave. An Edwardian byword for elegance and style, it was home to President Calvin Coolidge and provided guest accommodations to many foreign dignitaries, but was driven to closure by the 1968 riots. Now, however, its lavish renovation is one of the central elements in a huge scheme for the revitalization of the entire Downtown area, from the White House to Union Station and from Pennsylvania Ave. to M St., a joint venture between the DC Government and private enterprise.

Downtown Washington is now poised to become the city its founders promised through their planning two centuries ago. The biggest single development is the *Washington Convention Center* occupying an entire block bounded by 9th, 11th and H St. and New York Ave. Opened at the beginning of 1983, it acts as a catalyst, bringing other forms of new life to the area: hotels, restaurants, stores, places of entertainment. On the block adjacent to it another huge complex has taken shape. Called **Techworld**, it is a technological conference and exhibition center incorporating two new hotels.

The rebirth of Old Downtown includes 7th St., which bisects the area. Designated in the redevelopment plan as an "Arts Spine," it links the Old Patent Office (containing the *National Portrait Gallery* and *National Museum of American Art*) with the *National Gallery of Art* to the s. Smaller galleries are opening along this street. The remainder of the area can be divided into three sections: Downtown, E Downtown and Pennsylvania Ave. The western part, concentrated around F and G St. between 9th and 15th St., has a burgeoning new "Retail Core," dominated by the three largest stores: **Woodward and Lothrop**, **Garfinkel's** and the recently relocated **Hecht's** flagship store (see *Shopping*).

A pedestrian mall stretches along G St. by the Martin Luther King Memorial Library, and pedestrian access will be made easier by the widening of sidewalks. Although many new buildings are springing up, older ones of quality are not being neglected. *Ford's Theatre* at 511 10th St. was restored in the 1960s and functions once again as a stage as well as a museum. The graceful *Church of the Epiphany* at 1317 G St. has likewise been restored. The **National Press Club** at 14th and F St. has reopened its refurbished doors to the club, to office suites and to a shopping arcade on the three lowest levels. The old Masonic temple at New York Ave. and 13th St. is currently being transformed into the *National Museum of Women in the Arts*, which opened in 1987.

The area E of 7th St. similarly contains a mixture of fine buildings that are gradually coming into their own again as the surrounding areas are redeveloped. **Judiciary Sq.**, for example, is an attractive townscape, surrounded by municipal and federal buildings, with the splendid *Old Pension*

Building (now the National Building Museum) on its N side.
The axis of the square has been extended to the S with the
creation of **John Marshall Park** leading down to
Pennsylvania Ave. Farther to the E a new park and a cluster of
office and hotel developments are planned for the area along
New Jersey Ave. *Chinatown* (roughly 6th to 9th St. at H and I
St.) is a tiny enclave of Chinese restaurants and businesses.
What remains of the once much larger neighborhood is now
undergoing a needed facelift.

The S boundary of Downtown, Pennsylvania Ave., is a noble
thoroughfare connecting the White House with the Capitol.
Like the Champs-Elysées in Paris, it seems expressly designed
for parades and has often been.used for this purpose.
Unfortunately, however, the earlier decay of Downtown had
left it rather moth-eaten on the N side, in contrast to the
somewhat monotonous Neoclassicism of the Federal Triangle
to the S. For years it had been barren of restaurants and
places to linger on a sunny day. As with the rest of
Downtown, however, this has almost all changed.

Traveling E down the avenue from 15th St. you will pass
Pershing Sq., with its sunken park, pool and outdoor café.
Facing the National Theater is Western Plaza, which has been
lovingly and expensively restored to its Federal period
elegance. (Notice the plan of Washington set into the paving
of the plaza.) A little farther E, on the S side, contrasting
strikingly with the Federal Triangle buildings surrounding it,
is the **Old Post Office**, a splendid piece of Victorian
Romanesque, resembling a cross between Neuschwanstein
Castle and the Palazzo Vecchio in Florence, whose 315ft
(96m) clock tower is the third tallest structure in the city. This
fine building, saved from demolition by a vigorous
conservationist campaign, has been remodeled to serve two
functions. The seven upper floors house the **National
Endowment for the Arts** and its twin the **National
Endowment for the Humanities**. The focal point of the
three lower floors, known as **The Pavilion**, is a dramatic
skylit atrium; here there are stores, restaurants, bars, cafés
and a stage for everything from ballet to jazz.

At the front of the building the cafés spill out onto
Pennsylvania Ave., adding a Parisian touch to the
environment. Another feature of the building is the dramatic
view of the city from the top of the tower. The Pavilion has
given a tremendous boost to Downtown and the whole city.

Across the avenue, and a little farther E, is the FBI
headquarters. The remainder of the avenue, on its Downtown
side, is in a state of flux, with new parks and plazas being
created, new buildings constructed and old ones, such as the
twin-towered, red sandstone **Apex Building**, restored. If all
continues to go according to plan, Pennsylvania Ave. and all
of Downtown, for too long prospering only in political
promises, should emerge as one of the liveliest parts of the
whole city — as L'Enfant himself envisaged.

Old Pension Building *(National Building Museum)*
G St. between 4th and 5th St. NW, DC 20001 ☎ 272-2448.
*Map 7F8▣ ✗ Open Mon-Fri 10am-4pm, Sat, Sun, hols
noon-4pm. Closed major hols. Metro: Judiciary Square
(F St. exit).*
Despite its rather sober name this is one of the most
astonishing buildings in the city. Based on the Palazzo

Farnese in Rome and completed in 1885, the exterior is imposing in its own right, with a ¼ mile-long (500m) encircling frieze in low relief of Civil War scenes added in 1887. But the interior is yet more impressive — rather the product of a Roman emperor's folie de grandeur than, as it was, the creation of an army engineer named General Meigs. Once inside you are dwarfed by a vast courtyard divided by eight columns the size of giant redwood trees. A fountain dominates the center, and around the sides several stories of arched galleries rise to a row of windows high above. This spectacular hall, as it was intended, is used for grand festivities and has been the setting for several presidential inaugural balls, including President Reagan's second in January 1985. It would take the length of a waltz to dance once around the floor!

In 1926 the building ceased to house the Pension Bureau, and at one time was threatened with demolition. Now, securely protected as a National Historic Landmark, it houses the **National Building Museum**, a privately funded organization founded to commemorate and encourage the American building arts. The museum mounts temporary exhibitions on architectural and building themes. A museum shop sells books and items of architectural interest.

This is one of the many Washington buildings reputed to be haunted; a number of strange apparitions have been seen including a transparent horseman and malevolent skulls hovering around the pillars.

Pentagon

Department of Defense, DC 20301 ☎ 695-1776. Map 5I-J4
⊡ ⚑ ⚓ at 10.30am, 1.30pm, 3pm ⟵ Open Mon-Fri
8.30am-3.30pm. Closed Sat, Sun, hols. Metro: Pentagon.
Headquarters of the Department of Defense, the Pentagon is one of the world's largest office buildings, with three times the floor space of New York's Empire State Building. The architects who designed it seem to have measured its dimensions by the fingers of one hand. It has five sides, five floors and five concentric rings, and the center courtyard covers 5 acres (2ha). It was all built with incredible speed in 16 months and completed in 1943 to meet the sudden expansion of the armed forces caused by World War II. Intended as a temporary solution, the Pentagon has instead become a permanent fixture, and its design is now recognized as brilliant. Although there are 17½ miles (26km) of corridors and nearly 4 million sq.ft (372,000 sq.m.) of office space, it takes no more than 7mins to walk from one side to the other — if you know the quickest route. There are some surprising statistics; for example, 23,000 people work here, drinking 30,000 cups of coffee and making 200,000 telephone calls every day.

Guided tours of the building are very popular, so it is advisable to reserve in advance. Following a film presentation, the walking tour begins; it takes approximately 1½hrs and is conducted by a guide who walks backward so that he can keep an eye on his group. Exhibited in the corridors are examples of war art and photography, militaria such as army banners, and memorabilia of army, navy and air force heroes. The **Hall of Heroes** commemorates recipients of the Medals of Honor.

The building has a shopping mall but no restaurants or café

open to the general public. There is, however, a bakery in the mall, which sells sandwiches, drinks and snacks.

Petersen House

516 10th St. NW, DC 20004 ☎ 426-6830. Map 6F7 ⊡ Open 9am-5pm. Closed Christmas. Metro: Gallery Place, Metro Center.

After President Lincoln was shot in **Ford's Theatre** on April 14, 1865, he was carried across the street to a modest house built in 1849 by a Swedish tailor named William Petersen, who used the basement for his business and rented out the other rooms. The house, like the theater, is now owned by the National Park Service, and the ground floor is open to the public. The present furnishings are not original but are based on a study of contemporary inventories. Between visits to her husband's bedside, Mrs Lincoln spent the anguished night, consoled by her son and friends, in the front parlor. In the back parlor, Edwin M. Stanton, Secretary of War, at once launched an investigation into the shooting. The room where Lincoln died, nine hours after the shooting, is a small, low-ceilinged back bedroom. The only original object is one of the blood-stained pillows from his bed, now reverentially glassed over.

The Phillips Collection

1600 21st St. NW, DC 20009 ☎ 387-2151. Map 3D5 ⊡ (donations solicited) ⬛ Open Tues-Sat 10am-5pm, Sun 2-7pm. Closed Mon, most major hols. Metro: Dupont Circle.

This gallery bears the highly personal stamp of its founder, Duncan Phillips (1886-1966), a remarkably individual collector who refused to operate through dealers and followed only his personal judgment. The works he collected were "modern" in the broadest sense, including great innovative artists of the past as well as those of the 20thC. In 1921 he opened his collection to the public on three afternoons a week in the Neo-Georgian house he had inherited off Massachusetts Ave. This, the first permanent museum of modern art in the country, was such a popular success that Phillips and his wife, who was herself a painter, turned the whole house into a gallery and moved to another home.

In his book *A Collection in the Making*, Phillips described his type of gallery: "We plan to try the effect of domestic architecture, of rooms small or at least livable, and of such an intimate, attractive atmosphere as we associate with a beautiful home. To a place like that I believe people would be inclined to return once they have found it and to linger as long as they can for art's special study and its special sort of pleasure."

Although many extensions have been added to the house, it retains this intimate, private atmosphere.

In keeping with the eclectic scope of Phillips' taste, there are works here by artists as early as Giorgione and as avant-garde as Robert Cartwright. A highlight of the collection is Renoir's supremely joyful painting, *Luncheon of the Boating Party.*

Temporary exhibitions, concerts and poetry readings are also held here. As Phillips intended, his gallery is a place where you will want to linger.

Pierce Mill

Beach Dr. and Tilden St., DC 20008 ☎ 426-6908 ⊡ ☀ Open Wed-Sun 8am-4.30pm. Closed Mon, Tues, hols. Grinding Sat, Sun 1pm. Lectures second Sat of each month 11am.
This simple stone building, nestling snugly in a leafy dip in **Rock Creek Park**, is the only survivor of eight water mills that operated on the Creek during the 18th and 19thC. Completed in about 1829, Pierce Mill was technically advanced for its time, using conveyor belts and other labor-saving machinery. It ceased functioning in 1879 and is now run by the National Park Service. Milling has been revived, and visitors can buy corn, whole-wheat, rye, buckwheat and oat flour in traditional cloth sacks from a miller in authentic dress. The millstones, chutes and machinery are still here, and a friendly miller will always be happy to tell you about the mill's history.

There are regular authentic craft demonstrations given by artisans in period costumes, and monthly lectures on the techniques and economics of 18thC milling.

The **Art Barn** is just across the road from here (see **Rock Creek Park**). The setting of these buildings is tranquil and rustic, a delightful place in which to stroll on a fine day and perhaps picnic by the creek.

Potomac Park

S of Independence Ave., w of 14th St., DC ☎ 426-6700. Map 5&6. Tourmobile.
This park is divided into two sections: **West Potomac Park** has the **Lincoln Memorial** and reflecting pool, playing fields and landscaped areas; **East Potomac Park**, extending in a long peninsula between the Potomac and the Washington Channel, has a golf course and facilities for swimming and tennis. **Hains Point**, at the southern tip of the park, is a great place to take the kids; it has a playground, picnic tables and a startling piece of outdoor sculpture entitled *The Awakening*, a metal figure of a giant struggling up out of the earth from a horizontal position with only his head and part of his limbs visible. Between the two parks is the **Tidal Basin** (where paddleboats can be rented in season), overlooked by the **Jefferson Memorial** and ringed by cherry trees, which also extend down the side of E Potomac Park. Access to the latter is difficult unless you have a car. From both parks there are splendid views across the Potomac.

Renwick Gallery

17th St. and Pennsylvania Ave. NW, DC 20560 ☎ 357-1300 (info.), 357-2531 (guided tours). Map 3F6 ⊡ ✠ temporary exhibitions only ✗ by arrangement. Open 10am-5.30pm. Closed Christmas. Metro: Farragut West.
Amid the bustle of Pennsylvania Ave. this branch of the Smithsonian's **National Museum of American Art** comes as a delightful surprise. The building, originally constructed to house the Corcoran collection, is in the French Second Empire style with a high mansard roof and an ornate brick and sandstone facade. Named after the architect, James Renwick, it was saved from demolition in 1965 and beautifully renovated. Frequent temporary exhibitions are organized here, the emphasis being on American design, crafts and decorative arts.

A permanent display of painting and sculpture can be seen

in the second-floor **Grand Salon** and **Octagon Room**, both exquisitely furnished in opulent Victorian style with padded velvet sofas. Luxuriously seated on one of these, you can admire works by such artists as G. F. Watts, Pierre Puvis de Chavannes and William Sartain.

Films, concerts, lectures and craft demonstrations are held at the National Museum of American Art (*apply there for the calendar of events*).

Rock Creek Cemetery
Rock Creek Church Rd. and Webster St. NW, DC 20007.
A tranquil place on rolling terrain, farther E than Rock Creek itself. **St Paul's Church**, within its grounds, is the oldest in DC. The cemetery contains some fine sepulchral art, notably the figure by Augustus Saint-Gaudens called *The Peace of God*, or *Grief*.

Rock Creek Park
Map 2&3&5F4.
The Washington equivalent of Hampstead Heath or the Bois de Boulogne, this park consists of 1,754 acres (710ha) of beautiful woodland. There are many different things to see and do: riding stables, tennis courts, a golf course, 30 picnic areas, playing fields, and an extensive system of routes for walking, jogging, riding and cycling. The **Carter Barron Amphitheater** (*16th St. and Colorado Ave. NW* ☎ *829-3200*) is a 4,000-seat outdoor theater which offers a variety of performing arts in an attractive rural setting during the summer months.

Washington weather, in the early fall, blew hot and cold. On the cool days people went horseback riding in Rock Creek Park and tired gentlemen, strangulating in red tape, took a new lend-lease on life. The multitudes ... found that they could walk to work without frying. The crowded buses seemed less crowded, somehow, when there was more air to breathe. And in a mellow, more benevolent sunlight the working boys and girls of Mecca-on-the-Potomac went outside in the luncheon hour and ate their sandwiches under a pale blue sky.

Faith Baldwin, *Washington, USA*

Other attractions of the park include *Pierce Mill*; **Art Barn** (*2401 Tilden St. NW* ☎ *426-6719*), formerly a carriage house and now a lively gallery showing the work of local artists, where classes and artists' demonstrations are also held; and **Rock Creek Nature Center** (*5200 Glover Rd.* ☎ *426-6829* 🔲 𝄞 *open Tues-Fri 9.30am-5pm, Sat, Sun noon-6pm, Dec-Apr Sat, Sun noon-5pm; closed Mon*). Information on Rock Creek Park can be obtained from the Park Headquarters (☎ *426-6832*), and a useful leaflet on the park is published by the National Park Service.

St Matthew's Cathedral
1725 Rhode Island Ave. NW, DC 20005 ☎ *347-3215. Map 3E6* 🔲 𝄞 *Sun 2.30-4.30pm. Open 6.30am-6.30pm. Metro: Farragut North.*
This is the Roman Catholic church that President Kennedy attended and where his funeral mass was held on November 25, 1963. In Oct 1979, during his American visit, Pope John

Paul II celebrated the Eucharist here. Designed in the
Renaissance style with a central dome, the cathedral has a
remarkably rich interior, vibrant with colored marble, mosaics
and murals.

Smithsonian Institution Building
1000 Jefferson Dr. SW, DC 20560 ☎ *357-2700. Map 6G7* ☑
Open 10am-5.30pm. Closed Christmas. Metro:
Smithsonian.

On the s side of the Mall stands a many-turreted, red
sandstone building in a vaguely Romanesque style, which
was built in 1849 to a design by James Renwick. Popularly
known as the **Castle**, this is the headquarters of the
Smithsonian Institution, the largest complex of museums and
art galleries in the world. Its empire includes not only a dozen
museums in Washington as well as the *National Zoological
Park* but other facilities elsewhere in the USA and abroad. It
also conducts and sponsors research in science and the arts
and issues a wide range of publications. An introductory slide
presentation and talk, giving a bird's-eye view of all the
Smithsonian museums in Washington, is held daily in the
Great Hall on the first floor of the Castle (*check at the
information desk in the Great Hall or* ☎ *in advance for the
schedule*).

This extraordinary institution owes its existence to the
English scientist James Smithson, who died in 1829 and left a
large fortune to the USA to found an institution in Washington
bearing his name, "for the increase and diffusion of
knowledge among men." Today, James Smithson's tomb rests
in a little room off the entrance lobby to the Castle, along
with his portrait and a few mementoes. The **Visitors'
Information and Reception Center** offers information on
all parts of the Smithsonian.

In the space behind the Castle an exciting addition to the
Smithsonian has taken shape. Known as the **Quadrangle**, the
new museum complex includes the *National Museum of
African Art*, the *Arthur M. Sackler Gallery*, devoted to
Asian and Near Eastern Art, and the **International Center**,
which will sponsor research, hold symposia and mount large
exhibitions on themes that embrace many countries and
cultures, especially those of the non-Western world. These
three facilities, which opened in the summer of 1987, are
located largely underground. At ground level is the **Enid A.
Haupt Garden**, 4.2 acres (1.7ha) beautifully planted and laid
out in the manner of a Victorian garden and in keeping with
the style of the Castle.

The Castle's main tower looks like a good home for owls,
and that is exactly what it is. A colony was introduced there
some years ago by Dr Ripley, Secretary of the Smithsonian.

State Department
*Tour Office FMAS/GS, Room 7493, 2201 C St. NW, DC
20520* ☎ *647-3241. Map 5F5* ☑ ✗ *by appt only 4-6 weeks in
advance. Mon-Fri, tours at 9.30am, 10.30am, 3pm. Closed
Sat, Sun, hols. Metro: Foggy Bottom.*

One of the less widely advertised attractions of Washington is
the collection of art objects and furniture housed in the
sumptuous reception rooms on the eighth floor of the State
Department, the federal agency that handles foreign policy
and relations. Most of the antique furnishings and decorative

objects were given to the government in lieu of tax and are beautifully displayed in a series of interiors created in the 1960s in the gracious style of old American stately homes. One of the most attractive rooms is the John Quincey Adams State Drawing Room, with its portraits of Adams, Jefferson, Washington, Benjamin Franklin and others. The room also contains the desk on which the Treaty of Paris, which ended the War of Independence, was signed.

Supreme Court

1st and E Capitol St. SE, DC 20543 ☎ 479-3000. Map 8G10 ☷ Ⅹ by appt only ☞ Open Mon-Fri 9am-4.30pm. Closed Sat, Sun, hols. Hearings 10am-noon, 1-3pm, first come first seated. Courtroom lectures when Court is not in session every hour on the half-hour. Metro: Capitol South, Union Station.

The function of the Supreme Court is to prevent infringements of the US Constitution by reversing any unconstitutional laws or decisions that are referred to it. There are nine members: a Chief Justice and eight Associate Justices. The court sits on alternate fortnights from the first Mon in Oct until May or June. Sessions are 10am-3pm with a lunch break noon-1pm. These are open to the public on Mon, Tues and Wed; Mon is the most popular day for observing, as the court's decisions are usually pronounced then. Visitors to either the morning or afternoon sessions must be prepared to arrive ahead of time and, if allowed to enter, to remain the entire session.

Proceedings are carried out with great solemnity in an imposing room, ringed with Ionic columns, the black-robed justices sitting in a row behind a raised bench against the backdrop of a red velvet curtain — a formidable array for the counsel who stand facing them to argue their cases. Certain quaint traditions are cherished by the court; for example, white quill pens are placed, in crossed pairs, on the counsel tables every day. It is legal theatricality at its most fascinating.

As befits the highest court in the land, the building is extremely imposing. Completed in 1935, it is a gleaming, white marble, Corinthian-columned temple, approached by an apparently endless flight of steps, with the words "Equal Justice Under Law" inscribed over the portico. The interior is equally splendid and has two unusual self-supporting spiral staircases, rising through five stories in an elegant ellipse.

On the ground floor is a **museum** illustrating some of the Court's history. A film about the Court and how it works is shown in the small auditorium.

Textile Museum

2320 S St. NW, DC 20008 ☎ 667-0441. Map 2D4 ☷ Ⅹ Sat 1-3pm. Open Tues-Sat 10am-5pm, Sun 1-5pm. Closed Mon, hols. Metro: Dupont Circle.

Founded by George Hewitt Myers in 1925, this museum, occupying two handsome early-20thC brick houses in the Embassy Row area, contains more than 1,000 rugs and over 10,000 other textile items, from South American ponchos to Indian shawls. In addition to the permanent displays, there are three major temporary exhibitions each year. The museum shop offers for sale some lovely textiles, as well as books on the subject. The museum also has a library and runs a program of lectures, demonstrations and courses.

Theodore Roosevelt Island and Memorial
George Washington Memorial Parkway, Mclean, Va. 22101
☎ *285-2601. Map 4F-G3* 🔲 *✗ by appt a week in advance*
🔊 *Open 8am-sunset.*
This island in the Potomac is appropriately dedicated to
Theodore Roosevelt, President of the USA from 1901-9 and
early champion of wildlife and nature conservation. The 88
acres (36ha) of swamp, marsh and forest contain a rich
variety of native plants and provide a refuge for kingfishers,
turtles, frogs, muskrats, squirrels, chipmunks and many other
fauna. The island boasts 2½ miles (4km) of trails and an
impressive memorial to Roosevelt: a 17ft (5m) bronze statue
of him, larger than life, like the man himself.

Treasury Building
15th St. and Pennsylvania Ave. NW, DC 20220 ☎ *566-2000.*
Map 6F6 🔲 🔊 *Open Mon-Fri 9am-6pm. Closed Sat, Sun,*
hols. Metro: McPherson Square, Metro Center.
The US Treasury Department is a huge empire whose
branches include Internal Revenue, the Mint, the *Bureau of
Engraving and Printing*, Customs, the Bureau of Alcohol,
Tobacco and Firearms, and the Secret Service — surprisingly,
those "heavies" protecting the President are Treasury men,
not police or FBI. There was once a small museum in the
basement of the impressive Greek Revival building, but it is
now closed and much of the collection moved to the *Bureau
of Engraving and Printing*.

Truxtun-Decatur Naval Museum
1610 H St. NW, DC 20006 ☎ *842-0050. Map 6F6* 🔲 *Open*
10am-4pm. Closed hols. Metro: Farragut West.
A small museum in the former carriage house of the *Decatur
House*, around the corner. The exhibits relate to naval history
and include models, relics, photographs, paintings, prints and
other memorabilia, all of particular interest to naval buffs.

Union Station
Massachusetts and Delaware Ave. NE ☎ *269-3020 (general*
info.), 484-7540 (Amtrak info.). Map 7F9 🔲 *Open 7 days* 🔊
═ *✗* 🔊 *Metro: Union Station.*
Designed by Daniel H. Burman, this station was completed in
1908 when rail journeys between big cities were rituals that
began and ended in temples of awesome magnificence. This
one has, as its main entrance, a portico based on the Arch of
Constantine in Rome, surmounted by allegorical figures
sculpted by Louis Saint-Gaudens (son of the more famous
Augustus). The plaza in front is dominated by a great white
marble fountain, its focal point a 15ft-high (4.5m) figure of
Christopher Columbus standing in the prow of a ship.
By the 1970s, with the national decline in rail travel, the
station had been allowed to deteriorate severely. An attempt
to transform it into a National Visitor Center was a costly
failure. Beset with crumbling walls and a leaking roof, it was
closed while the authorities argued over its fate. Even the
railroad tracks were moved to a new adjacent building.
Happily, the decision was made to rehabilitate the building, a
course that has saved many fine old edifices in the District.
After a reported expenditure of $100 million, at least
$500,000 just for gold leaf, it reopened in 1988. Even a
cursory look at the interior reveals that it does not merely

réclaim its past glory: it surpasses it. The coffered, barrel-vaulted main concourse now soars above two fountains and a round two-floor central café, and the space has already been used for a Presidential inaugural ball. While the station continues to serve its original purpose, with Capitol Hill commuters and Amtrak passengers scurrying through, it also shelters scores of upscale retail stores, theaters, and a number of eating establishments that run from simple and fast to almost unimaginably grand. (See **Adirondacks** in *Restaurants*.) Union Station has been returned to the people, vibrant, exciting, and a superb foretaste for arriving travelers.

Free half-hour tours (*Wed and Fri at 10am, 11am, 1pm*) leave from the kiosk of the **National Trust for Historic Preservation** at the E end of the concourse. Sign up at the information desk nearby.

United States Botanic Garden

1st St. and Maryland Ave. SW, DC 20024 ☎ *225-8333. Map 7G9* ▣ ✗ *by arrangement* ☎ *225-7099. Open June-Sept 9am-9pm, Oct-May 9am-5pm. Metro: Federal Center.*
There is something irresistibly romantic about plant houses. In their steamy greenness it is easy to imagine once again playing a childhood game of jungle exploration where snakes and crocodiles lie hidden in the shadows. The central palm house in this building, complete with stream, lends itself to such flights of fancy. There are also sections for orchids, cycads, ferns, cacti, bromeliads and other types of plant. And there are areas for temporary flower shows, notably the **Easter Show** (*Palm Sun-Easter Sun*), the **Summer Terrace Display** on the patio in front of the building (*late May-Sept*), the **Chrysanthemum Show** (*mid-Nov to Thanksgiving*), and the **Poinsettia Show** (*mid-Dec through the Christmas hols*).

There is a bustle to Washington at the approach of fall, the Indian summer briskness that slowly sheds the torpid layers of August and deepens somehow the hopes and renewals of the official city, as if the health of the Republic itself depends on such simple cycles. Washington at the first touch of fall was like the new school years of one's childhood, when even the most perfunctory rituals are for a time fraught with possibility.

Willie Morris, *The Last of the Southern Girls*

The building, just to the SW of the Capitol, is in the grand manner of the great Victorian conservatories, but surprisingly it was built in the 1930s. The Botanic Garden also administers a public park on Independence Ave. opposite the rear entrance to the conservatory, which is used as a display garden for spring and summer flowering plants. The focal point of the park is the **Bartholdi Fountain**, named after its creator, the French sculptor Frederic Auguste Bartholdi, who also designed the Statue of Liberty.

United States Naval Observatory

34th St. and Massachusetts Ave. NW, DC 20390 ☎ *653-1543 (tour info.), 653-1541 (public affairs). Map 2B-C3* ▣ ✗ *compulsory Mon night only.*
When glancing at your watch or dialing the speaking clock you probably forget that all measurement of time is ultimately

determined by astronomical observations. The US Naval Observatory is the source of all standard time used in the country. Special telescopes monitor the positions and movements of the heavenly bodies, while some 30 atomic clocks record an average time reading accurate down to one trillionth of a second. In addition, the observatory has conventional telescopes for astronomical research. It also publishes the official almanacs for astronomers and navigators.

A visit to the observatory for one of the Monday night tours is a fascinating experience. The scientific complexities are well explained by the guides, and a slide show illustrates the work of the observatory. The 26in (65cm) refracting telescope and the 6in (15cm) transit circle telescope are available for celestial viewing.

Walking up the driveway from the observatory gates, you can see, behind a railing to the left, the official residence of the US Vice-President.

Vietnam Veterans Memorial
Constitution Gardens, w end of Mall. Map 5G5 🗺
Tourmobile.
This memorial, in Constitution Gardens to the w of the Lincoln Memorial, aroused much controversy when it was unveiled in 1982. Designed by Maya Ying Lin, it consists of a long tapering cliff of black polished stone set into a bank. It is inscribed with the names of all dead or missing combatants — over 58,000 — listed in order of their deaths from 1959 to 1975. There are alphabetical directories to help visitors find the names they seek. Many still-mourning survivors make paper rubbings of the names of friends and relatives; others leave flags, flowers, wreaths and votive candles. In answer to the original protests, a more traditional statuary group was positioned nearby in 1984. By then, however, opinion about the monument had shifted dramatically to its favor. It is a memorial of moving simplicity, testimony to a deeply traumatic episode in recent American history.

Voice of America
330 Independence Ave. SW, DC 20547 ☎ *485-6231. Map 7G8* 🗺 𝄃 *last tour 2.45pm.* 🚶 *Open Mon-Fri 8.30am-5.30pm. Closed Sat, Sun, hols. Metro: Federal Center.*
The Voice of America is a broadcasting division of the United States International Communication Agency. Its radio programs, designed to convey a positive image of the USA, are listened to by approximately 75 million people, a large proportion of them in the Soviet Union and Eastern Europe. The station broadcasts 24hrs a day in English and some 35 other languages. Visitors touring the building are shown staff at work and can hear a program being transmitted.

Washington Cathedral ★
Mount Saint Alban, DC 20016 ☎ *537-6200. Map 2A2* 🗺 𝄃 ➤ 𝄃€ *Open Mon-Sat 10am-4.30pm, Sun 8am-4.30pm* 𝄃 *Mon-Sat 10am-3.15pm, Sun 12.30-2.45pm, except during services.*
Washington Cathedral (officially the Cathedral Church of St Peter and St Paul and known also as the National Cathedral), seat of the Episcopal Bishop of Washington, is a glorious anachronism: a great medieval Gothic church built in the

20thC, indeed probably one of the last of its kind that will
ever be constructed. The foundation stone was laid in 1907,
and completion is now in sight. The principal architect was
Philip Hubert Frohman, who worked on the building from
1921 until his death in 1972.

Superbly located on Mount St Alban in NW DC, it is laid out
in the traditional form of a cross. At the intersection of nave,
choir and transept rises the **Gloria in Excelsis Tower**, 676ft
(206m) above sea level and having the unique feature of two
sets of bells, one above the other. At the w end of the church
are the two smaller **towers of St Peter and St Paul**. The
observation gallery below these twin towers affords a good
view of Washington and its environs, as well as some of the
building's exterior stonework — pinnacles, gargoyles and
grotesques. Notice also from here the beautiful geometry of
the flying buttresses. Not only for show, they structurally
balance the outward thrust of the walls, so that no steel
reinforcement was necessary anywhere in the building.

Stand in the vast interior where the nave meets the
transepts, and the illusion of Chartres or Canterbury is
powerful. Three superb rose windows blaze from w, N and s,
and the proportions of column, arch, clerestory and soaring
ribbed vaulting sing out in exhilarating harmony. The
cathedral does have at least one advantage over its medieval
counterparts: central heating under the marble floors, so there
is no need to freeze while your spirit is nourished.

Other details also indicate that this is a 20thC cathedral: for
example, the **Space Window**, halfway along the s side of the
nave, commemorating the Apollo XI flight. It depicts the
spaceship's trajectory and contains a sliver of moon rock
brought back from the flight. The next bay to the E houses the
tomb of President Woodrow Wilson and has another striking
window, depicting war and peace, by Ervin Bossanyi. Notice
the quality of fine detail throughout the building. Every boss
and decorated column has been as lovingly carved as the
great pulpit, made of French limestone from Caen, or the high
altar with its assembly of prophets and saints.

Downstairs on the crypt floor is a Visitors' Center, a shop
selling books, souvenirs and gifts, a brass rubbing center, and
four small chapels, including the **Chapel of the Good
Shepherd**, which is open for private prayer 24hrs a day.
Services in the cathedral are memorable for their music and
choral singing; choirs from all over the country come here.
There are Sun afternoon organ recitals following evensong.
The carillon in the main tower is played on Sat at 4.30pm, and
a ten-bell peal is rung after the 11am service on Sun.

In the extensive **grounds** of the cathedral you can linger in
the Bishop's Garden, buy plants from the Greenhouse and
visit the Herb Cottage, where dried herbs, books, souvenirs
and a variety of gifts are on sale.

Washington Convention Center

*900 9th St. NW, DC 20006 ☎ 789-1600, 371-4200 (events).
Map 6E-F7 ▣ but ▣ for events ☎ events line for opening
times. Metro: Metro Center, Gallery Place.*
Convention centers have become a popular way for cities to
attract business and revenue. This one, opened at the
beginning of 1983, boasts an impressive range of facilities for
conferences and exhibitions: 378,000sq.ft (35,000sq.m) of
exhibition space; 40 meeting rooms, capable of holding

between 50 and 14,000 people; sophisticated security; closed-circuit television; and computerized air conditioning and heating. Its Downtown location is convenient for access, and the center is part of the massive revival scheme for the area (see *Old Downtown*).

Washington Monument ★
Center of the Mall, Constitution Ave. and 15th St. NW
☎ *426-6841. Map 6G6* 🔲 *K Sat and Sun 10am, 2pm. Open Mar 20-Labor Day 8am-midnight, rest of year 9am-5pm. Metro: Federal Triangle, Smithsonian. Tourmobile.*

The gleaming marble obelisk that rises from the center of the *Mall* has become as much a symbol of Washington as the Eiffel Tower has of Paris. It is strong, simple, majestic and exquisitely proportioned. It positively sings out over the skyline, sounding a clear note of Classical beauty that resonates powerfully with the rest of the city. So perfect is it as a visual focal point of the capital that it is impossible to imagine Washington without it.

When Pierre L'Enfant designed the city he intended to have a Washington Monument occupying the point at the intersection of the western axis of the Capitol and the southern axis of the White House. But the ground was too marshy, and another site had to be chosen some 360ft (110m) to the E and 120ft (36.5m) to the s. A stone marking the original site was placed there in 1884 by Thomas Jefferson and replaced in 1889.

Although a monument to George Washington had been mooted even before his death in 1799, it was not until 1833 that a National Monument Society was set up, largely by Washington's fellow freemasons. A competition was held, and the winning design by Robert Mills was for a great colonnaded circular mausoleum with an obelisk projecting from the center. Gradually, under financial pressure, the concept was whittled down until only a simple obelisk remained.

The cornerstone was laid in 1848, but by 1865 only about a quarter of the monument had been built, and the Corps of Engineers of the US Army took over the construction, with the help of federal funds. The able officer-in-charge, Lt.-Col. Casey (who also built the *Library of Congress*), reinforced the base, corrected a tilt, and altered the proportions to conform to those of the ancient obelisks. When Casey took over, a slightly different marble was used, and it is evident how the color changes about a quarter of the way up the shaft. The monument was finally finished in 1885 and opened to the public in 1888, equipped with a steam-driven elevator that took about 10mins to reach the summit.

Today you are whisked to the top in 70 seconds. Despite the rather small windows, there is a magnificent view of the city in all directions, and from here the full, formal grandeur of L'Enfant's town plan is revealed. Come here on a summer night when all the monuments and the great public buildings are floodlit. (During the day you may have to line up for 40mins or so to get in.)

At 555ft 5⅛in (169.29m), the monument was once the tallest building in the world. It has long since lost that title, but it remains an impressive tribute to the man who has been called "first in war, first in peace, and first in the hearts of his countrymen."

Washington Post
1150 15th St. NW, DC 20007 ☎ 334-7969. Map 3E6 ⬚ 🖈
✗ by arrangement Mon-Fri 10am-3pm every hr. Metro:
McPherson Square, Farragut North.
The public can tour the offices of this famous newspaper,
known worldwide for the journalistic investigation into the
Watergate scandal that led to President Nixon's resignation in
1974. The conducted tour, which includes the newsroom and
printing presses, gives a fascinating insight into the workings
of a modern newspaper. Be sure to reserve in advance.

Watergate Complex
Virginia and New Hampshire Ave. NW, DC 20037. Map 5F4.
Metro: Foggy Bottom.
In June 1972, five men working for the re-election of
President Nixon were caught burgling the headquarters of the
Democratic National Committee in the Watergate complex.
Since then the name "Watergate" has been associated with the
ensuing scandal that ultimately led to Nixon's resignation in
1974. To most Washingtonians, however, the Watergate is
primarily a big shopping, residential and office complex near
the Kennedy Center, with smart boutiques and a high-class
hotel. The sweeping curves of the building are striking. The
sixth-floor offices, where the burglary took place, are no
longer occupied by the Democratic National Committee.

The Watergate Complex is not to be confused with the
Watergate itself, which is a broad flight of steps leading down
to the Potomac near the Lincoln Memorial.

The White House ★
1600 Pennsylvania Ave. NW, DC 20500 ☎ 755-7798. Map
6F6 ⬚ 🖈 ✗ Open Tues-Sat 10am-noon. Closed Mon, Sun,
major hols. Metro: McPherson Square.
Theodore Roosevelt christened the mansion the "White
House." It is the only residence of a head of state, anywhere
in the world, that is open regularly to the public and free of
charge, with more than 1½ million visitors each year. That fact
makes necessary a discussion of the practicalities of a visit.

Advance planning is rewarded. Residents of the USA can
write to their senators or congresspersons to request passes
for VIP tours, which are given at hours other than those listed
above. Since the supply is very limited and demand is high,
requests should be made six months or more in advance.
Foreign citizens might be able to obtain passes at their
consulates. All others must line up. And line up. No tickets
are required for regularly scheduled tours from Labor Day to
Memorial Day, when visitors simply join the line at the
entrance on the E side of the White House. But from
June-Aug, they must first obtain tickets from the booth on the
Ellipse, the greensward stretching S from the White House.
The daily quota melts away quickly, so 8am is not too soon to
arrive. They then must line up at the entrance itself. Even in
bitterly cold, muggy or rainy weather, lines are long, with a
2hr wait far from unusual. Once inside, the tour covers only
five rooms, which do not include the Oval Office or the First
Family's living quarters. And finally, the building can be
closed on short notice for occasions of state. For all these
reasons, the elderly and parents with children or impatient
teenagers in tow may wish to consider whether the time
might be more comfortably and profitably spent at one of

Washington's more accessible attractions. The White House gardens, by the way, are open to the public on certain days during the year (☎ *for details*).

All that said, the most striking thing about the President's official residence is that it is rather modest. It is elegant, distinguished but unostentatious — and all the better for that. For this we have to thank George Washington; he chose the site in 1791, and approved the simple dignity of the design by the Irish architect James Hoban. But Washington never lived

WHITE HOUSE FLOOR PLAN

1 Vermeil Room	14 East Room	
2 Library	15 Green Room	
3 China Room	16 Truman's Balcony	
4 South Portico	17 Blue Room	
5 Diplomatic Reception Room	18 Cross Hall	
6 Ground Floor Corridor	19 North Portico	
7 Curator	20 Red Room	
8 White House Staff Office	21 Usher's Office	
9 Map Room	22 State Dining Room	
10 Doctor's Office	23 Family Dining Room	
11 Housekeeper's Office	24 Lincoln Bedroom	
12 Kitchen	25 Queen's Bedroom	
13 President's Oval Office and Executive Offices	26 Treaty Room	
	27 Yellow Oval Room	
	28 First Family's Private Quarters	

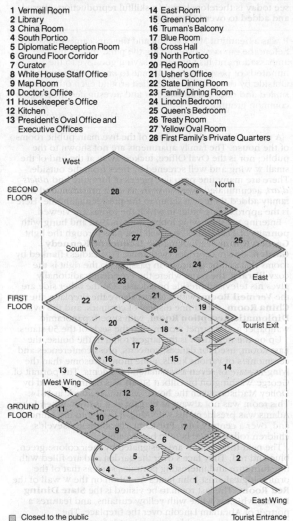

☐ Closed to the public

here, and John Adams was the first to move into the house referred to as the "President's Mansion" or "President's Palace" in 1800, while it was still unfinished.

In 1814, during the War of 1812, the British burned the house, leaving only the shell. It was rebuilt, and the Virginia sandstone exterior walls were painted white to obliterate the fire marks. By the 1940s it was discovered to be so unsound that it had to be almost completely reconstructed around a new steel skeleton. During the rebuilding, from 1949 to 1952, President Truman and his family lived across the street in Blair House at 1651-3 Pennsylvania Ave. NW. The house you see today is therefore largely a skillful reproduction, altered and added to over 132 years.

It was a beautiful May evening and the cars came and went before the embassy overlooking the park. Inside, the ambassador and his wife stood saying goodbye to the hundreds of people they had come to know in Washington. Outside by the pool, guests eddied around each other and smiled and nodded, investigator and investigatee meeting on common ground.

Abigail McCarthy, *Circles*

A normal visit includes a tour of the five main public rooms of the house. The family apartments are not shown to the public; nor is the Oval Office, tucked away at the end of the small W wing and well screened by trees from the outside. There are many fine portraits, pieces of furniture and *objets d'art*, accumulated over the years as each president and his family added their own stamp to the presidential home. Here is the approximate order in which the rooms are viewed.

Entering via the E wing lobby, built in 1942 and hung with portraits of First Ladies, you will first pass through the light **Garden Room** overlooking the **Jacqueline Kennedy Garden**, down a corridor (with more First Ladies) flanked by rooms that can be glimpsed in passing. To the right is the cozy **library**, the room where the President traditionally gives his televised fireside broadcasts. On the other side are the **Vermeil Room**, with a Monet above the fireplace, the **China Room**, with a fine display of ceramics, and the oval **Diplomatic Reception Room**, with superb panoramic wallpaper and a carpet woven with the seals of the 50 states.

Up on the next floor is the largest room in the house, the East Room, used for dances, concerts, press conferences and ceremonies of various kinds, none more awesome than the lying-in-state of seven assassinated presidents. The portrait of George Washington by Gilbert Stuart was daringly saved by Dolley Madison when the house was under attack in 1814. This room was not always as elegant as it is now. When John Adams was president, his wife Abigail used it to dry laundry, and, over a century later, President Theodore Roosevelt's children roller-skated here in bad weather.

The next three rooms are designated by their colors: green, blue and red. They face S over the garden and are filled with fine furniture and interesting portraits, such as that of the ornithological artist John James Audubon on the W wall of the **Red Room**. The last room to be visited is the **State Dining Room**, which is white with yellow curtains, and features a portrait of Abraham Lincoln over the fireplace. The inscription on the marble mantelpiece is from a letter by John

Adams, written on his first night in the mansion to his wife Abigail, who was still in Massachusetts: "I pray heaven to bestow the best of blessings on this house and all that shall hereafter inhabit it. May none but honest and wise men ever rule under this roof." Here sometimes as many as 140 guests dine. Passing the long Cross Hall and Entrance Hall, hung with portraits of recent presidents, you emerge from the house on the N side under the great main portico.

Although Abigail Adams, first of the First Ladies to attempt to make a home out of the White House, was most concerned simply to see the structure completed, other presidential wives have made the improvement of their executive residence a national priority. (It was not until 1902 that the First Families could enjoy total privacy in their second-floor quarters, although they continued to take their meals in the first-floor dining room for another 60yrs.) Mary Todd Lincoln spent compulsively (criminally, her critics said) on lavish French furnishings for the mansion while the nation was on the brink of the Civil War. A century later, Jacqueline Bouvier Kennedy spearheaded a worldwide campaign for private and public contributions to return to the White House those historically accurate and original furnishings that had been looted, loaned or moved during 34 administrations.

This massive restoration has been carried on by successive First Ladies, so that today the White House is a treasure trove of significant American furnishings and decorative objects, as well as the stately home of the nation's highest statesman.

Woodrow Wilson House

2340 S St. NW, DC 20008 ☎ 673-4034. Map 2D4 ▨ ✗ Open Tues-Sun 10am-4pm. Closed major hols. Metro: Dupont Circle.

"An unpretentious, comfortable, dignified house, fitted to the needs of a gentleman's home" is how Mrs Woodrow Wilson described the house that she and her husband settled into in 1921, following his retirement from the Presidency. The handsome brick Georgian revival house, designed in 1915, is preserved much as it was when the Wilsons lived there. Mementoes include the typewriter on which Wilson drafted the League of Nations proposal, and the projector and screen that enabled him to enjoy silent movies at home.

Where to stay

Hotels are concentrated in various parts of town. After a period of decline, the area near Union Station has once again, with the revival of rail travel, become a thriving hotel district. In Old Downtown the burgeoning new hotels around the Convention Center compete with the gracious establishments of the **Willard** and the **Washington**, both recently renovated. New Downtown has such *grande dame* hotels as the **Hay-Adams**, **Sheraton-Carlton** and **Mayflower**. In the West End and Foggy Bottom there is a colony of new luxury hotels: the **Grand**, **Westin**, **Park Hyatt**, **Wyndham Bristol**, **Ramada Renaissance** and **Watergate**. The embassy area is catered to by the **Embassy Row** and **Ritz Carlton**.

Options are not limited to such costly choices as these, by any means. The District and its close-in suburbs spread a panoply of options to suit every need and budget. One laudable trend is the all-suite hostelry, in which all accommodations include living room, bedroom and kitchen. They are generally priced at or below standard double rooms in first-class hotels, making them spacious alternatives for business people on long stays or for families intent on cutting costs. Since the kitchens typically have refrigerators, stoves or hot plates, and at least minimal crockery, glassware and utensils, substantial savings can be made compared to restaurant fare and room service. Exemplary of the breed are the **River Inn** and economical **Carlyle Suites**.

Guesthouses and bed-and-breakfasts are increasingly visible. While they tend to be somewhat away from the center of things, they represent excellent value and the opportunity to meet natives and fellow travelers in a cozy atmosphere reminiscent of European *pensions*. The **Kalorama Guest Houses** and **Tabard Inn** are representative. Two organizations function as referral agencies for scores of private homes that take in as many as 12 guests at a time (see pages 108-9). Some of them are as luxuriously furnished as any top hotel, others are merely plain and clean. Most constitute significant travel bargains.

On that subject, bear in mind that most hotels in the greater Washington area offer reduced rates on weekends and often during vacation periods, and tariffs can then be as much as 50 percent less than usual. Be certain to inquire when reserving. These packages frequently carry bonuses ranging from free parking to complimentary breakfast (the price does not usually include breakfast). For further details of such offers or for general hotel information, contact the **Washington Convention and Visitors Association** (*1575 I St. NW, DC 20005* ☎ *789-7000*) or the **Hotel Association of Washington** (*1219 Connecticut Ave. NW, DC 20036* ☎ *833-3350*).

A useful service is provided by **Washington D.C. Accommodations** (*1720 20th St. NW, DC 20009* ☎ *289-2220 or toll-free 1-800-554-2220*). Once they are given the salient facts — length of stay, size of party, particular needs — they suggest hotels in the requested price range, describing them in as much detail as required. When a choice is made, so is the reservation, often right away. Follow-up materials and confirmations arrive by post shortly thereafter. No fee is charged.

Many hotels have sprung up in the immediate suburbs of Washington, including the big new commercial colonies at Rosslyn and Crystal City. Prices are generally lower than in the District, and there is usually quick and easy Metro access.

The following list of hotels is a selective one, covering a broad spectrum with regard to size, price, area and character. In the major hotels all rooms have private bathrooms.

Hotels classified by area

Capitol Hill
Holiday Inn Capitol 📖▯
Hyatt Regency Washington on
  Capitol Hill 📖📖 to 📖📖
Phoenix Park 📖📖
Quality Inn Capitol Hill 📖▯
Washington Court on Capitol Hill
  📖📖 to 📖📖

Dupont Circle
Canterbury 📖📖
Carlyle Suites 📖▯
Embassy Row 📖📖 to 📖📖
Holiday Inn Connecticut Avenue 📖▯

Omni Georgetown 📖📖
Ritz Carlton 📖📖
Embassy District
Normandy Inn 📖▯
Washington Hilton and Towers 📖▯
  to 📖📖
Foggy Bottom
River Inn 📖📖
Watergate 📖📖
Georgetown
Four Seasons 📖📖
Georgetown Inn 📖📖 to 📖📖
Georgetown Marbury House 📖📖

Maryland
Bethesda Marriott *IIII*
Hyatt Regency Bethesda *IIII*
New Downtown
Capital Hilton *IIII to IIII*
Hampshire *IIII*
Hay-Adams *IIII to IIII*
Governors House Holiday Inn *III to
     IIII*
Jefferson *IIII*
Madison *IIII*
Mayflower *IIII to IIII*
Ramada Renaissance *IIII*
Sheraton Carlton *IIII*
Tabard Inn *I□ to IIII*
North of the Convention Center
Morrison-Clark Inn *III to IIII*
Northeast of the White House
Henley Park *IIII*
Holiday Inn Central *III□*
Holiday Inn Thomas Circle *I□ to III□*
Vista International *IIII to IIII*
Old Downtown
Grand Hyatt *IIII*
J. W. Marriott *IIII*
Morrison-Clark *III to IIII*
Washington *IIII*
Willard Inter-Continental *IIII*
Southwest
Channel Inn *III□*
Loews L'Enfant Plaza *IIII*
Upper Northwest
Holiday Inn Georgetown *III□*
Howard Johnson's Wellington *III□*
Kalorama Guest Houses *I□*
Omni Shoreham *III to IIII*
Rock Creek *I□*
Sheraton Washington *IIII to IIII*
Virginia
Best Western — Rosslyn Westpark
     III□
Hyatt Regency Crystal City *IIII*
Marriott — Key Bridge *IIII*
Morrison House *III□*
West End
Grand *IIII*
Washington Marriott *IIII*
Westin *IIII to IIII*
Wyndham Bristol *IIII*

**Best Western — Rosslyn
Westpark**
*1900 North Fort Myer Dr.,
Arlington, Va. 22209* ☎ *527-4814.
Map 4F2 III□ 308 rms* ⊷ ⇄ *AE*
CB *S* *◑* *◐* *VISA Metro: Rosslyn.*
*Location: Across the river from
Georgetown.* A very friendly hotel
whose 17th-floor dining room
commands exciting views.
& ⟨€ ⇝

Bethesda Marriott
*5151 Pooks Hill Rd., Bethesda,
Md. 20814* ☎ *228-9290 IIII 407
rms* ⊷ *AE CB S ◑ ◐ VISA Metro:
Medical Center.*
*Location: 6 miles (10km) NW of the
city center, off the Beltway.* Set in 18

acres (7.3ha) of attractively
landscaped grounds, this hotel has
three restaurants in addition to
extensive sports facilities. There is a
complimentary shuttle service for the
Medical Center Metro station.
& ⥥ ⇝ ⟟

Canterbury
1733 N St. NW, DC 20036
☎ *393-3000 ◑ 892669. Map 3E6
IIII 99 rms* ⊷ ⇄ *AE CB S ◑ ◐*
VISA Metro: Dupont Circle.
*Location: Near the lively Dupont
Circle area and six blocks from the
White House.* A fairly small,
attractive hotel, where the amenities
are modern, with kitchenettes in
every room, although the overall
style is old-world, with paisley
fabrics and some four-poster beds.

Capital Hilton
1001 16th St. NW, DC 20036
☎ *393-1000 ◑ 7108229068. Map
3E6 IIII to IIII 533 rms* ⊷ ⇄ *AE*
*CB ◑ ◐ VISA Metro: McPherson
Square, Farragut North.*
*Location: Three blocks N of the White
House.* Built in 1943, this de luxe
hotel with its marvelous Art Deco
finery was recently totally renovated
at a cost of $44 million and the
rooms reduced from 800 to 533,
making them among the most
spacious in Washington. The hotel
is a pick-up point for airport buses.
& ⟨€ ⟟

Carlyle Suites
*1731 New Hampshire Ave. NW,
DC 20009* ☎ *234-3200. Map 3D6
III□ 176 suites* ⇄ *AE ◑ ◐ VISA
Metro: Dupont Circle.*
*Location: Near Dupont Circle and
the galleries and stores of
Connecticut Ave.* The authentic Art
Deco styling of both exterior and
interior won designation as a
historic landmark for this engaging
stopover. The surroundings are a
bonus, for its primary appeal lies in
the friendly (if occasionally harried)
staff and the roominess of the
lodgings, all of which are suites with
kitchenettes. They are ideal for
families hoping to keep food costs
down. The pleasant **Jimmy K's** has
a super Sunday brunch at
surprisingly low cost.

Channel Inn
650 Water St. SW, DC 20024
☎ *554-2400 ◑ 6971708. Map 7I8
III□ 100 rms* ⊷ ⇄ *Metro:
L'Enfant Plaza.*
Location: On the SW waterfront.
More than half these comfortable
nests overlook the water and

marina; all have balconies. The
swimming pool occupies children in
the humid summer, and those under
12 sleep free in their parents' rooms.
Pier 7, the on-premises restaurant,
has good views and a popular bar,
but ordinary food.

Embassy Row
*2015 Massachusetts Ave. NW,
DC 20036* ☎ *265-1600* ⊙ *892650.
Map 3D5* IIII *to* IIII *194 rms* ⊷
AE CB ⊙ CD VISA *Metro: Dupont
Circle.*
*Location: In the embassy district, a
stone's throw from Dupont Circle.*
Hungarian-born Gabor Olah, the
original manager of the Watergate
Hotel, was lured out of retirement in
Florida to manage this hotel in the
embassy district. He has brought
great polish to the hotel, and his
staff have been carefully trained in
the European tradition of courteous
and efficient service.
↝

Four Seasons
*2800 Pennsylvania Ave. NW, DC
20007* ☎ *342-0444* ⊙ *904008.
Map 2E4* IIII *197 rms* ⊷ ⥰ AE
CB ⊙ CD VISA *Metro: Foggy
Bottom.*
*Location: On the edge of
Georgetown, backing directly onto
the C&O Canal.* Paeans and kudos
are routinely accorded what many
believe is not only the finest
hostelry in the region, but quite
possibly in the land. Showbiz
satraps and folk of noble birth
mingle happily with the world's
movers and shakers. All are
accorded the regal treatment they
rank as their due, but hardly more
than that given unknowns with
sufficient credit ratings. Guests are
whisked directly to their rooms,
without tedious delays at the
registration desk. The **Aux Beaux
Champs** restaurant is up to the
challenge of its surroundings, and
there is an exclusive private disco to
which registered guests are
admitted. One glitch: some rooms
are a trifle snug for these princely
tariffs. Ask for another, preferably
overlooking the Canal.
&

Georgetown Inn
*1310 Wisconsin Ave. NW, DC
20007* ☎ *333-8900* ⊙ *4970926.
Map 2E3* IIII *95 rms* ⊷ ⥰ AE
CB ⊙ CD
*Location: In the heart of
Georgetown.* Handy to Georgetown
clubs and bistros, this mature,
self-effacing brick building is

decorated in attractive Colonial style
with four-poster beds in all rooms.
&

Georgetown Marbury House
3000 M St. NW, DC 20007
☎ *726-5000. Map 2E4* IIII *164
rms* ⊷ AE CB ⊙ CD VISA
Location: Central Georgetown. A
pleasant, comfortable hotel in the
liveliest part of Georgetown. The
building is new but the decor and
furnishings are in Colonial style.
& ↝

Grand
2350 M St. NW, DC 20037
☎ *848-0016* ⊙ *904282. Map 3E5*
IIII *265 rms* ⊷ ⥰ AE CB ⊙ CD
VISA *Metro: Foggy Bottom.*
*Location: West End, a 10min walk
from Georgetown.* The hallowed
Regent empire knows how to
soothe its monied multinational
clientele. A serene, circular, domed
lobby sets the tone. Privacy is
strictly observed, the better to wrap
up in the robes provided and sip
brandy before one of the working
fireplaces. Style and service are
decidedly Continental, with such
comforting amenities as impossibly
lavish baths and a romantic pocket
courtyard. Ensuing sloth can be
worked off in the health club.
& ❦ ↝

Grand Hyatt
1000 H St. NW, DC 20001
☎ *582-1234* ⊙ *897118. Map 6F7*
IIII *to* IIII *907 rms* ⊷ *Metro:
Metro Center.*
*Location: Directly opposite the
Convention Center.* Understatement
is not a corporate goal of the Hyatt
chain. Yes, that is a sunken pool
beneath the tables of the three-tier
lobby lounge, with a special round
island for the cocktail pianist. They
call it the "Lagoon." Waterfalls feed
it. And bubble elevators do swoop
up the sides of the trademark atrium
past the vertiginous walkways at
each floor. Few comforts are
neglected in the relatively restrained
bedrooms, however, and the staff is
surprisingly solicitous for so large a
place. Weekend discount packages
are especially attractive.
&

Hampshire
*1310 New Hampshire Ave. NW,
DC 20036* ☎ *296-7600*
⊙ *7108229343. Map 3E5* IIII *82
rms* ⊷ ⥰ AE CB ⊙ CD VISA
Metro: Dupont Circle.
*Location: Two blocks sw of Dupont
Circle.* A former apartment block

converted into a small hotel with a good reputation for comfort and service. Guests have free use of a health center nearby. The restaurant, **Lafitte**, is known for its New Orleans Creole cooking.

Hay-Adams
1 Lafayette Square NW, DC 20006 ☎ *638-6600* ✆ *7108229543. Map 3F6* ▥▥ *to* ▥▥ *155 rms* ⬠ ⬠ ▱▱ ▱▱ ▱ ▱ ▱ *Metro: McPherson Square, Farragut West.*
Location: Directly across Lafayette Park from the White House. A Rolls-Royce of a hotel, fairly small, quiet, intimate and elegant in an old-world way. The handsome building occupies the site of two earlier houses, one lived in by the historian Henry Adams, the other by John Hay, diplomat, statesman and author of a biography of Lincoln.
✦

Henley Park
926 Massachusetts Ave. NW, DC 20001 ☎ *638-5200* ✆ *904059* ▥▥ *96 rms* ⬠ ⬠ ▱▱ ▱▱ ▱ ▱ ▱ *Metro: Gallery Place, Metro Center.*
Location: On the N edge of Old Downtown. An exceptionally attractive, quiet, small hotel with a calming Old World atmosphere and carefully chosen furnishings to match, a stone's throw from the *Washington Convention Center*.

Holiday Inn Capitol
550 C St. SW, DC 20024 ☎ *479-4000. Map 7G8* ▥▥ *530 rms* ⬠ ⬠ ▱▱ ▱▱ ▱ ▱ ▱ *Metro: L'Enfant Plaza.*
⬠ ⬠

Holiday Inn Central
1501 Rhode Island Ave., DC 20005 ☎ *483-2000. Map 3E6* ▥▥ *214 rms* ⬠ ⬠ ▱▱ ▱▱ ▱ ▱ ▱ *Metro: Farragut North.*
⬠ ⬠

Holiday Inn Connecticut Avenue
1900 Connecticut Ave. NW, DC 20009 ☎ *332-9300. Map 3C5* ▥▥ *149 rms* ⬠ ⬠ ▱▱ ▱▱ ▱ ▱ ▱ *Metro: Dupont Circle.*
⬠ ✦ ⬠

Holiday Inn Georgetown
2101 Wisconsin Ave. NW, DC 20007 ☎ *338-4600. Map 2C2* ▥▥ *300 rms* ⬠ ⬠ ▱▱ ▱▱ ▱ ▱ ▱
⬠ ⬠

Governors House Holiday Inn
1615 Rhode Island Ave, NW, DC 20036 ☎ *296-2100. Map 3E6* ▥▥ *to* ▥▥ *152 rms* ⬠ ⬠ ▱▱ ▱▱ ▱ ▱ ▱ *Metro: Farragut North.*

Holiday Inn Thomas Circle
1155 14th St. NW, DC 20005 ☎ *737-1200. Map 3E7* ▥▥ *to* ▥▥ *208 rms* ⬠ ⬠ ▱▱ ▱▱ ▱ ▱ ▱ *Metro: McPherson Square.*
⬠ ⬠

The Washington Holiday Inns vary slightly in price but are all broadly similar in character. They do not pretend to offer great luxury or superior service, but you can rely on a good standard of comfort and efficiency.

Howard Johnson's Wellington
2505 Wisconsin Ave. NW, ,DC 20007 ☎ *337-7400* ▥▥ *147 rms* ⬠ ⬠ ▱▱ ▱▱ ▱ ▱ ▱
Location: Upper Northwest. A converted building in a pleasant location near the upper end of Embassy Row. Much of its business is connected with the embassies. It has an attractive restaurant called **The Gazebo**.
⬠ ⬠

Hyatt Regency Bethesda
1 Bethesda Metro Center, Bethesda, Md. 20814 ☎ *(301) 657-1234* ▥▥ *383 rms* ⬠ ⬠ ▱▱ ▱▱ ▱ ▱ ▱ *Metro: Bethesda.*
Location: Directly above Bethesda Metro station, 5 miles (8km) from central Washington. Opened in Nov 1985, this hotel is located in the business and shopping area of downtown Bethesda.
⬠ ⬠ ⬠

Hyatt Regency Crystal City
2799 Jefferson Davis Highway, Arlington, Va. 22202 ☎ *486-1234* ✆ *901943* ▥▥ *685 rms* ⬠ ⬠ ▱▱ ▱▱ ▱ ▱ ▱ *Metro: Crystal City.*
Location: Next to National Airport. A handsome hotel, recognizably Hyatt in style with its 5-story atrium, which is full of greenery and glassed-in elevators. Most of the clientele is corporate.
⬠ ✦ ⬠

Hyatt Regency Washington on Capitol Hill
400 New Jersey Ave, NW, DC 20001 ☎ *737-1234* ✆ *897432. Map 7F9* ▥▥ *to* ▥▥ *842 rms* ⬠ ⬠ ▱▱ ▱▱ ▱ ▱ ▱ *Metro: Union Station.*
Location: Near Union Station. The most striking feature of this hotel is its huge skylit atrium with a fountain and forest of trees. The usual Hyatt standard of comfort and facilities prevails. There is a good view from the rooftop dining room.
⬠ ⬠

Jefferson

1200 16th St. NW, DC 20036
☎ 347-2200 ❿ 248879. Map 3E6
IIIII 104 rms ⇌ ⊒ AE CB ⊙ ⊙
VISA Metro: Farragut North.
Location: Five blocks N of the White House. The Jefferson in its present form is the creation of one of Washington's most gifted hoteliers, Mrs Rose Narva, who also masterminded the renovation of the **Hay-Adams** and the **Sheraton Carlton**. At the Jefferson she has created a highly civilized environment. The prevailing style is 18thC English. Mrs Narva and her staff go out of their way to ensure that their guests feel at home in this unique hotel.
& ⊄

Kalorama Guest House

1854 Mintwood Pl., DC 20009
☎ 667-6369. Map 3C5. 31 rms.
Also *2700 Cathedral Ave., DC
20008* ☎ 328-0860. Map 3B5. 19
rms. Both ☐ to ⊓ AE ⊙ ⊙
Metro: Woodley Park-Zoo.
Location: The first near the sprightly Adams-Morgan district, the second near the Zoo. Here is a top choice for those willing to swap color TV and room service for a companionable sherry by the fire in the parlor. Closely resembling a London B&B of the sort furnished by judicious shopping in flea markets and garage sales, each of the six turn-of-the-century townhouses is clean and tidy, with no costly frippery. All are air conditioned, though, and about a third have private baths. The breakfast buffet has muffins, bagels, fruit and juices, with tea available 24hrs. Guests are welcome to use the refrigerator and laundry machines. Think of vacations at Grandma's house.

Loews L'Enfant Plaza

*480 L'Enfant Plaza East SW, DC
20024* ☎ 484-1000 ❿ 89657. Map
6H7 IIIII 372 rms ⇌ ⊒ AE CB ⊙
⊙ VISA Metro: L'Enfant Plaza.
Location: Between the Mall and the SW waterfront. In a somewhat stark and characterless environment but well placed for the Smithsonian museums on the S Mall. Rooms have mini-bars and closed-circuit movies. Pets are allowed, and children under 14 are welcome to stay free with parents.
⊄ ⇝

Madison

15th and M St. NW, DC 20005
☎ 862-1600 ❿ 64245. Map 3E6 IIIII

368 rms ⇌ ⊒ AE CB ⊙ ⊙ VISA
Metro: McPherson Square.
Location: Five blocks N of the White House. One of Washington's top hotels. Each room has an individual touch, and the furnishings and decoration are comprised of items from the proprietor's own collection, including many Oriental *objets d'art*.

J. W. Marriott

*1331 Pennsylvania Ave. NW, DC
20004* ☎ 393-2000 ❿ 7108229638.
Map 6F7 IIIII 774 rms ⇌ ⊒ AE
CB ⊙ ⊙ VISA Metro: Metro
Center.
Location: Old Downtown, facing the Federal Triangle and next door to the National Theater. Opened in 1984 as part of the new National Place complex. The glum brown exterior compares unfavorably with the Willard, across the street, but the lobby is a striking 4-story atrium of pink marble and mahogany. Below are restaurants, meeting rooms and two grand ballrooms. Above are guest rooms, some with magnificent views.
& ⊄ ⇝ ⍹

Marriott — Key Bridge

*1401 Lee Highway, Arlington,
Va. 22209* ☎ 524-6400. Map 4F2
IIIII 558 rms ⇌ ⊒ AE CB ⊙ ⊙
VISA Metro: Rosslyn.
Location: Directly across the river from Georgetown. Built about 20yrs ago, this attractively furnished hotel is the second oldest of the Marriott chain. Its rooftop **View** restaurant commands a fine panorama.
& ⊄ ⇝

Mayflower

*1127 Connecticut Ave. NW, DC
20036* ☎ 347-3000 ❿ 892324.
Map 3E6 IIIII to IIIII 724 rms ⇌
⊒ AE CB ⊙ ⊙ VISA Metro:
Farragut North.
Location: New Downtown. One of the grandest of *grande dame* hotels. Opened in 1925, in time for President Coolidge's inaugural ball, it has recently undergone renovation and has re-emerged in all its finery. In the richly ornate lobby there is a model of the ship after which the hotel was named. It has two restaurants: **Nicholas**, a high-class, formal dining room, and the **Café Promenade** for more casual meals. The latter has some charming murals of garden scenes painted by Edward Lanning under the auspices of the Works Progress Administration in the 1930s. They were covered in the 1950s and only

rediscovered during the recent extensive restoration.
&

Morrison-Clark Inn
Massachusetts Ave. and 11th St., NW, DC 20001 ☎ *898-1200* ▥ *to* ▥▥ *54 rms and suites* ⇌
▣ ▣ ▣ ▣
Location: N of Techworld and the Convention Center. No effort has been spared to make this a new benchmark in elegant urban inns. Built in 1864 and long known to Washingtonians as home of the Soldiers & Sailors Club, it burst its glum cocoon and emerged a radiant butterfly in 1989. No two of its always bright and airy rooms are precisely alike, with their lace curtains or wicker or armoires or monumental headboards, many of them antiques. Unobtrusive modernity adds computer-access data ports to such customary gadgets as remote-control TV. The smashing dining room, with its crystal chandeliers and marble fireplaces, showcases one of the District's hottest young chefs. A limo is available to guests.

Morrison House
116 S Alfred St., Alexandria, Va. 22314 ☎ *838-8000* ❹ *3792672* ▥▯ *47 rms* ⇌ ▣ ▣ ▣ ▣ ▣
Metro: King Street.
Location: Near the center of Alexandria. Undisputed front-runner among Alexandria hostelries, this is in the same rarefied league as the similarly named **Morrison-Clark Inn** (above). In fact, the owners of that estimable establishment dropped by during their planning stage to pick up pointers. Although the brick building just off King St. is of recent construction, here too are superbly furnished rooms featuring brass chandeliers and high four-poster beds, an extremely cordial and helpful staff, and a restaurant with an enviable reputation for its contemporary Gallic cuisine. Take afternoon tea in the firelit parlor, or savor a cognac to piano music in the **Grill** room.

Normandy Inn
2118 Wyoming Ave. NW, DC 20008 ☎ *483-1350. Map 3C5* ▯▯ *72 rms* ⇌ ▣ ▣ ▣ ▣ ▣
Metro: Dupont Circle.
Location: NW of Dupont Circle, in the embassy district. Although the bland modern exterior doesn't look promising, the Irish owners have instilled an open-hearted attitude in

its employees and added such niceties as a weekly wine reception. Most of the so-called "Queen" rooms have VCRs and unstocked mini-refrigerators. Continental breakfast is extra, but inexpensive, and is served on the patio in fine weather. There is a secure underground garage.

Omni Georgetown
2121 P St. NW, DC 20037 ☎ *293-3100. Map 3D5* ▥▥ *300 rms* ⇌ ▣ ▣ ▣ ▣ ▣
Metro: Dupont Circle.
Location: Just w of Dupont Circle and near, but not in, Georgetown. The building is a former apartment block with spacious rooms, all recently refurbished. Middle-level and middlebrow rather than flashy, it provides expectable comforts and an attentive staff.
& ⇌ ▾

Omni Shoreham
2500 Calvert St. NW, DC 20008 ☎ *235-0700* ❹ *7108220142. Map 2B4* ▥▥ *to* ▥▥ *884 rms* ⇌ ▣ ▣ ▣ ▣ *Metro: Woodley Park-Zoo.*
Location: Upper Northwest, near the Zoo. A large and imposing 1930s Art Deco-style building, which has been recently renovated. It is in a pleasant residential part of town with expansive grounds and direct access to **Rock Creek Park.** There is dancing nightly in the **Marquee Lounge** and a comedy cabaret Fri-Sun evenings as well as a Sun matinée.
⇌ ⮿

Phoenix Park
520 North Capitol St. NW, DC 20001 ☎ *638-6900* ❹ *904104. Map 7F9* ▥▥ *84 rms* ⇌ ▣ ▣ ▣ ▣ ▣ *Metro: Union Station.*
Location: Close to Union Station Named after the famous Dublin park, this is a small luxury hotel with an atmosphere as warm as the Irish accents that can often be heard here. Its high-class restaurant, the **Powerscourt,** is much frequented by members of Congress. Next door, under the same management, is the **Dubliner** pub.
&

Quality Inn Capitol Hill
415 New Jersey Ave. NW, DC 20001 ☎ *638-1616* ❹ *7108220153. Map 7F9* ▥▯ *341 rms* ⇌ ▣ ▣ ▣ ▣ ▣ *Metro: Union Station.*
Location: Near Union Station and the Capitol. A modern 10-story

hotel, not in the luxury class, but functional and comfortable.
&. 🛏

Ramada Renaissance
1143 New Hampshire Ave. NW, DC 20037 ☎ *755-0800*
🖂 *7108229209. Map 3E5* ⅢⅢ *355 rms* 🍴 ⚌ AE CB ⬤ CD VISA
Metro: Dupont Circle, Foggy Bottom.
Location: W side of New Downtown, within easy walking distance of Georgetown, the Kennedy Center and Dupont Circle. One of the better representatives of an elite subdivision of the ubiquitous motel chain, this ambitious Ramada spent much of its budget on the impressive lobby. The bright, marble-floored space has a forest of potted plants and a large glass front.
&.

Ritz Carlton
2100 Massachusetts Ave. NW, DC 20008 ☎ *293-2100* 🖂 *263758. Map 3D5* ⅢⅢ *250 rms* 🍴 ⚌ AE CB ⬤ CD VISA *Metro: Dupont Circle.*
Location: Embassy Row, near Dupont Circle. One of the District's premier haunts of the power elite, the **Fairfax** lounge and deceptively rustic **Jockey Club** restaurant are feasts for political junkies. Sooner or later, all of Washington's most influential media people and Congressional leaders put in appearances. The rest of us are made quite welcome, from ingratiating reception to nightly turn-down. Sister Parish, the designer, preferred lots of chintz, pencil-post beds and furnishings reminiscent of British country estates. Bathrooms boast not only powerful hairdryers and water temperature gauges on the showers, but telephones and TV sets. If price is no object, choose one of the suites overlooking Massachusetts Ave. If it is, and there are children along, stay elsewhere. With its air of knowing formality, this is a haven for CEO's, diplomats, senators and businessmen.
&. 👜

River Inn
924 25th St. NW, DC 20037 ☎ *337-7600. Map 2F4* ⅢⅢ *127 suites* ⚌ AE ⬤ CD VISA *Metro: Foggy Bottom.*
Location: A short walk from Watergate and Kennedy Center. This paradigm of all-suites hotels rises above a tranquil block of neat 2-story terraces. To the left of the

entry is the **Foggy Bottom Café**, where even soups and sandwiches are notches above the norm. Rooms are in soothing desert tones, with Oriental prints and vases of silk flowers. The kitchens have microwave ovens and refrigerators. In many, a canister of fresh coffee beans stands next to a grinder and percolator. A weather report accompanies the wake-up call, and the morning newspaper is delivered to the door. All this, and blessed space to sprawl or organize stacks of reports. The "Potomac" suites have views of the river.
&.

Rock Creek
1925 Belmont Rd. NW, DC 20009 ☎ *462-6007. Map 2C4* ☐ *54 rms* 🍴 *Metro: Woodley Park-Zoo.*
Location: Upper Northwest, on the edge of Rock Creek Park. A low-priced hotel, where the rooms are simply furnished and clean, yet manage to avoid being poky. The location is pleasant and convenient.

Sheraton Carlton
923 16th St. NW, DC 20009 ☎ *638-2626* 🖂 *440650. Map 3E6* ⅢⅢ *250 rms* 🍴 ⚌ AE CB ⬤ CD VISA *Metro: Farragut North, McPherson Square.*
Location: Two blocks N of the White House. A gracious hotel built in 1926, which was extensively renovated under the supervision of Mrs Rose Narva, who runs the **Jefferson** hotel. It is now one of the most opulent of Washington hotels.

Sheraton Washington
2660 Woodley Rd. NW, DC 20008 ☎ *328-2000* 🖂 *892630. Map 2B4* ⅢⅢ *to* ⅢⅢ *1,500 rms* 🍴 ⚌ AE CB ⬤ CD VISA *Metro: Woodley Park-Zoo.*
Location: Upper Northwest, near the Zoo and Rock Creek Park. A huge hotel incorporating two modern buildings and a historic former apartment house. It has three restaurants, two lounges (one with live music Mon-Sat evenings) and a variety of shops including a hairdresser, beauty parlor and post office. On Sun there is a gargantuan American buffet with over 175 items.
&. 🛏

Tabard Inn
1739 N St. NW, DC 20036 ☎ *785-1277. Map 3E6* ☐ *to* ⅢⅢ *40 rms* ⚌ ⬤ VISA *Metro: Dupont Circle.*
Location: Two blocks SE of Dupont Circle. A jolly Buddha greets guests

in the tiny lobby, in which no interior designer can have had a hand. Scattered about are well-used oddments of furniture and bric-à-brac that might be encountered in a Cotswolds inn. Beyond that is a dim paneled sanctum where residents chat over drinks beside a crackling fire. The decorative non-scheme carries through to the bedchambers, some of which share baths. A restaurant serves all three meals daily. The three mid-19thC townhouses that comprise the Tabard enhance the quiet residential street, yet are only a short walk from Dupont Circle.
♨

Vista International
1400 M St. NW, DC 20005
☎ *429-1700* ☎ *440237. Map 3E6*
||||| *to* ||||| *396 rms* 🚗 🍽 AE CB
⊕ CD VISA *Metro: McPherson Square.*
Location: Five blocks N of the White House. Glassed-in atriums have become popular features in American hotels. This hotel has a particularly striking one that is 14 stories high — a delightful place in which to listen to the chamber orchestra that plays in the evenings.
♨ ♨ ♨

Washington
15th St. and Pennsylvania Ave. NW, DC 20004 ☎ *638-5900*
☎ *7108220105. Map 6F6* ||||| *370 rms* 🚗 🍽 AE CB ⊕ ⊕ VISA
Metro: Metro Center.
Location: Close to the White House. A fine old hotel in a prime position, it has been in operation since 1918 and recently was totally renovated. From the top floor, with its restaurant and open-air terrace bar, there is an unparalleled view of central Washington.
♨ ♨

Washington Court on Capitol Hill
525 New Jersey Ave. NW, DC 20001 ☎ *628-2100* ☎ *4970525.*
Map 7F9 ||||| *to* ||||| *272 rms* 🚗
🍽 AE CB ⊕ ⊕ VISA *Metro: Union Station.*
Location: Near Union Station and the Capitol. The salient feature of this former Sheraton is its striking 3-story atrium. Some $150,000 was spent on the greenery alone, brought from all over the world. The mezzanine café in the atrium makes a delightful spot for a light meal, and there is also a more formal restaurant. Guests have the use of the **Capitol Hill Squash Club.**
♨

Washington Hilton and Towers
1919 Connecticut Ave. NW, DC 20009 ☎ *483-3000* ☎ *248761.*
Map 3C5 ||||| *to* ||||| *1,154 rms* 🚗
🍽 AE CB ⊕ ⊕ VISA *Metro: Dupont Circle.*
Location: N of Dupont Circle. This large, modern hotel commands fine views out over the city. Popular with conferences and tour groups, it has the largest ballroom in Washington.
♨ ♨ ♨ ♨ ♨ ♨

Washington Marriott
1221 22nd St. NW, DC 20037
☎ *872-1500* ☎ *7108221195. Map 3E5* ||||| *350 rms* 🚗 🍽 AE CB ⊕
⊕ VISA *Metro: Foggy Bottom.*
Location: A 10min walk from Georgetown, in New Downtown. A comfortable, modern hotel (opened in 1981) with rooms furnished in contemporary style.
♨ ♨

Watergate
2600 Virginia Ave. NW, DC 20037 ☎ *298-4450* ☎ *904994.*
Map 2F4 ||||| *238 rms* 🚗 🍽 AE
CB ⊕ ⊕ VISA *Metro: Foggy Bottom.*
Location: Foggy Bottom, near the Kennedy Center. Part of a large conglomeration of buildings overlooking the Potomac (see **Watergate Complex**), this luxurious hotel, set in attractively landscaped grounds, is run with tremendous style and polish. It has two restaurants, one of which is the well-known **Jean-Louis** (see **Restaurants**).
♨ ♨ ♨ ♨ ♨

Westin
2401 M St. NW, DC 20037
☎ *429-2400* ☎ *4979800. Map 3E5* ||||| *to* ||||| *416 rms* 🚗 🍽 AE CB
⊕ ⊕ VISA *Metro: Foggy Bottom.*
Location: N of Washington Circle. Opened at the end of 1985, this is a luxury hotel of very attractive design, focusing on a charming garden courtyard with trees, shrubs and a stone Italian fountain in the center. The accent throughout is on traditional elegance coupled with modern convenience.
♨ ♨ ♨ ♨

Willard Inter-Continental
1401 Pennsylvania Ave. NW, DC 20008 ☎ *628-9100* ☎ *3725559.*
Map 6F7 ||||| *395 rms* 🚗 🍽 AE
CB ⊕ ⊕ VISA *Metro: Metro Center.*
Location: Close to the White House and the Mall. Not just a hotel but

one of Washington's great historic landmarks, in existence since 1850 and rebuilt in its present palatial Beaux-Arts form around the turn of the century. Presidents, senators, heads of state, diplomats and tycoons have all gathered and conferred in its sumptuous rooms. The building was threatened with demolition, but was fortunately saved and entirely renovated. It has now re-emerged in all its ornate glory as a jewel of the resurrected Old Downtown.
&. ◁€

Wyndham Bristol
2430 Pennsylvania Ave. NW, DC 20037 ☎ 955-6400 ◉ 292024. Map 2E4 ▥ 240 rms ⇌ ═ AE CB DC ◑ VISA Metro: Foggy Bottom.
Location: In the West End, a 5min walk from Georgetown. As the name suggests, this elegant hotel has adopted an English style, right down to the mahogany four-poster bed in every room. Each room also has a kitchen attached. The excellent **Bristol Grill** is famous for its mesquite-grilled dishes.

Bed-and-breakfast lodgings

Alternatives to conventional hotels in Washington fall roughly into two categories. First are guesthouses in transformed private homes comparable to London B&Bs or to Florentine *pensioni*. These solicit trade by advertising or merely hanging out signs. Some are described above. Another, far larger group can be located only through co-operative referral agencies. Prominent among these is **Bed 'n' Breakfast Ltd of Washington, DC** (*P.O. Box 12011, DC 20005 ☎ 328-3510*).

This organization acts as a clearing house and reservation center for about 60 or 70 member "hosts." These are private individuals with one or more rooms available to guests in their homes. Most of them — a remarkably energetic lot — pursue full-time careers unrelated to innkeeping. The lodgings they offer range from astonishingly ornate to nearly spartan, in century-old buildings or modern high-rise towers.

It represents, for example, a couple identified only as "Host #135." The 1890s structure has a magnificent parlor with fireplace and bay windows. Floral sprays are everywhere. Sit-down breakfast is served at a communal table set with silver flatware beneath a crystal chandelier. One of the four upstairs bedrooms is done in grand Art Deco-Moderne style; another has a canopied four-poster with wing chairs. All have TV, clock radios and telephones. Host #100 has a flamboyant Victorian residence that would have amused Auntie Mame, with a player piano and giant antique theatrical posters. A one-bedroom basement apartment has an equipped kitchen, while five other rooms have shuttered windows and colorful throw pillows. Full breakfasts are provided on Wednesdays and Saturdays. Host #112 is located in a 1910 Georgian-style house behind the Washington Hilton. An author of books on recent history, he is proud of his extensive library and Oriental carpets.

Obviously, a certain spirit of adventure is required of those deciding to use one of these agencies. Rooms may or may not have the gadgets to which Americans are accustomed in hotels. Most must share bathrooms with other guests, although usually with only one other room. The hosts have a variety of idiosyncrasies they enforce, since these are their homes. Many forbid smoking entirely, few allow pets, and many restrict their properties to children above certain ages. Conversely, they are knowledgable about their city, are invariably outgoing, take pride in their hospitality, and rarely charge more than $90 a night for their best rooms, with some going as low as $30. A number of unhosted apartments are also available, which amount to short-term rentals.

Reservations are made by contacting one of the agencies by mail or phone. In addition to Bed 'n' Breakfast Ltd of Washington, there is the **Bed & Breakfast League, Ltd** (*3639 Van Ness NW, DC 20008* ☎ *363-7767*). It recently combined with a third agency, **Sweet Dreams and Toast, Inc.** After determining requirements, they match prospective guests with appropriate hosts. An advance deposit must then be sent to secure lodging. Major credit cards are accepted, but money orders or travelers cheques are preferred.

Where to eat

In the days when Washington was a federal government "company town," it was as hard to discover an interesting restaurant as it was to find an intelligent person who could converse about anything other than politics. Steak and potatoes and Southern fried chicken were the staple diet, and foreign cuisine meant little more than a handful of Italian, French and Chinese restaurants. Tight government expense accounts exacerbated the situation, and cuisine was generally a low priority. Circumstances have now changed, partly thanks to the large corporations that have recently moved their headquarters into the Washington suburbs, bringing with them a huge influx of expense-account customers who demand both quality and variety.

There are now about 150 different nationalities of cuisine represented in the city, the only notable exception being Scandinavian. Successful ethnic restaurants of all types cluster in Adams-Morgan, Georgetown and the suburbs. Take the Metro to Arlington and it's like being in little Saigon; the Chinese stronghold is still in its Old Downtown position around H St. Regional differences have also become important. Exciting northern Italian cooking has largely replaced spaghetti and meatballs, and Chinese no longer means just Cantonese but also Hunan and Szechuan. At the same time Washingtonians still relish their local specialties: the fresh bounty of Chesapeake Bay, the cornucopia of products from Maryland and Virginia farms (ham, game, fruit, vegetables, dairy products), and beef from America's heartland.

Today the diner seeking interesting experiences will find Indian, Creole, Cuban, Spanish, Ethiopian, Guatemalan, Mexican, Brazilian, German, Hungarian and French restaurants in various parts of Washington. Meanwhile tradition still reigns along "Restaurant Row" — K St. w of Connecticut Ave. — where prices tend to match the elaborately stylized menu designs.

Power lunches are a Washington specialty, and for many people the place and the customers are more important considerations than the menu. Status comes with a center table at the **Maison Blanche**, close to the White House, or at **Duke Zeibert's** on Connecticut Ave. Media moguls even gather for power breakfasts at **Joe and Mo's**, also on Connecticut Ave. On Capitol Hill, places where you may catch a glimpse of a member of Congress or two include **The Monocle**, **La Colline**, the **Sheraton Grand** hotel, **La Brasserie** and the **American Café** — or you could sample the famous Senate bean soup in the *Capitol* cafeteria.

Waterfront restaurants seem to blossom as regularly as the cherry trees around the Tidal Basin. The grandiose Potomac On The River, in the handsome Washington Harbour complex, was an expensive flop. But less ambitious enterprises thrive — the Tex-Mex yuppie haven **Jaimalito's** and **Hisago**, for two. Instant success attended the openings of **Adirondacks** in Union Station, cacophonous **Twenty-One Federal** and Tuscan tribute **i Ricchi**. They seem likely to survive in a business with a daunting mortality rate; but even if they do not, other gastronomic gamblers will race to fill the void.

With the renaissance of *Old Downtown* has come a mushrooming of restaurants in that area, and several new hotels with first-class restaurants have upgraded the standard of dining in the West End. Furthermore, at any high-class restaurant you can now count on an excellent selection of wines, usually from America and Europe. So today you need never go far in Washington to find an acceptable place to eat and drink.

When reading a menu, bear in mind that prices do not include tax. A basic tip is about 15 percent and up to 20 percent in the smartest establishments.

Restaurants classified by area

Adams-Morgan
Fasikas *I❏* Ethiop
New Orleans Emporium *II❏* Creole
Capitol Hill
Adirondacks *IIII❏* Am
American Café (1) *II❏* Am
La Brasserie *II❏* Fr
La Colline *II❏* Fr
The Monocle *IIII* Am
Dupont Circle
El Bodegon *II❏* Sp
Galileo *IIII* It
The Jockey Club *IIII* intnl
Foggy Bottom/West End
Jean-Louis *IIII* Fr
Maison Blanche *IIII* Fr
Georgetown
American Café (3) *II❏* Am
Au Pied de Cochon *II❏* Fr
Aux Fruits de Mer *II❏* Fr fish
Bamiyan (1) *II❏* Afghan
Clyde's *II❏* Am
Madurai *I❏* Ind veg
Martin's Tavern *II❏* Am
Maryland
O'Brien's Pit Barbecue (1) and (2)
I❏ S Am
New Downtown
Bacchus *II❏* Leb
Bombay Palace *II❏* Ind
Charley's Crab *IIII* fish
Dominique's *IIII* Fr
Duke Zeibert's *IIII* Am
i Ricchi *II to III❏* It
Joe and Mo's *IIII* Am fish
Le Lion d'Or *IIII* Fr
Le Pavillon *IIII* Fr
Prime Rib *IIII* Am
Takesushi *IIII* Jap
Tiberio *IIII* It
Old Downtown
Big Wong *❏* Ch
Café Mozart *I❏* Ger

Dutch Mill Deli *❏* Am
Hunan Chinatown *II❏* Ch
Marrakesh *II❏* Moroc
Occidental *II❏* Am
Old Ebbitt Grill *II❏* Am
Pavilion at the Old Post Office *I❏ to*
IIII intnl
Southwest
Hogate's *II❏* Am fish
Phillips Flagship *IIII* Am fish
Upper Northwest
American Café (2) and (4)
II❏ Am
Dancing Crab *II❏* fish
Thai Taste *I❏* Thai
Virginia
L'Auberge Chez Francois
IIII Fr
Bamiyan (2) *II❏* Afghan
Le Chardon d'Or *IIII* Fr
East Wind *I❏ to II❏*
Viet
O'Brien's Pit Barbecue (3) *I❏*
S Am
Potowmack Landing *II❏* Am

Key to types of cuisine
Am	American
Ch	Chinese
Ethiop	Ethiopian
Fr	French
Ger	German
Ind	Indian
intnl	international
It	Italian
Jap	Japanese
Leb	Lebanese
Moroc	Moroccan
S Am	South American
Sp	Spanish
veg	vegetarian
Viet	Vietnamese

Adirondacks
50 Massachusetts Ave. NE
☎ *682-1840. Map 7F9* ▥ ➤ *AE*
⊙ ⊙ ▥ Closed major hols.
Metro: Union Station.
The name suggests a setting
imitative of the vast timbered lodges
of upstate New York. Instead, the
space at the E end of Union Station,
echoing the vaulted halls of the
main concourse, more nearly
resembles the ballroom of a Beaux
Arts Manhattan hotel. Huge vats of
flowers in the sleek marble bar and
dining room are in keeping with the
vast scale. The food is eclectic
American and unsolemn. A playful
kitchen sends out plates with
Post-Modernist arrangements of
triangles, squares and
parallelograms of fried polenta,
each a different color. Swordfish
arrives rare, in steakhouse style. The
menu is changed daily. Apart from
an occasional minor fumble, servers
are adroit and cheery. Good wines,
not plonk, are available by the glass.
Note that a 15 percent service
charge is added to the bill, still an
infrequent practice in these parts.

American Café (1)
227 Massachusetts Ave. NE
☎ *547-8500. Map 7F9* ▥ *AE CB*
⊙ ⊙ ▥ Closed Christmas,
Thanksgiving. Metro: Union
Station.
American Café (2)
1300 F St. NW ☎ *626-0770. Map*
6F7 ▥ *AE CB ⊙ ⊙ ▥ Closed*
Christmas, Thanksgiving. Metro:
Metro Center.
American Café (3)
1211 Wisconsin Ave. NW
☎ *944-9464. Map 2E3* ▥ *AE CB*
⊙ ⊙ ▥ Closed Christmas,
Thanksgiving.
American Café (4)
5252 Wisconsin Ave. NW
☎ *363-5400* ▥ *AE CB ⊙ ⊙ ▥*
Closed Christmas, Thanksgiving.
Metro: Friendship Heights.
This chain has four restaurants in
the District. Dishes rotate
seasonally, but the food is basically
light, standard American fare. It is
variable in quality, but pasta,
quiches and salads — especially the
chicken and tarragon salad — are
good. The wines are all American.

L'Auberge Chez Francois
322 Springvale Rd., Great Falls,
Va. ☎ *(703) 759-3800* ▥ ➤ *AE*
⊙ ▥ Closed Mon, Christmas,
New Year's Day.
About 15 miles (22.5km) up the
Potomac from central Washington,
this French country inn has a
long-standing and devoted
following. The menu is *prix fixe*
only, with a choice of such entrées
as peppered swordfish steak,
salmon soufflé and duck
choucroute. Reservations essential.

Au Pied de Cochon
1335 Wisconsin Ave. NW
☎ *333-5440. Map 2E3* ▥ *AE CB*
⊙ ⊙ ▥ Closed Mon 2.30-
11.30am.
This amiable French bistro drew a
touch of notoriety when a KGB
defector to the CIA left his meal to
defect back to the Soviet Union.
That flurry of unwanted attention
aside, its durability is sustained by
its round-the-clock hours and the
availability of such sturdy
retro-comfort food as *coq au vin*
and onion soup. Dinner servings are
appropriately substantial, but lighter
fare can be chosen for
after-midnight snacks following a
Georgetown pub crawl. They only
close for a few hours Mon morning.

Aux Fruits de Mer
1329 Wisconsin Ave. NW
☎ *333-2333. Map 2E3* ▥ ➤ *AE*
CB ⊙ ▥
A suitably nautical decor
complements the wide range of
seafood on offer at this busy
Georgetown restaurant. It shares a
kitchen with the adjacent **Au Pied
de Cochon**, but the menu is
different.

Bacchus
1827 Jefferson Pl. NW
☎ *785-0734. Map 3E5* ▥ ➤ *AE*
⊙ ▥ Closed Sun, major hols.
Metro: Dupont Circle.
A small, elegant Lebanese
restaurant, serving consistently good
food. The menu includes such
exotic-sounding dishes as *ouzi*
(lamb served on a bed of spiced rice
with minced meat, almonds and
pine kernels) and *warak inab
mahshi* (stuffed vine leaves).

Bamiyan (1)
3320 M St. NW ☎ *338-1896. Map*
2E3 ▥ ➤ *AE ⊙ ▥ Closed*
Thanksgiving and for lunch.
Bamiyan (2)
300 King St., Alexandria, Va.
☎ *548-9006* ▥ ➤ *AE ⊙ ▥*
Closed Christmas, Thanksgiving.
The two branches of this restaurant
have won fervent converts to
Afghan food among
Washingtonians. As well as
wonderfully spicy kebabs and other
meat dishes, there is a choice of
vegetarian fare.

Big Wong
*610 H St. NW ☎ 638-0116. Map
7F8 ⬚ AE CD VISA Metro: Gallery
Place.*
Located in Chinatown, this simply
decorated restaurant offers a wide
range of delicious Cantonese dishes
at very reasonable prices. Bear in
mind that no wine is served here,
only beer and soft drinks. Popular
for a *dim sum* Sun brunch.

El Bodegon
*1637 R St. NW ☎ 667-1710. Map
3D6 ⬚ AE CB CD VISA Closed
Sun. Metro: Dupont Circle.*
Veteran Hispanophiles are here
transported to a Madrid *taberna*.
Authenticity is promoted by the
hams and garlands of garlic and
dried peppers hanging from the
ceiling. *Aficionados* nibble on the
traditional bar snacks called *tapas*,
from a changing list of up to 40 tasty
dishes. In the main room, such
staple Spanish recipes as seafood
paella and *zarzuela* are
understandable favorites.
Middling-good flamenco music and
dancing enliven dinners Mon-Sat.

Bombay Palace
*1835 K St. NW ☎ 331-0111. Map
3E6 ⬚ to ⬚ AE CD CD VISA
Closed major hols. Metro:
Farragut West.*
Not all K St. restaurants require a
thick billfold or gold credit card.
Patrons willingly line up for up to an
hour for the bargain all-you-can-eat
weekend brunches at this outpost of
the international chain. They
descend from street level past brass
figurines in lighted niches. The large
basement rooms are in pale green,
rose and pink, with a few vaguely
Art Moderne filigrees no doubt left
over from an earlier tenant.
Tandoori breads and fowl and, of
course, curries lead the card. While
prices are higher than usually
encountered at ethnic eateries, they
seem a relief after dinner at one of
the neighborhood's expense
account emporia.

La Brasserie
*239 Massachusetts Ave. NE
☎ 546-9154. Map 7F8 ⬚ AE
CD CD VISA Metro: Union Station.*
La Brasserie offers *nouvelle cuisine*,
exquisitely prepared in tiny portions
at vast prices. The decor is intimate
and recherché.

Café Mozart
*1331 H St. NW ☎ 347-5732. Map
6F6 ⬚ AE CB CD CD VISA
Closed Christmas, New Year's*

*Day. Metro: Metro Center,
McPherson Square.*
The best place in Washington for
excellent German food at
reasonable prices. The atmosphere
is enriched by music — a different
program every evening, usually of
piano or accordion, sans singing.

Le Chardon d'Or
*Morrison House hotel, 116 S
Alfred St., Alexandria, Va.
☎ (703) 838-8000 ⬚ AE
CD VISA Metro: King Street.*
The luster of Alexandria's best hotel
glows even brighter with the
presence of this, its most
accomplished restaurant.
Contemporary cuisine *français* is
the bias, with creative domestic
flourishes from the young American
chef. The arena for his delicate,
artful presentations is a formal room
in which the Sun King's courtiers
would feel at home. If the
admittedly stiff tariffs deter, there is
a fixed-price Sun brunch, and the
same kitchen prepares the
lower-cost food for the adjacent
Grill. Or, go for the proper English
tea, served daily from 3-5pm.

Charley's Crab
*1101 Connecticut Ave. NW
☎ 785-4505. Map 3E6 ⬚ ⚋ AE
CB CD CD VISA Closed lunch Sat
and Sun. Metro: Farragut North.*
Located in the middle of the busy
New Downtown area, within an
office and shopping complex linked
to Farragut North Metro station, this
big restaurant is good for clam
chowder, crab meat cakes, broiled
fish and other seafood.

Clyde's
*3236 N St. NW ☎ 333-9180. Map
2E3 ⬚ ⚋ AE CB Closed
Christmas for lunch. Metro:
Foggy Bottom.*
Funky, colorful and animated, this is
one of the most fashionable of
Georgetown haunts. Standard
American dishes such as
hamburgers and fried chicken are
recommended. In the omelet room
only egg dishes are served.

La Colline
*400 North Capitol St. NW
☎ 737-0400. Map 7F9 ⬚ ⚋ AE
CB CD VISA Closed major hols.
Metro: Union Station.*
A French restaurant that looks like a
cheerful brasserie, and boasts an
imaginative menu, including such
dishes as shrimp Toulouse-Lautrec
(with lobster sauce and a dash of
pernod) and suprême of duckling

with blackcurrants. There is a very reasonable *prix fixe* dinner.

Dancing Crab
4611 Wisconsin Ave. NW
☎ 244-1882 ⅢⓁ AE CB ◉ ⓒ VISA
Closed Christmas.
A highly individual restaurant where you roll up your sleeves and attack steamed crabs on brown paper tablecloths and can make as much mess as you like. A good place to taste the varied produce of the Chesapeake Bay.

Dominique's
1900 Pennsylvania Ave. NW
☎ 452-1126. Map 3F5 ⅢⅢ ➤ AE
CB ◉ ⓒ VISA *Closed Sun on Sat and Sun. Metro: Farragut West.*
A huge, elegant restaurant with a formidably long menu. Owner Dominique d'Erno is a showman and specializes in highly exotic meat dishes. Appetizers include kangaroo *bourguignon,* buffalo sausages, sautéed alligator tail and rattlesnake salad. But mostly the menu has standard French dishes plus a good range of seafood.

Duke Zeibert's
1050 Connecticut Ave. NW
☎ 466-3730. Map 3E6 ⅢⅢ ➤ AE
CB ◉ ⓒ *Closed Sun in summer, major hols. Metro: Farragut North.*
In the glossy new Washington Sq. complex, this large second-floor restaurant is a favorite with politicians and executives of professional associations. Hearty American fare — steaks, roast beef, chicken-in-the-pot — is on offer.

Dutch Mill Deli
639 Indiana Ave. NW
☎ 347-3665. Map 7F8 ☐ *Closed Sun, most major hols; closes Mon-Fri 7pm, Sat 4pm. Metro: Archives.*
Housed in a very old building in the blossoming **Old Downtown** area, this self-service cafeteria is excellent for breakfast, a sandwich or a wholesome deli meal.

East Wind
809 King St., Alexandria, Va.
☎ (703) 836-1515 Ⅲ☐ to ⅢⅢ AE ◉
ⓒ VISA *Closed Sat and Sun lunch. Metro: King Street.*
This mecca for Vietnamese food has a cooking style both exotic and familiar. Its storefront venue has two rooms with a bar in the middle, at which a few minutes must inevitably be passed on popular weekend

evenings. Pine walls and Breuer chairs underline the jolly informality, the better to concentrate on the subtle and complex seasonings of *bo'dun* (marinated beef strips roasted on a skewer) and stuffed squid. While it is packed at both lunch and dinner, the suave maitre d' keeps things moving briskly along.

Fasikas
2447 18th St. NW ☎ 797-7673.
Map 3B5 ⅢⅢ AE ◉ ⓒ VISA *Closed for lunch.*
The multitudinous options presented by the welter of ethnic restaurants in the bustling Adams-Morgan district can be bewildering. Venturesome diners can hardly go wrong by selecting this comfortable Ethiopian. Prices are low and the surroundings — Victorian armchairs and large woven baskets — undeniably comfortable. The often fiery meat-and-vegetable stews are scooped up with slabs of bread, accounting for the lack of utensils. This gives fastidious souls pause, but they deny themselves the treats of *poro wat* (lemon chicken in red pepper sauce) and *yebeg wat* (marinated lamb).

Galileo
2014 P St. NW ☎ 293-7191. *Map 3D5* ⅢⅢ AE CB ◉ ⓒ VISA *Closed Sun. Metro: Dupont Circle.*
A small, crowded restaurant, which has attained a high reputation for authentic Italian cuisine, prepared by chef and co-owner Roberto Donna from Turin.

Hogate's
9th St. and Maine Ave. SW
☎ 484-6300. *Map 6H7* ⅢⅢ ➤ AE
CB ◉ ⓒ VISA *Closed Christmas. Metro: L'Enfant Plaza.*
A waterfront seafood restaurant with a 550-seat dining room overlooking the Potomac. A popular dish is "mariner's platter," a combination of flounder, oyster, scallops, clam, shrimp and crab cake, which is served with coleslaw and potatoes.

Hunan Chinatown
624 H St. NW ☎ 783-5858. *Map 7F8* ⅢⅢ AE ◉ ⓒ VISA *Metro: Gallery Place.*
The principal virtues of the District's Chinese enclave are its restaurants. If there is time for only one, pick this. Recently done over in placid brown and beige, its only concession to the usual Chinatown decorative conceits is a fierce

113

ceramic dragon near the door. The clientele is usually rather sedate, too, another deviance from the standard clamor. One of the pricier dishes is also one of the kitchen's best: "Crispy Whole Fish," a sea bass in tangy Hunan sauce. They're open 12hrs a day, until 1am on Fri and Sat.

i Ricchi
1220 19th St. NW ☎ *835-0459* ▥▥
▤ ▣ ▣ ▨▨ *Closed Sat lunch, Sun. Metro: Dupont Circle.*
President Bush and the First Lady anointed this Tuscan newcomer by attending a party there shortly after his own inaugural. It was already enjoying extravagant word of mouth, although it had opened only a few weeks before. The spare interior of quarry tiles and suggestions of arches has as its focal point an exhibition kitchen with an imported woodburning oven. In an age of culinary hyperbole, it produces dishes of gratifying simplicity. An example is the appetizer called *la fettunta*, garlic bread heaped with white beans. Among the pastas is *pappardelle sulla lepre* — noodles dressed with hare sauce — while many of the main courses are merely herbed and grilled, as are the baby goat chops with lemon and rosemary. Judging by the crowds, long will it live. Reservation 2 or 3 days ahead is wise.

Jean-Louis
Watergate Hotel, 2650 Virginia Ave. NW ☎ *298-4488. Map 2F4* ▥▥ ▥ ▤ ▣ ▣ ▣ ▨▨ *Closed Aug, some major hols. Metro: Foggy Bottom.*
Jean-Louis Palladin was lured from the South of France in 1979 to become chef at this small, hushed sanctum in the basement of the Watergate Hotel (see *Hotels*). Jean-Louis applies his masterly French cuisine to the local produce with great success, and each dish is a delight to both the eye and the taste buds. Prices at dinner are commensurately high, but the lunch menu is a good bargain. All menus are fixed-price.

Jockey Club
Ritz Carlton Hotel, 2100 Massachusetts Ave. NW ☎ *659-8000. Map 3D5* ▥▥ ▥ ▣ ▣ ▣ ▨▨ *Metro: Dupont Circle.*
One of Washington's prestige restaurants, this is a place to see and be seen in. Prices are predictably high, but so is the standard of food. The chef is an Italian-trained

Japanese, Hede Yamamoto, who practices a sophisticated French cuisine with a touch of *nouvelle*. He is strong on fresh seafoods, including fish imported from France. The decor has the wood-paneled coziness of an English country inn, and the walls are hung with prints of horse-racing scenes. (See *Hotels*.)

Joe and Mo's
1211 Connecticut Ave. NW ☎ *659-1211. Map 3E6* ▥▥ ▥ ▤ ▣ ▨▨ *Closed Sat lunch, Sun, hols. Metro: Dupont Circle, Farragut North.*
A steak and seafood restaurant that has become one of *the* fashionable places in Washington. Breakfast is popular, not only for the food but also for spotting the media moguls who often start the day here. There is no Joe, but the host, Mo Sussman, runs the place with great panache.

Le Lion d'Or
1150 Connecticut Ave. NW ☎ *296-7972. Map 3E6* ▥▥ ▥ ▤ ▣ ▣ ▣ ▣ ▨▨ *Closed Sat lunch, Sun, most major hols. Metro: Farragut North.*
The inconspicuous location of this restaurant — downstairs in a large office building — does not prepare you for the château-style elegance of its decoration, nor for the superb cuisine, generally rated as among the best of its kind in Washington. This is French *haute cuisine* with some interesting innovations, such as duck sausages, as well as standard dishes, always prepared with great finesse and subtlety of flavoring. Reserve in advance.

Madurai
3318 M St. NW ☎ *333-0997. Map 2E3* ▥▯ ▤ ▣ ▣ ▣ ▨▨
A restaurant that proves how delicious and endlessly varied Indian vegetarian food can be. Portions are generous, and the restaurant is very good value, especially the Sun fixed-price buffet lunch, where you help yourself to as much as you want.

Maison Blanche
1725 F St. NW ☎ *842-0070. Map 6F6* ▥▥ ▥ ▤ ▣ ▣ ▣ ▨▨ *Closed Sun, some major hols. Metro: Farragut West.*
Where you are seated at this restaurant can be more important than what you eat, as it is a haunt of politicians, lobbyists and White House staff. The decor re-creates old-world elegance, with tapestries and crystal chandeliers. The food is

best described as "modern" French
– that is, classical with some
innovative touches, such as duck
with blackcurrant sauce.

Marrakesh
617 New York Ave. NW
☎ 393-9393. Map 7E8 Ⅲ Closed
lunch, Christmas, Thanksgiving.
Metro: Gallery Place.
A colorful corner of Morocco in the
Old Downtown area. The
fixed price dinner menu is excellent
value.

Martin's Tavern
1264 Wisconsin Ave. NW
☎ 333-7370. Map 2E3 Ⅲ AE CB
● ● VISA Closed Christmas.
Metro: Foggy Bottom.
A bar-restaurant with a welcoming
wood-paneled interior decorated
with sculptures and English racing
prints from President Madison's
collection. Opened in 1933 on the
very day prohibition was repealed,
Martin's is renowned for its hearty
meat dishes. It's an excellent place
too for a substantial breakfast.

The Monocle
107 D St. NE ☎ 546-4488. Map
7I9 Ⅲ ☎ AE CB ● ● VISA
Closed Sun. Metro: Union
Station.
A Capitol Hill institution that has
been in the hands of the same
family since 1960. It comprises both
a cozy pub and a quietly elegant
restaurant with a good selection of
seafood and standard meat dishes.

New Orleans Emporium
2477 18th St. NW ☎ 328-3421.
Map 3C5 Ⅲ AE CB ● ● VISA
Closed Christmas, Thanksgiving.
The name is descriptive, for there
are several distinct enterprises under
the same roof and management. All
concern themselves with North
America's most distinctive native
cookery, Creole-Cajun, but
approach it from different
directions. At the main address is a
semiformal restaurant and a food
store featuring take-out dishes and
Louisianan condiments. Next door is
a tavern peddling brews from the
Deep South. One floor below is an
oyster bar and seafood café. And
around the corner, at 1790 Columbia
Rd., is the **New Orleans Café**. It
purveys cheaper versions of Cajun
standards, as well as those
traditional New Orleans delectables,
beignets (a kind of cruller) and
chicory coffee. Prices are a trifle
high for the scruffy but vibrant
Adams-Morgan district in which the

Emporium is located, at least in the
main dining room. That's the reason
for the alternative operations.

O'Brien's Pit Barbecue (1)
7305 Waverly St., Bethesda, Md.
☎ (301) 654-9004 Ⅲ ● VISA
Closed major hols. Metro:
Bethesda.
O'Brien's Pit Barbecue (2)
1314 E Gude Dr., Rockville, Md.
☎ (301) 340-8596 Ⅲ ● VISA
Closed major hols. Metro:
Rockville.
O'Brien's Pit Barbecue (3)
6820 Commerce St., Springfield,
Va. ☎ (703) 569-7801 Ⅲ AE ●
VISA Closed major hols.
At the three suburban locations of
this local institution, barbecued
meat is prepared in the authentic pit
style, served with delicious spicy
sauces and accompanied by potato
salad and coleslaw. People come
here for the food rather than the
decor, which is plastic and modern.

Occidental
147 Pennsylvania Ave. NW
☎ 783-1475. Map 6F6 Ⅲ to Ⅲ
AE ● ● VISA Metro: Metro
Center, Federal Triangle.
Adjacent to the Willard Hotel, but of
independent management, this
stunning throwback to a grander
age shares the same late 19thC
sensibility. At street level is a
popular bar and grill, where dressy
informality rules. Up the stairs is a
vast pillared room with soaring
ceiling, etched glass, dark paneling,
crimson drapes and tufted velvet
booths. A large model of a schooner
takes center stage. On the walls are
gilt framed portraits of former
presidents. The already ample menu
is supplemented by a long roster of
daily specials, which tests the
memory banks of the well-trained
service staff. Most are updated
variations of American classics,
which arrive in attractive, not
precious, presentations. If the food
is not quite up to the opulent
surroundings, it's close enough.
Save this one for special events.

Old Ebbitt Grill
675 15th St. NW ☎ 347-4801.
Map 6F6 Ⅲ ☎ AE CB ● ● VISA
Metro: Metro Center.
Housed in a converted movie
theater and fitted out with style and
opulence, this establishment has
basically the same type of American
menu as **Clyde's** in Georgetown,
except that there is no omelet room.
Located near the National Theater,
National Press Club, Willard

Inter-Continental (see *Hotels*) and White House, it is much patronized by the young executive class.

Pavilion at the Old Post Office

1100 Pennsylvania Ave. NW. Map 6F7. For ☎ and prices see individual restaurants below. Metro: Federal Triangle.

The multiple facilities here are divided into two basic categories. On the lower level, counters serve a variety of foods of different nationalities, including Indian, Greek and Chinese. The idea is to buy a tray and carry it to a table in the atrium in front of a stage, where there is often live entertainment. On the floors above there are a number of restaurants, including **Enrico's Trattoria**, which concentrates on pasta and pizzas, featuring "all you can eat" specials Mon-Sat 4-7pm; **Blossoms** (☎ 371-1838 ▥▢), a brasserie-style restaurant with an oyster bar as well; **Fitch, Fox and Brown** (☎ 289-1100 ▥▥), serving upscale American fare; and **Hunan** (☎ 371-2828 ▢), where you can eat good Chinese food at reasonable prices in an attractive dining room.

Le Pavillon

1050 Connecticut Ave. NW ☎ 833-3846. Map 3E6 ▥▥ ▤ ▦ ▣ ▥▥ Closed Sat lunch, Sun, major hols. Metro: Farragut North.

One of the contenders for top spot among Washington restaurants. The cuisine is vaguely *nouvelle*, but chef-owner Yannick Cam prefers to call it "*cuisine personalisée*." His combinations are interesting, for example, breast of duck with a wild honey and vinegar sauce.

Phillips Flagship

900 Water St. SW ☎ 488-8515. Map 6H7 ▥▥ ➡ ▤ ▦ ▣ ▥▥ Closed Christmas, Thanksgiving. Metro: L'Enfant Plaza.

This enormous waterfront restaurant opened at the end of 1985. The menu covers a wide range of seafood dishes, which prove to be serviceable, if not exactly trend-setting.

Potowmack Landing

George Washington Memorial Parkway, Alexandria, VA. ☎ 548-0001 ▥▥ ➡ ▤ ▦ ▣ ▥▥ Metro: National Airport.

A restaurant to visit as much for the setting as for the food. From the glass-walled dining room there is a fine view across the river. The decoration is appropriately nautical

and the fare includes steak and fish cooked over a mesquite grill.

Prime Rib

2020 K St. NW ☎ 466-8811. Map 3E6 ▥▥ ▤ ▦ ▣ ▥▥ Closed Sat lunch, Sun. Metro: Farragut West.

Cole Porter might have kicked up his heels here, especially since the piano-bass duo plays much of his songbook. Definitely a suit-and-tie place, this quintessential steakhouse turns in a polished door-to-tab performance. Ebony walls with brass accents are backdrops for pictures of 1920s flappers languishing on settees and in inglenooks. Even with reservations, there is almost certain to be a wait in the crowded bar, at least in the evenings. Appetites are thus whetted for manly salads and 20-ounce portions of prime beef. Patrons are overwhelmingly men on the gray side of 40.

Takesushi

1010 20th St. NW ☎ 466-3798. Map 3E5 ▥▥ ▤ ▦ ▣ ▥▥ Closed Sat lunch, Sun, hols. Metro: Farragut North.

If you are attracted by the Japanese style of eating, with its multitude of exquisitely presented small dishes, this popular *sushi* bar is unbeatable. At lunchtime there is a special selection of seafood and other attractive morsels.

Thai Taste

2606 Connecticut Ave. NW ☎ 387-8876. Map 2B4 ▢ to ▢ ▤ ▦ ▣ ▥▥ Closed Sun lunch. Metro: Woodley Park-Zoo.

Local consensus elects this as the cream of the burgeoning Thai crop. No one accuses it of lush decor. The gaggle of waiters and waitresses chatter animatedly at the back when not rushing steaming platters to customers. There are almost as many Chinese dishes as Thai, most of them unintimidatingly mild in seasoning. Believe any choice designated as either "spicy" or "hot and spicy," however, especially as applied to the curries.

Tiberio

1915 K St. NW ☎ 452-1915. Map 3E5 ▥▥ ▤ ▦ ▣ ▥▥ Closed Sat lunch, Sun, major hols. Metro: Farragut West.

High-quality Italian cuisine with a northern regional bias in the K St. expense-account belt. Specialties include hearty meat dishes, and more than 1,000 wines are listed.

Nightlife and the arts

Washington's nightlife and performing arts menu, like its gastronomic one, has greatly increased in variety and scope in recent years. There is something here for everyone, whether they want a classical concert, a cabaret with dinner, or an evening of frenzied dancing and laser lights.

In DC nightspots, live entertainment usually begins between 9 and 9.30pm and continues until 1.30 or 2am during the week and until 2.30 or 3am on weekends. Due to stricter licensing laws in the Virginia and Maryland suburbs, the entertainment in clubs there tends to start at about 8pm and finish at midnight or 1am throughout the entire week.

Many of the clubs will charge a "cover," a "minimum" or both, depending on the caliber and celebrity of the featured entertainers. "Cover" is simply an admission fee. "Minimum" is an additional charge that can be offset by ordering an equivalent value in food or drink.

While after-dark entertainment is found in many parts of the city and suburbs, the greatest concentration is in Georgetown along Wisconsin Ave. and M St. NW. Other havens are found on Connecticut Ave. NW, N and S of Dupont Circle in the region of 19th St. in New Downtown and 7th St. NW in Old Downtown. Certain areas are rich in particular styles of music or entertainment. For example, many bluegrass and country-and-western venues are located near the Interstate 495 section of the Capital Beltway in the Maryland and Virginia suburbs. The red-light district along DC's 14th St. has virtually disappeared, owing to extensive redevelopment, and where it re-emerges remains to be seen.

Celebrity-spotting is rather haphazard, except on gala opening nights at the opera, symphony or ballet. Washington's mighty meet publicly at business lunches in exclusive restaurants, then retreat to private dinner parties.

The following is only a selective list, divided into very broad categories. For a full weekly briefing on the current nightlife agenda, read the *Weekend* section of the Fri *Washington Post*, or the free *City Paper*, which appears every Thurs.

Two ticket-buying services are useful and convenient. **Ticketplace** (*12th and F St. NW* ☎ *842-5357*) sells cut-price tickets for cash only on the day of the performance. **Ticketron** (*1101 17th St. and other locations* ☎ *659-2601*) and **Ticket Center** (*Metro Center, 13th and G Sts. and other locations* ☎ *432-0200*) are computerized agencies that sell tickets in person or over the telephone. All three accept credit cards, but only for full-price advance tickets. Students, the elderly, the disabled, and/or lower ranks of military personnel are offered discounts by some theaters.

Ballet, contemporary dance and opera

Although Washington hardly matches London, New York or Moscow for ballet, it nevertheless mounts a significant share of high-level performances. The two main venues for ballet are supplemented by smaller stages that offer more modern dance.

The Dance Place
3225 8th St. NE ☎ *269-1600.*
Map 7F8.
Troupes such as Liz Larman and the

Dance Exchange and Toe Jam and Jelly perform in a variety of dance idioms, many ethnically rooted. Classes are held during the week.

117

Nightlife and the arts

John F. Kennedy Center for the Performing Arts
New Hampshire Ave. and Rock Creek Parkway NW ☎ *254-3600. Map 5F4. Metro: Foggy Bottom.*
Many distinguished visiting ballet companies such as the New York City Ballet, the American Ballet Theater and the Joffrey Ballet come here to perform anything from *Swan Lake* to works by Balanchine, in the 2,300-seat Opera House. The Kennedy Center is also home to the Washington Performing Arts Society.

Lisner Auditorium
21st and H St. NW ☎ *822-4757. Map 3F5. Metro: Foggy Bottom.*
This auditorium in the George Washington University complex is,

among other things, the home of the Washington Ballet, a company with a wide repertoire whose brilliant Singapore-born choreographer Choo-San Goh has won international acclaim.

The Washington Opera
Kennedy Center ☎ *994-6800. Map 5F4* AE CD VISA *Metro: Foggy Bottom.*
A small but well-regarded company, The Washington Opera struggles yearly to raise enough funds to see itself through a short four-opera season. It performs Nov-Feb and productions are usually sold out. With the Metropolitan Opera of New York no longer touring, this is the only opportunity to see opera.

Cabarets, comedy theaters and supper clubs
Cabaret flourishes in Washington in many restaurants, cafés and cabaret theaters that also serve food and drink. Here are some of the places where you can test the proposition that laughter is good for the digestion.

Anton's 1201 Club
1201 Pennsylvania Ave. NW ☎ *783-1201. Map 6F7* AE CD VISA *Open lunch and dinner daily, shows at 8.30 and 10.45pm. Metro: Federal Triangle, Metro Center.*
A new Art Deco entry in the old-fashioned supper club tradition, it brings on such name performers as George Shearing, Helen Reddy and the Four Freshmen. That constitutes a canny mix of glitz and nostalgia, so the crowd tends to be older than in the usual nightclub. After all, they can dine, listen to the music of their salad days, and still be home by 10.30.

Comedy Café
1520 K St. NW ☎ *638-JOKE. Map 3E6* CD VISA *Shows Thurs 8.30pm; Fri 8.30pm, 10.30pm; Sat 7.30pm, 9.30pm, 11.30pm. Cover. Metro: McPherson Sq.*
At street level is a spacious bar called **Jonathan's**, with its own disc jockey. Full meals are available upstairs, in a long, thin room with a small stage in the middle. National and more successful local comedians give their all on weekends. The Walter Mittys who would like to join their ranks get their chance at "open mike" every Thurs. On those nights, only bravery and apparent disregard for humiliation can be assured. Sometimes, though, the unknowns are actually funny.

d.c. space
443 7th St. NW ☎ *347-1445. Map 6F8* AE CD VISA *Closed Sun. Metro: Gallery Place.*
Jammed nightly with a punkish, avant-garde crowd, which can never be entirely certain what will happen. The management has put on poetry readings, comedians, cabaret, movies, and musical groups covering the spectrum from jazz and classical to folk and reggae. Part of the space functions as an art gallery, too. Eccentric American food meets medium standards. Eating isn't the point, anyway.

Garvin's Laugh Inn
Between 13th and 14th Sts. NW, off L St. ☎ *726-1334. Map 3E7* AE CD VISA *Two shows Fri, Sat 8.30pm, 10.30pm. Cover and minimum.*
More local and national comedy performers. Go Thurs-Sat, as it is likely to be dead other nights. There is another Garvin's at the **Ramada Hotel** in Alexandria.

Marquee Lounge
Omni Shoreham Hotel, 2500 Calvert St. NW ☎ *234-0700. Map 2B4* AE CB CD VISA *Open 8pm-2am. Shows Thurs, Fri, Sat. Metro: Woodley Park-Zoo.*
The long-running character "Mrs Foggy Bottom," created and performed by Joan Cushing, delivers her jaundiced and satiric view of Washington's influential elite.

Old Vat Room
*Arena Stage, 6th and Maine St.
SW ☎ 488-3300. Map 718* ≡ ▣
▣ *Shows Thurs, Fri 8pm; Sat
7pm, 10pm. Metro: L'Enfant
Plaza.*
This 180-seat auditorium at Arena
Stage is the home of one of the

longest-running and most popular
shows in Washington: Stephen
Wade's one-man *Banjo Dancing*.
Wade plays five different types of
banjo, performs clog-dancing and
tells stories full of folksy humor.
Two bars sell drinks and light
snacks.

Cafés and bars

A convivial atmosphere and, occasionally, live entertainment can
be found in a number of Washington's cafés and bars. **The
Dubliner** also appears under *Nightclubs*.

Brickskeller
*1523 22nd St. NW ☎ 293-1885.
Map 3D5* ▣ ▣ ▣ ▣ ▣ *Open
5pm-2am. Metro: Dupont Circle.*
A mecca for drinkers of beer, with
over 500 varieties on sale. Similar to
a British neighborhood pub in
atmosphere and locale.

Clyde's
*3236 M St. NW, Georgetown
☎ 333-0294. Map 2E3* ≡ ▣ ▣
▣ ▣ *Closes Mon-Thurs
2am, Fri-Sat 3am, Sun 6pm.*
A stylish Georgetown bar-restaurant,
with a new branch in Tyson's
Corner, Va. (☎ (703) 734-1901).

The Dubliner
*520 N Capitol St. NW ☎ 737-
3773. Map 7F9* ≡ ▣ ▣ ▣ ▣
▣ *Open Sun-Thurs 11.30am-
2am, Fri, Sat noon-3am. Metro:
Union Station.*
An attractive evocation of a Dublin
pub, with two bars and a restaurant
that serves hearty pub food. Irish
folk groups or other live entertainers
perform every evening.

Fairfax Bar
*Ritz-Carlton Hotel, 2100
Massachusetts Ave. NW
☎ 293-2100. Map 3D5* ▣ ▣ ▣
▣ *Open 11am-2pm. Metro:
Dupont Circle.*
With its burnished wood sheathing
and equestrian oils, it might be the
retreat of British landed gentry.

Instead, it routinely hosts the mighty
of Washington media, politics and
society. The rooms of the lounge
serve several purposes, with light
meals throughout the day, afternoon
tea 2-5pm, and restrained jazz most
evenings back near the fireplace.
Men must wear jackets after 5pm.

F. Scott's
*1232 36th St. NW, Georgetown
☎ 965 1789. Map 2E2* ≡ ▣ ▣
▣ ▣ *Closes Mon-Thurs
2am, Fri, Sat 3am, Sun 10.30pm.*
Named after the famous American
novelist, author of the *Lost
Generation*, this cozy, mirrored bar,
poised on the edge of Georgetown
University's campus, is filled with
Art Deco chic. The 18thC
townhouse is also home of the **1789**
restaurant and the **Tombs Bar**, all
owned and managed by the same
organization as **Clyde's**.

**Kramerbooks and Afterwords
Café**
*1517 Connecticut Ave. NW
☎ 387 1462. Map 2D5* ≡ ▣ ▣
▣ *Open Sun-Thurs 8am-1am,
Fri, Sat for 24hrs. Metro: Dupont
Circle.*
This bookstore-cum-café is one of
the most civilized features of the
Dupont Circle area. After browsing
in the well-stocked front section,
you can repair to the back for a
drink or a meal. Occasionally there
is live entertainment.

Cinema

In spite of the meteoric rise of home video movie rentals,
Washington is still very much a cinema city. Its *aficionados*
can find anything from first-run Hollywood hits to
foreign-language releases, martial-arts flicks to evergreen
movie classics.
    Many of the theaters have several showings daily, beginning
in the afternoon (often at a reduced matinée price), and
several have multiple theaters under one roof. There are one
or two of the grand old movie palaces left, but

generally the interior decor is disappointingly utilitarian rather than awe-inspiring.

Attractions generally change on Fri; the *Weekend* section of the *Washington Post* carries synopses of those films currently playing, as well as their location. Only cash is accepted by theater box offices and refreshment counters, and smoking is forbidden by District law.

American Film Institute Theater
John F. Kennedy Center, 2700 F St. NW ☎ 254-3600 (recorded). Map 5F4 ═ Metro: Foggy Bottom.
This national nonprofit organization, formed to preserve the best in American film, regularly presents classic movies in a well-designed auditorium. Nightly showings offer several films.

American Theater
10th and D St. SW ☎ 554-2111. Map 6H7. Metro: L'Enfant Plaza.
Occasional venue for experimental theater. More usually a showcase of martial arts movies.

Bethesda Cinema 'N' Drafthouse
7719 Wisconsin Ave. NW, Bethesda, Md. ☎ 656-3337. Metro: Bethesda.
Current movies at half-price, with the civilizing touch of sitting at café tables, sipping beer or wine. (Also in Arlington.)

Biograph
2819 M St. NW, Georgetown ☎ 333-2969. Map 2E4. Metro: Foggy Bottom.
Frequently runs mini film festivals.

Cineplex Odeon Dupont Circle
1350 19th St. SW ☎ 872-9555. Map 3D5. Metro: Dupont Circle.
First-run releases with reduced-price matinée showings.

Cineplex Odeon Outer Circle
4849 Wisconsin Ave. NW ☎ 244-3116. Map 2D3.
First-run movies, primarily by American producers.

Cineplex Odeon West End Theaters
23rd and L St. NW ☎ 293-3152. Map 3E5. Metro: Foggy Bottom.
Seven screens showing first-run releases. Low-priced first showings.

Georgetown
1351 Wisconsin Ave. NW, Georgetown ☎ 333-5555. Map 2E3.
Second-run releases; X-rated midnight movie on weekends.

K-B Cerberus
3040 M St. NW, Georgetown ☎ 337-1311. Map 2E4. Metro: Foggy Bottom.
First-run offerings on three screens.

K-B Fine Arts
1919 M St. NW ☎ 223-4438. Map 3E5. Metro: Farragut North.
New releases at reduced prices.

K-B Janus
1660 Connecticut Ave. NW ☎ 232-8900. Map 3D5. Metro: Dupont Circle.
First-run releases and classics.

Key
1222 Wisconsin Ave, NW, Georgetown ☎ 333-5100. Map 2E3.
Four screens showing major movies.

Library of Congress
1st St. and Independence Ave. SE ☎ 287-5502. Map 8G10. Open Tues, Thurs, Fri at 7.30pm. Metro: Capitol S., Union Station.
Regular showings in the Mary Pickford Theater from the library's extensive film archive.

Classical music

Although the Kennedy Center, with its program of large orchestral performances, dominates the musical scene in Washington, music can also be heard in many other places in the city and its environs, such as concert halls, churches, museums, galleries, libraries and historic houses. Many of these concerts are free. Indeed, few cities in the world offer so much free music every day of the week. A selection of venues where a range of music can be heard is listed here. For a full list, consult the sources given on p.117. Another source of information for major performances is the

Washington Performing Arts Society (*1029 Vermont Ave. NW, Suite 1100, DC 20005* ☎ *393-3600*), which will send a schedule on request.

Anderson House (Society of the Cincinnati)
2118 Massachusetts Ave. NW
☎ 785-0540. Map 3D5. Metro:
Dupont Circle.
Occasional free concerts in this historic Palladian townhouse full of treasured art and furnishings.

Church of the Epiphany
1317 G St. NW ☎ 347-2635. Map 6F7. Metro: Metro Center.
Free organ recitals every Fri at noon, except during Lent.

Corcoran Gallery
17th St. and New York Ave. NW
☎ 638-3211. Map 6F6. Metro:
Farragut West.
Frequent free classical concerts (☎ *for weekly program*). Also a Contemporary Music Forum at 8pm on the third Mon of every month Sept-May.

DAR Constitution Hall
18th and D St. NW ☎ 638-2661.
Map 6F6. Metro: Farragut West.
The hall where for racial reasons the great soprano Marian Anderson was once forbidden to perform is now occasionally the venue for rock bands, as well as other musical groups. The 4,000-seat auditorium has been somewhat eclipsed by the Kennedy Center, but its handsome Beaux-Arts appearance is unique.

John F. Kennedy Center
New Hampshire Ave. and Rock Creek Parkway NW ☎ 254-3600.
Map 5F4 ═ Metro: Foggy Bottom.
The Concert Hall at the Kennedy Center is the scene of many concerts by distinguished orchestras. The National Symphony Orchestra's concert series runs Oct-Apr.

Library of Congress
1st St. and Independence Ave. SE ☎ 287-5502. Map 8G10. Metro: Capitol South.
The library has a fine collection of musical instruments, including several Stradivarius violins, which require constant exercise to keep them fit — one reason for the regular concerts held in the library's **Coolidge Auditorium**. Tickets are available on the Mon morning preceding the concert. Performances are Oct-Apr Fri at 8pm, Sat at 5.30pm.

Lisner Auditorium
21st and H St. NW ☎ 994-6800.
Map 3F5. Metro: Foggy Bottom.
The 1,500-seat auditorium, part of the George Washington University, is the site of occasional free concerts, and home of the Washington Ballet (☎ *for program information*).

National Gallery of Art
6th St. and Constitution Ave. NW ☎ 737-4215. Map 7G8. Metro: Gallery Place.
Free Sun concerts at 7pm.

New York Ave. Presbyterian Church
1313 New York Ave. NW
☎ 393-3700. Map 3F7. Metro:
Metro Center.
Free Fri morning concerts are held at this church in Old Downtown.

Phillips Collection
1600 21st St. NW ☎ 387-2151.
Map 3D5. Metro: Dupont Circle.
Sun eve concerts at 5pm in this superb collection of Impressionist art, now a public museum.

Smithsonian Museums
☎ 357-1300.
The Smithsonian's Division of Performing Arts is responsible for concerts held frequently in various museums. For details consult the Smithsonian bulletin of events in the *Washington Post* on the last Sun of every month (see **Sights** for individual museum addresses).

Washington Cathedral
Wisconsin Ave. and Massachusetts Ave. NW
☎ 537-6247. Map 2A2.
After nearly 80yrs, this magnificent example of Gothic ecclesiastical architecture is still under construction using the medieval craft of stone carving. The cathedral has regularly scheduled recitals after Sun evensong, and carillon performances on Sat afternoons; other music is frequently scheduled.

Wolf Trap Farm Park
1624 Trap Rd., Vienna, Va.
☎ (703) 255-1800.
This national performing arts center is set amid almost 120 acres (49ha) of gently rolling Virginia farmland. The permanent stage and wooden 3-sided auditorium of the **Filene**

121

Center are surrounded by grassy terraces where you can picnic while listening to the New York City Opera or Charley Pride. Many Sun afternoon concerts are free. The principal season is May-Sept, but there are occasional performances at the Barns in winter.

Lectures and literary events

You can usually find an interesting lecture in Washington on any day of the week, whether the subject is astronomy at the *National Air and Space Museum*, Japanese embroidery at the *Textile Museum* or Renaissance painting at the *National Gallery of Art*. There are also guided walks in parts of the city. For information, consult the *City Paper* or *Smithsonian Calendar* in the *Washington Post*, or phone Smithsonian Resident Associates (☎ *357-3030*) for a bulletin of lectures.

For anyone with a literary bent, Washington offers many lectures and readings by visiting authors and members of the city's own growing band of poets and creative writers. A strong focus of activity is the **Writer's Center** (*7815 Old Georgetown Rd., Bethesda, Md.* ☎ *654-8664*). The *Washington Post* publishes a *Literary Calendar* on the last Sun of each month.

Nightclubs and music venues

The following list is subdivided by type of music, although of course many venues present a variety of styles.

Country/folk/ethnic

Birchmere
3901 Mount Vernon Ave., Alexandria, Va. ☎ *549-5919*
This rustic outpost in a converted supermarket between Arlington and Alexandria is a real mecca for bluegrass fans (the Seldom Scene play on Thurs eve). Also a venue for folk, Celtic and cowboy artists.

The Dubliner
520 N Capitol St. NE ☎ *737-3773. Map 7F9* AE CB VISA *Metro: Union Station.*
See *Cafés and bars.*

Discos

Cities
2424 18th St. NW ☎ *328-7194. Map 2B5* AE CB VISA *Open Wed-Sat. Cover charge. Metro: Woodley Park-Zoo, then a 15min walk.*
The Adams-Morgan disco-of-the-nanosecond sports a large lounge and restaurant at ground level, two more bars, large dance floor and separate VIP room one flight up. Although New American fare is the kitchen's preference, the whole place is redecorated every four months to celebrate another world city.

East Side
1824 Half St. SW ☎ *488-1206. Map 7I9* CB VISA

Gallagher's Pub
3391 Connecticut Ave. NW ☎ *686-9189* 🍴 AE CB VISA
The original Gallagher's, where Irish stew is mixed with Irish folk ballads and plenty of Irish spirits. Young musicians play acoustic guitars, small harps and flutes.

Ireland's Four Provinces
3412 Connecticut Ave. NW ☎ *244-0860* 🍴 AE CB VISA
Folk balladeers perform every weekend in this neighborhood pub.

Once a gay disco called The Pier that also welcomed straights, this nightspot in the warehouse district has become a determinedly heterosexual dance club with a slick lightshow, sophisticated sound system and refurbished decor.

Kilimanjaro
1724 California St. NW ☎ *328-3838. Map 2C5* 🍴 AE CB VISA *Open 7 nights. Cover charge. Metro: Woodley Park-Zoo, then a long walk.*
Live groups and recorded music keep the insistent beat thumping 'way past midnight, with African, reggae and calypso rhythms augmented frequently by Motown sounds. The food is derived mainly

from Africa and the Caribbean. Young to middle-aged blacks predominate, but everyone with the price of admission is made welcome. The fringe Adams-Morgan location is away from convenient Metro stops, so a taxi or private car are preferable, and essential in the early morning hours, when Metro is closed.

Jazz

Blues Alley
1073 Wisconsin Ave. NW (½ block S of M St.) ☎ *337-4141, 337-2338 for group rates. Map 2E3* ☰ AE ⬤ VISA *Dinner at 6.30pm. Shows Sun-Thurs 8.10pm, Fri, Sat midnight. Cover and minimum.*

One of the last regular venues for top jazz performers — Sarah Vaughan, Buddy Rich, Mel Torme, Charlie Byrd and the like. Restaurant seating with dinner available; sandwich menu for midnight shows. Well worth the substantial cover and minimum charge.

Café Lautrec
2431 18th St. NW ☎ *265-6436. Map 2C5* ☰ ⬤ AE VISA *Open 7 nights. Minimum, no cover. Metro: Woolley Park-Zoo, then a 15min walk.*

Decent bistro food, they have, and live jazz or related music every night of the week. But the extra added attraction that has customers assembling on the street hoping to enter is the tap dancer. He displays his quick-silver artistry Thurs-Sat, and he does it on the long bar, not on the floor. There isn't any room for him down there.

Mr. Henry's
1836 Columbia Rd. NW ☎ *797-8882. Map 2C5* ☰ AE ⬤ ⬤ VISA *Cover charge. Metro: Woolley Park-Zoo, then a 15min walk.*

In Adams-Morgan again, this chummy restaurant-lounge arranges its tables in snug ranks perpendicular to the stage, with a room-length bar on one side. It's difficult *not* to meet your neighbors. Sun-Thurs are "open mike" nights, abetted by a piano

and singer. On Fri and Sat, jazz and soul groups with five or six performers hold the spotlight. The Sun brunch is popular.

One Step Down
2517 Pennsylvania Ave. NW ☎ *331-8863. Map 2E4* AE ⬤ ⬤ VISA *Closes Sun-Thurs 2am, Fri, Sat 3am. Cover. Metro: Foggy Bottom.*

An authentic jazz bar featuring some of the East Coast's most talented musicians. Three sets a night and jam sessions Sat and Sun afternoons.

Potter's House
1658 Columbia Rd. NW ☎ *232-5483. Map 3B6* ⬤ VISA

In the Adams-Morgan neighborhood, which has a strong Latin influence and is dotted with emerging art galleries. You can enjoy anything here from open auditions to ethnic performances.

Tucson Cantina
2605 Connecticut Ave. NW ☎ *462-6410. Map 2B4* ☰ AE ⬤ VISA *Metro: Woolley Park-Zoo.*

Live entertainment with a country rock flavor, aimed at a clientele in their 30s. Frequented by many regulars as well as tourists from nearby hotels. Tex-Mex food.

The Wintergarden
Embassy Row Hotel, 2015 Massachusetts Ave. NW ☎ *265-1600. Map 3D5* AE CB ⬤ ⬤ VISA *Metro: Dupont Circle.*

John Eaton, Washington's premier jazz pianist, performs current hits plus his own evergreen arrangements of oldies, in this small, pricey hotel. Reservations are strongly advised Thurs-Sat.

Pop/Rock/New Wave

The Bayou
3135 K St. NW, Georgetown ☎ *333-2897 (recorded concert listings). Map 2E3* AE ⬤ VISA *Admission by ticket only. Metro: Foggy Bottom.*

Down by the Potomac at the foot of Georgetown, this is one of the few showcases for live rock by well-known performers in the city.

Fifth Column
915 F St. NW ☎ *393-3632. Map 7E8* AE ⬤ ⬤ VISA *Open Wed-Sun. Cover charge. Metro: Gallery Place.*

At least the second disco to operate on the premises of this century-old former bank, this incarnation strives to provoke and amuse. The three levels are hung with sculptures and

123

other artworks, and each has a different function. Up top is a VIP lounge, down below is recognizable rock, and in between they play what the management call "high energy progressive music."

9.30 Club
930 F St. NW ☎ 393-0930. Map 6F7. Metro: Gallery Place.
Every garage band in the metropolitan area dreams of getting its big break at this showcase for new music. Incredibly smoky, crowded and loud. Not for the

faint-hearted nor the claustrophobic. Tickets can be obtained through Ticketron.

The Roxy
1214 18th St. NW ☎ 296-9292. Map 3E6 ▨ Cover. Metro: Dupont Circle, Farragut North.
The management has spent far more on the acoustic system than on the seating arrangements, which are benches at tables and unpadded accountants' stools. Expect anything from reincarnations of folk groups to would-be acid rock stars.

Theater

Washington has several theaters of national stature, presenting performances by either resident or touring professional companies. Performances are listed in the *Washington Post.*

Arena Stage
6th St. and Maine Ave. SW ☎ 488-3300. Map 7I8 ▨ ▨ ▨ Metro: L'Enfant Plaza.
Washington's original theater-in-the-round and first professional repertory company is nationally regarded for its acting, directing and producing talents. The founders, Zelda and Tom Fichandler, oversee the 800-seat Arena Stage, the 500-seat **Kreeger Theater** and the 180-seat **Old Vat Room**, stocking them with a full range of exciting drama and entertainment each season.

The Folger Shakespeare Theater
201 E Capitol St. SE ☎ 547-7070. Map 8G10 ▨ ▨ ▨ Metro: Capitol South.
Not only the Bard, but other classic dramatists such as Molière are presented in an authentic 16thC theater. The library also has an excellent collection of manuscripts and memorabilia from Shakespeare's time.

Ford's Theatre
511 10th St. NW ☎ 347-4833. Map 6F7 ▨ ▨ ▨ Metro: Gallery Place, Metro Center.
Our American Cousin, the play during which President Lincoln was shot, may have been their most notorious production, but these days Ford's Theatre offerings range from current musicals to political satire. Local theater-goers applaud the new reproduction theater seats that replaced the uncomfortable "authentic" period pieces.

Kennedy Center Eisenhower Theater
New Hampshire Ave. and Rock Creek Parkway ☎ 254-3670. Map 5F4 ▨ ▨ ▨ ▨ Metro: Foggy Bottom.
Director Peter Sellars has mounted some startling productions of Chekhov classics and modern-day angst in this 1,200-seat jewel box of a theater. Not the type of drama the local supporters of the arts had in mind for a national arts center, but the adventurous can't wait for another controversial season.

The National Theater
1321 E St. NW ☎ 628-6161. Map 6F7 ▨ ▨ ▨ Metro: Federal Triangle, Metro Center.
The *grande dame* of Washington theaters, established in 1835, has recently emerged from a multimillion dollar renovation by renowned theater designer Oliver Smith. Now owned by the Schubert Organization, the 1,672-seat house shows Broadway musicals and other lavish productions.

The Source Theater
1835 14th St. NW ☎ 462-1073. Map 3D7 ▨ ▨ ▨
Three stages present a range of drama from American classics to experimental plays.

Warner Theater
513 13th St. NW ☎ 626-1050. Map 6F7 ▨ ▨ ▨ Metro: Federal Triangle, Metro Center.
Once a vaudeville palace, this 2,000-seat auditorium has been splendidly renovated and now serves as a concert hall.

Shopping

Washington provides myriad opportunities to buy anything from souvenir T-shirts sold by grizzled street vendors to *haute couture* reluctantly offered by disdainful store assistants. What Washington does not provide, however, is a major geographic concentration of elegance such as that found in midtown Manhattan, for example.

In this sprawling metropolitan area convenient public transportation did not arrive until the late 1970s with the opening of the Metro; the car is therefore historically the vehicle of choice for many local residents. The downtown department stores and specialty shops dwindled to a paltry few as more and more local and regional merchants relocated in vast shopping malls in the Maryland and Virginia suburbs, conveniently near an interstate highway off-ramp, inconveniently 10-25 miles (15-37km) from downtown.

However, there are still old pockets of urban retail sophistication, and indications of a revived interest in serving all the shopping needs of Washington's inhabitants as well as the city's frequent visitors. **Hecht's**, a local department store chain, relocated its flagship store in 1985 to Metro Center (the square encompassed by 11th and 12th, F and G St.), an area that is well served by the Metro and is currently undergoing renovation. Other local landmarks include the department stores, **Garfinkel's** and **Woodward and Lothrop. Georgetown Park**, a "vertical" mall with Victorian overtones and a recent addition to Georgetown, has begun a major expansion that will include a market garden among its furniture, fashion, confectioners and craftsmen.

Comfortably shod window shoppers will be rewarded in browsing along Connecticut Ave. between K St. and R St. (*Metro: Dupont Circle and Farragut North*), crowded with boutiques, bookstores, galleries, jewelers, shoe stores, record stores, street musicians and restaurants. The avenue provides a delightful day's shopping, and you are sure to find something here you never knew you needed.

Another part of Georgetown that is attractive to shoppers lies about 2½ miles (4km) w of Metro Center. To preserve the community's narrow streets, its citizens decided that they did not want their roads destroyed during the years of Metro construction, so there is no underground stop, but buses run frequently to and from this district; the cab ride is only one zone from downtown, so the fare is modest. Wisconsin Ave. and M St. and its offshoots offer contemporary and antique furnishings, rare books and prints, fine fabrics, jewelry, and clothes for all the family from running gear to evening wear. Restaurants are varied both in character and price.

Fortunately the citizens of upper Wisconsin Ave. in Chevy Chase did not veto a Metro stop at Friendship Heights (*5400 Wisconsin Ave. NW*). Exit here and you will find yourself in a shopper's paradise that includes **Mazza Gallerie** to the E and **Saks-Jandel** and **Saks Fifth Avenue** to the w. Here decidedly upscale local retailers have a long-established, luxury-conscious clientele that has attracted like-minded retailers from New York, Texas and California. Browsers are welcome, and there are always surprisingly inexpensive, yet desirable, small items at the most exclusive boutiques.

Tyson's Corner Mall, near McLean, Va., and **White Flint Mall**, close to Bethesda, Md., are the two nearest large shopping centers, each with close to 200 shops, as well as movie theaters, cafés and amusement arcades, under one roof. The malls are served by Metrobus routes, and White Flint has an underground stop.

At the other end of the scale are the cut-price stores that sell manufacturers' seconds. Beware the "suggested retail price" that is listed above "our sales price." It may bear no relation to the real economic world. You usually get what you pay for; the question is, how much is it worth? If you loathe paying retail for anything, visit **Potomac Mills Mall**, a collection of stores that sells well-priced merchandise ranging from family clothing to European furniture. The mall is 30 miles (45km) s of Washington on I-95, and can only be reached by car.

Each of the many museums in Washington has a gift shop, where reasonably priced mementoes and some astonishing bargains may be found, and where shoppers gain the satisfaction of knowing they have contributed something to the ongoing upkeep and development of the museum.

Antiques
While there are no bargains in Washington's antique stores, you can find a host of beautiful and rare examples of decorative furniture, silver, jewelry, art and fabrics from Amish quilts to Chinese silks.

Antiques By Plain Jane
222 N. Lee St., Alexandria, Va. ☎ (703) 546-2457 🆎 💳
A rich array of restored Victoriana is in stock, from electrified lamps to large furniture pieces.

Peter Mack Brown
1742 Wisconsin Ave. NW, Georgetown ☎ 338-8484. Map 2D3 🆎
Elegant displays of 18thC French, English and American furniture.

GKS Bush Company
2828 Pennsylvania Ave. NW ☎ 965-0653. Map 2E4.
The place for original American antiques.

Georgetown Antiques Center
2918 M St. NW ☎ 338-3811 🆎 💳 💳
Four stores under one roof present an entrancing variety of old silver, jewelry, furniture and prints from the early 19thC to 1930s Art Deco. Not far from the Four Seasons Hotel.

Susquehanna Antiques
1319 Wisconsin Ave. NW ☎ 333-1511 💳 💳
Fine American furniture from the Colonial and Federal periods.

Tiny Jewel Box
1143 Connecticut Ave. NW ☎ 393-2747. Map 3E6 🆎 💳 💳
This shop specializes in diamonds, precious gems and antique jewelry.

Beauty parlors and hairdressers
The leisurely day at the hairdresser is all but forgotten in large American cities. The customers, both male and female, are hard at work in downtown offices, dashing in after work or in their lunch hour for a quick cut and blow dry at a convenient "no appointment necessary" unisex salon. But bastions of luxury still exist, where, for a price, women and men can enjoy a "day of beauty," including a skin treatment and massage. Also, some hotels and major department stores have hairdressers.

Walk-in shops
Daniel's   1831 M St. NW ☎ 296-4856. Map **3**E5 ⬛ 💳 Open
Sun.
The Hair Loft   1716 I St. NW ☎ 298-7228. Map **3**E6.
Raphael of Montreal Coiffures   1821½ L St. NW ☎ 785-0474.
Map **3**E5.
Shears   822 15th St. NW (at I St.) ☎ 842-4070. Map **3**E6.
Luxury parlors
Elizabeth Arden Salon   5225 Wisconsin Ave. NW
☎ 362-9890 ⬛ ⬛ 💳
Robin Weir and Co.   2134 P St. NW ☎ 861-0444. Map **3**D5
⬛ ⬛ 💳 Hairdressers to former First Lady, Nancy Reagan.
Suissa Hair & Skin Salon   3068 M St. NW, Georgetown
☎ 833-1066. Map **2**E4 ⬛ ⬛ 💳
Watergate Salon   2532 Virginia Ave. NW ☎ 333-3488. Map
2F4.

Books and records
Washington is blessed with a huge selection of book and
record stores catering to any taste from the classical to the
avant-garde.

Booked Up
1209 31st St. NW, Georgetown
☎ *965-3244. Map 2E3.*
A store devoted to first editions,
fine, rare and unusual books.

Crown Books
4400 Jennifer St. NW ☎ 966-
8784 and 1155 19th St. NW
☎ *659-4172* ⬛ ⬛
This local chain sells every book at a
discount. Hard-cover and paperback
bestsellers, popular consumer and
specialized magazines sell for 15-40
percent off the retail price.

B. Dalton
Mazza Gallerie, Wisconsin Ave.
and Military Rd. ☎ *362 7055* ⬛
⬛
This nationwide chain carries
national and local bestsellers.

Globe Book Shop
1700 Pennsylvania Ave. NW
☎ *393-1490. Map 3F6* ⬛ ⬛ 💳
Foreign-language publications and
recordings are available here.

Kramer Books and Afterwords
1517 Connecticut Ave. NW
☎ *387-1462. Map 3D5* ⬛ ⬛ 💳
A Dupont Circle institution, this
cozy bookstore-café welcomes
browsers and bibliophiles alike. The
café serves excellent soups, salads
and desserts, plus beer and wine,
and keeps late hours.

Olsson's
1239 Wisconsin Ave. NW,
Georgetown (and other
branches) ☎ *338-6712. Map 2E3*
⬛ ⬛
An extensive inventory of books,
from bestsellers to scholarly tomes,
as well as a treasure-trove of classic
and jazz recordings and tapes.

Penguin Feather Records and Tapes
3225 M St. NW, Georgetown
(and other branches) ☎ *965-*
7172. Map 2E3 ⬛ 💳
Funk, punk, reggae or retro-rock in
a trendy setting.

Second Story Books
2000 P St. NW ☎ *659-8884. Map*
3D5 ⬛ ⬛ 💳
If it's old, out of print,
custom-bound or a small press
publication, this is where to find it.

Tower Records
2000 Pennsylvania Ave. ☎ *331-*
2400. Map 3E5 ⬛ ⬛ 💳
A gigantic store with a wide choice
of records, cassettes and compact
discs in every category.

Waldenbooks
12th St. and Pennsylvania Ave.
NW ☎ *638-0225 and 1700*
Pennsylvania Ave. NW ☎ *393-*
1490. Map 6F7, 3F7 ⬛ ⬛ 💳
Another bestseller chain.

Cameras and photographic equipment
A wide range of services and supplies, from inexpensive
point-and-shoot cameras to de luxe German and Japanese

equipment, is available at competitive prices. Some stores offer repair services and have multilingual staff.

Baker's Photo Supply
4433 Wisconsin Ave. NW ☎ 362-9100 [AE] [CB] [VISA]
Hasselblad, Nikon, Graflex, Beseler and other less expensive equipment are on sale. There is also a repair service.

Congressional Photo
209 Pennsylvania Ave. SE (2nd floor) ☎ 543-3206. Map 8G10 [AE] [CB] [VISA]
The professionals' choice for custom finishing. A full camera repair service and budget processing are available.

Embassy Camera Center
1709 Connecticut Ave. NW ☎ 483-7448. Map 3C5 [CB] [VISA]
Assistants are fluent in Spanish, French and German, and the range includes American and Japanese cameras, accessories and film.

Potomac Photo
1819 H St. NW ☎ 822-9001. Map 3F5 [AE] [CB] [VISA]
Same-day slide service, and national brand cameras and accessories.

Clothes and shoes for men
Like much else in Washington, men's clothes — and clothes shops — have become more cosmopolitan and adventurous in recent years. The following list covers a wide range, from traditional three-piece suits to jeans and safari jackets.

Arthur A. Adler Inc.
1101 Connecticut Ave. NW
☎ 628-0131. Map 3E6 [AE] [CB] [VISA]
Tailored menswear geared to the tastes of Washington executives.

Athlete's Foot
3222 M St. NW, Georgetown
☎ 965-7262. Map 2E3 [AE] [CB] [VISA]
Exercise gear and footwear for almost every sport.

Banana Republic
14th and F St. NW ☎ 783-1400.
Map 6F7 [AE] [CB] [VISA]
Safari styling in casual shirts, jackets, sweaters, pants and accessories. (There is another branch in Georgetown.)

Britches of Georgetown
1219 Connecticut Ave. NW
☎ 347-8994. Map 3E6 [AE] [CB] [CB] [CB] [VISA]
The downtown branch offers trim tailoring in tuxedos, tweed jackets, traditional suits and casual wear, as well as shoes and accessories. (There is another branch in Georgetown.)

The Gap
1217 Connecticut Ave. NW
☎ 638-4603. Map 3E6 [AE] [CB] [CB] [VISA]
Blue, white, gray and striped jeans, sweaters and sports shirts.

Georgetown University Shop
1248 36th St. NW, Georgetown
☎ 337-8100. Map 2E2 [AE] [CB] [CB] [VISA]
On the edge of campus, this store features Ivy League styles designed for the student or the still-slim graduate.

Raleigh's
Mazza Gallerie, Wisconsin Ave. and Military Rd. ☎ 785-7011 [AE] [CB] [VISA]
A long-standing local source for correct menswear, now featuring European designers as well. Shoes and accessories too.

Watergate Men's Wear
2520 Virginia Ave. NW ☎ 333-0299. Map 2F4 [AE] [CB] [VISA]
A good range of expensive imported menswear, knitwear and executive gifts.

Clothes and shoes for women
Geoffrey Beene, Bill Blass, Liz Claiborne, Perry Ellis, Alexander Julian, Donna Karan, Ann Klein, Calvin Klein and Ralph Lauren are the top names in American design. Their

clothes, from leisure to luxurious evening wear, are characterized by simple, unfussy lines and natural fabrics. They are stylish, yet at the same time practical and comfortable.

At the stores listed below will be found a wide selection of daywear, evening wear, sportswear, shoes and accessories by these and other American designers, as well as by European and Oriental designers. Many of the men's stores also feature a large selection of women's clothing.

Alcott and Andrews
2000 Pennsylvania Ave. NW
☎ *822-9476. Map 3E5* AE ◎
Office and leisure wear designed for the contemporary executive woman.

Jos. A. Bank Clothier
1118 19th St. NW ☎ *466-2282. Map 3E5* AE ◎ VISA
Traditional suits and accessories for successful women executives.

Commander Salamander
1420 Wisconsin Ave. NW, Georgetown ☎ *333-9599. Map 2D3* AE ◎ VISA
Funky clothes and accessories in a way-out setting.

Claire Dratch
1224 Connecticut Ave. NW
☎ *466-6500. Map 3E6* AE ◎ VISA
A well-established local designer boutique, selling sophisticated

clothing. (There are branches also downtown and in Bethesda, Md.)

Guy Laroche Boutique/Saint Laurent Rive Gauche
600 New Hampshire Ave. NW
☎ *333-8702. Map 2F4* AE ◎ VISA
Ready-to-wear clothes by the famous Parisian designers.

Saks-Jandel
5510 Wisconsin Ave. NW, Chevy Chase ☎ *652-2250* AE ◎ ◎ VISA
Elegant afternoon and evening wear.

Ann Taylor
Mazza Gallerie, Wisconsin Ave. and Military Rd. ☎ *244-1940* AE ◎ VISA
Chic clothing and footwear with the American look. (There is another branch in Georgetown Park.)

Department stores
Recently many new department stores have opened in the burgeoning shopping centers of Washington's suburbs. But if you prefer to shop in the city, the three stalwarts of Old Downtown — **Garfinkel's, Hecht's** and **Woodward and Lothrop** — are enjoying a new lease on life as the area revives.

Bloomingdale's
Tyson's Corner Mall, McLean, Va. ☎ *556-4600* AE CB ◎ ◎ VISA
Outpost of the famous New York-based chain featuring trendsetting fashions for men, women and children, shoes and accessories, household goods and soft furnishings.

Garfinkel's
14th and F St. NW ☎ *628-7730. Map 6F7* AE ◎ ◎ VISA
Long-standing local retailer with a select stock of fine clothing, jewelry, tableware and linen.

Hecht's
Metro Center, 12th & G St. NW
☎ *628-6661. Map 6F7* AE ◎ VISA
Anything from mattresses to video

cameras, children's socks to bridal gowns can be bought in this store, which has become a local institution. Central location.

Lord and Taylor's
5255 Western Ave. NW
☎ *362-9600* AE
Another New York shopping giant transplanted to Washington. (Another branch at Seven Corners.)

Neiman-Marcus
Mazza Gallerie, 5300 Wisconsin Ave. NW ☎ *966-9700.*
The great Texas institution whose his-and-hers Christmas gifts are exercises in conspicuous consumption. Remarkably good bargains at their "Last Call" half-yearly sales.

J.C. Penney's
Springfield Mall, Springfield, Va.
☎ 971-8850 AE ⦿ VISA
The century-old king of mail order companies now transformed into a store selling well-designed and keenly priced family clothing and the Rolls Royce-on-tea-cups that drew Princess Diana to this shop on her first American visit.

Saks Fifth Avenue
5555 Wisconsin Ave. NW,
Chevy Chase ☎ 657-9000 AE CB ⦿
The Washington branch of one of the loftiest names in New York retailing.

Woodward and Lothrop
11th and F St. NW ☎ 347-5300.
Map 6F7 AE ⦿ VISA
Much of the same merchandise as that found at Hecht's, although there are some slightly more expensive lines as well.

Food

Only lately has Washington developed a cosmopolitan restaurant presence, so it is no surprise that there are very few suppliers to the gastronome at home. But those that do exist can hold their own with other cities for variety, quality and price.

Cannon's Seafood
1065 31st St. NW, Georgetown
☎ 337-8366. Map 2E3.
The finest fresh seafood at prices to match. Often crowded at lunchtime with Georgetown shoppers.

Eastern Market
400 E Capitol St. SE ☎ 543-2444.
Map 8G10.
This farmers' market is so famous that there is a Metro stop named after it. Fresh turkeys, dewy vegetables, home-cured sausages, local color, bustle and bargains are all to be found here.

Neam's Market
3217 P St. NW, Georgetown
☎ 338-4694. Map 2D3.
Splash out here on such luxuries as white asparagus, caviar, Columbian coffee and French wines. A boy will carry your bags to your car.

Sutton Place Gourmet
3201 New Mexico Ave. NW
☎ 363-5800 AE ⦿ VISA
Stargaze on noted politicians and TV personalities as you shop for mouthwatering delicacies, including a splendid choice of wines and cheeses.

Jewelry

Luxurious, close-carpeted boutiques, brightly lit middle-price shops and bustling department stores feature a variety of precious and semiprecious jewelry from heirloom to souvenir quality. Prices range accordingly.

Bailey, Banks and Biddle   Tyson's Corner Mall, McLean, Va.
☎ 883-1400 AE ⦿ VISA

W. Bell   1901 L St. NW ☎ 881-2000. Map 3E5
⦿ VISA

J. E. Caldwell Co.   1140 Connecticut Ave. NW ☎ 466-6780.
Map 3E6 AE ⦿ VISA

Melart Jewelers   National Pl. NW ☎ 737-8772. Map 6F7 AE
CB ⦿ VISA

Les Must de Cartier   1127 Connecticut Ave. NW ☎ 887-5888.
Map 3E6 AE ⦿ VISA

Pampillonia Jewelers   Mazza Gallerie, Wisconsin Ave. and
Military Rd. ☎ 363-6305 AE ⦿ VISA

Pharmacies

The sensible traveler always carries a signed prescription form for any necessary medication. Luggage can be lost, medicines can be spilled or spoiled, and a trip to a private physician or clinic can cost precious time and money just for a replacement prescription. Pharmacies carry a wide variety of over-the-counter remedies, but some of those customarily

available overseas may only be obtained by prescription.
American pharmacies also stock perfume, cosmetics,
greetings cards, film, paperback novels and detergents.

Dart Drugs
1275 K St. NW ☎ *682-2155. Map 6E7.*
A major local chain, open daily.

Drug Fair
1501 K St. NW ☎ *638-5225. Map 3E6* ☐ ☐
One of several Drug Fair stores in the downtown area, open daily.

Foggy Bottom Apothecary
1118 22nd St. NW ☎ *296-9314. Map 3E6* ☐ ☐ ☐

Located in a hospital area, this pharmacy is good for unusual prescriptions.

Morgan Pharmacy
3001 P St. NW, Georgetown
☎ *337-4100. Map 2D4* ☐ ☐ ☐
Free delivery, open every Sun till noon.

People's Drug Store
1905 14th St. NW ☎ *234-9110. Map 3E7* ☐ ☐
The only 24hr pharmacy downtown.

Sports and camping

Name the sport and there will be a Washington merchant who
can supply the equipment or clothing. Favorite weekend
activities for Washingtonians are hiking, canoeing and
camping, so sports stores carry everything from tent stakes to
freeze-dried meals, trail boots and bed rolls.

Eddie Bauer   1800 M St. NW ☎ 331-8009. Map **3**E6 ☐ ☐
☐ ☐ ☐

Herman's World of Sporting Goods   800 E St. NW
☎ 638-6434. Map 7F8 ☐ ☐ ☐ ☐ ☐

Hudson Trail Outfitters   4437 Wisconsin Ave. NW.
☎ 363-9810. Map 6F7 ☐ ☐

Irving's Sports Shops   1203 Connecticut Ave. NW
☎ 466-8830. Map 3E6 ☐ ☐ ☐

Toys

Beatrix Potter books, snakes-and-ladder games and toys
remembered from the nursery vie with the latest movable
plastic cartoon monsters and video games on the shelves of
the modern metropolitan toy store. Some stores specialize in
handcrafted or educational toys.

Georgetown Zoo   3222 M St. NW, Georgetown Park
☎ 338-4182. Map 2E3 ☐ ☐ ☐

Red Balloon   1073 Wisconsin Ave. NW, Georgetown
☎ 965-1200. Map 2E3 ☐ ☐ ☐

FAO Schwarz   3222 M St. NW ☎ 342-2285. Map 2E4 ☐ ☐
☐ ☐

Toys "R" Us   8449 Leesburg Pike, Tyson's Corner, Va.
☎ 893-2223 ☐ ☐ ☐

Wine and spirits

The following liquor stores are among the best in the city for
choice and value.

Calvert Woodley Liquors   4339 Connecticut Ave. NW
☎ 966-4400. Map 2B4 ☐ ☐

Colonial Liquor Shoppe   1800 I St. NW ☎ 338-4500. Map 3E6
☐ ☐

Mayflower Wines and Spirits   2115 M St. NW ☎ 463-7950.
Map 3E5 ☐ ☐

Wagner's Liquor Shop   1717 Wisconsin Ave. NW,
Georgetown ☎ 232-1900. Map 2D3.

SPECIAL INFORMATION

Biographies

It would be an impossible task to list here all the famous people, politicians included, associated with Washington. The following is a selection of those who, either by birthright, noteworthy deed or influence, have contributed to the history of the city.

Adams, Henry (1838-1918)
Historian and philosopher. Grandson of President John Quincy Adams and son of the diplomat Charles Francis Adams. Although his best-known book is his autobiographical work *The Education of Henry Adams*, he also wrote a monumental *History of the United States*. He settled in Washington in 1877 in a house on the site of the present Hay-Adams Hotel.

Barry, Marion S., Jr (born 1936)
Mayor of Washington since 1979, second holder of the office, former civil rights activist. His administration has been clouded by allegations of official and private misbehavior.

Bradlee, Benjamin (born 1921)
Executive Editor of the *Washington Post*. He steered the *Post* through the period of the Watergate investigation (1972-4), conducted by journalists Carl Bernstein and Bob Woodward.

Buchwald, Art (born 1925)
Syndicated newspaper columnist living in Washington who writes with mischievous wit and humor about life and politics in the capital. His column appears in some 500 newspapers in many countries, and several collections of his articles have been published as books.

Douglass, Frederick (c.1817-95)
Pioneer advocate of black liberation. His real name was Frederick Augustus Washington Bailey, but he assumed the alias Douglass after escaping from the slavery into which he was born. He dedicated his life to writing, lecturing and campaigning for the cause of black freedom and equality. See **Frederick Douglass House**.

Ellicott, Andrew (1754-1820)
Surveyor who helped L'Enfant lay out the area that is now DC. He took over after L'Enfant's dismissal, and the map of the territory published in 1793 was in his name, although it was mostly L'Enfant's work.

Ellington, Duke (1899-1974)
Seminal jazz composer, band leader and pianist, born in Washington. His real name was Edward Kennedy Ellington.

L'Enfant, Pierre Charles (1754-1825)
The brilliant, temperamental French engineer and architect who, more than anyone else, is responsible for the shape of Washington today. Having come to America to fight in George Washington's army against the British, he was commissioned in 1791 to prepare a plan for the federal capital. The following year he was dismissed after quarreling with the Commissioners of the District of Columbia. He spent the latter part of his life fighting for greater compensation and died in poverty. Posthumous recognition came in 1909 when his remains were moved to **Arlington National Cemetery** and a monument to him was erected there.

Graham, Katharine (born 1917)
Chairman and Chief Executive Officer of the Washington Post Company. Her son, Donald E. Graham, is publisher of the *Washington Post* newspaper. See also *Benjamin Bradlee* above.

132

Hayes, Helen (born 1900)
Actress, born in Washington. Helen Hayes became a star after
appearing in James Barrie's play *Dear Brutus* in 1918.
Probably her most famous role was as Queen Victoria in the
play *Victoria Regina* (1935).

Hoban, James (1762-1831)
Irish-born architect who designed and supervised the
construction of the *White House*.

Hooker, General Joseph (1814-79)
A name that achieved a dubious immortality. Hooker was a
Union general during the Civil War who tried to restrict
prostitution in the capital by confining camp followers (nearly
4,000) to one part of the city. Hence the term "hooker."

Hoover, J. Edgar (1895-1972)
Director of the Federal Bureau of Investigation for 48yrs from
1924 until his death. Born in Washington and a graduate of
George Washington University Law School, Hoover built the
FBI into the powerful organization that it is today. A tough,
combative figure, he was both widely respected and much
disliked. For 20yrs he lunched regularly at the Mayflower
Hotel, and after his death his customary table was draped in
red, white and blue for a week, in mourning.

Jolson, Al (1886-1950)
Popular singer and actor. Originally named Asa Yoelson, he
was born in Russia and raised in SW Washington, where his
father was a rabbi.

Latrobe, Benjamin Henry (1764-1820)
English-born architect. He came to America in 1796 and
designed a number of buildings in Washington including
Decatur House and parts of the *Capitol* and *White House*.

Pope, John Russell (1874-1937)
Architect whose serene Neoclassical buildings are a major
feature of Washington. They include the *National Archives*,
the West Building of the *National Gallery of Art*, the
Jefferson Memorial and *House of the Temple*.

Shepherd, Alexander Robey ("Boss") (1835-1902)
Shepherd was to Washington what Baron Haussmann was to
Paris. He became Head of the Board of Public Works in 1871
and Governor of the District of Columbia in 1873. Under his
regime a vast program of public works was undertaken,
which bankrupted Washington but at last gave it adequate
sidewalks, water mains, sewerage, lighting and so on.

Smith, Captain John (1580-1631)
English adventurer who, in 1608, with "7 souldiers and 7
gentlemen," sailed up the Potomac. Where Washington now
stands he discovered a settlement of Algonquin Indians.
Charmed, he encouraged colonists to settle here.

Smithson, James (1765-1829)
Although Smithson never came to Washington, the city would
have been a very different place without him. He was a
British scientist whose bequest of $500,000 to the USA
resulted in the creation of the Smithsonian Institution.

Sousa, John Philip (1854-1932)
Bandmaster and composer. Born in a house on Capitol Hill,
Sousa was for many years leader of the US Marine Band
before forming his own. Composer of many styles of music,
he is most famous for his rousing marches, which include
Liberty Bell, Semper Fidelis, The Stars and Stripes Forever and
the *Washington Post* march, played every time a band passes
the newspaper's offices. He also wrote five novels and an

autobiography, *Marching Along*. Of Polish parentage, his real name was So, to which he later added the letters USA.
Thornton, William *(1759-1828)*
Scottish-born doctor, architect and inventor. He emigrated to the USA in 1787, won the competition for the design of the Capitol in 1792, and supervised the construction of the building until he was replaced by Latrobe.
Washington, George *(1732-99)*
First President of the United States, he chose the location of the city named in his honor. He selected a site far enough inland to be safe from surprise naval attack yet at the same time accessible to ocean-going vessels. His own home was nearby at Mount Vernon (see ***Excursions***).
Washington, Walter E. *(born 1915)*
What more appropriate name for the man who became the first mayor of Washington in 1975? A black, and a lawyer by profession, he held the office for four years.

Chronology of US presidents

Name	Party	Years in office
George Washington	None	1789-97
John Adams	Federalist	1797-1801
Thomas Jefferson	Democratic-Republican	1801-9
James Madison	Democratic-Republican	1809-17
James Monroe	Democratic-Republican	1817-25
John Quincy Adams	Democratic-Republican	1825-9
Andrew Jackson	Democrat	1829-37
Martin Van Buren	Democrat	1837-41
William H. Harrison	Whig	1841
John Tyler	Whig	1841-5
James K. Polk	Democrat	1845-9
Zachary Taylor	Whig	1849-50
Millard Fillmore	Whig	1850-3
Franklin Pierce	Democrat	1853-7
James Buchanan	Democrat	1857-61
Abraham Lincoln	Republican	1861-5
Andrew Johnson	National Union	1865-9
Ulysses S. Grant	Republican	1869-77
Rutherford B. Hayes	Republican	1877-81
James A. Garfield	Republican	1881
Chester A. Arthur	Republican	1881-5
Grover Cleveland	Democrat	1885-9
Benjamin Harrison	Republican	1889-93
Grover Cleveland	Democrat	1893-7
William McKinley	Republican	1897-1901
Theodore Roosevelt	Republican	1901-9
William H. Taft	Republican	1909-13
Woodrow Wilson	Democrat	1913-21
Warren G. Harding	Republican	1921-3
Calvin Coolidge	Republican	1923-9
Herbert C. Hoover	Republican	1929-33
Franklin D. Roosevelt	Democrat	1933-45
Harry S. Truman	Democrat	1945-53
Dwight D. Eisenhower	Republican	1953-61
John F. Kennedy	Democrat	1961-3
Lyndon B. Johnson	Democrat	1963-9
Richard M. Nixon	Republican	1969-74
Gerald R. Ford	Republican	1974-7
James E. Carter, Jr	Democrat	1977-81
Ronald W. Reagan	Republican	1981-1989
George H.W. Bush	Republican	1989-

Washington for children

An invaluable book is *Going Places with Children in Washington*, available from the publisher, **Green Acres School** (*11701 Danville Dr., Rockville, Md. 20852* ☎ *881-4100*). Also useful is *Kiosk*, a free monthly bulletin of events; to join their mailing list, write to the **Public Affairs Office** (*National Capital Parks, 900 Ohio Dr. SW, Washington DC 20242* ☎ *485-9874*).

Coming events for children are listed in the "Where and when" section of the *Washingtonian* monthly magazine and in the "Carousel" and "Saturday's Child" sections in the *Weekend* supplement of the *Washington Post*, published Fri. The *Post* publishes a *Calendar of the Smithsonian* toward the end of each month. See also *Telephone services* in **Basic information** for recorded information on a range of services, such as the **DC Recreation Department** (☎ *673-7660*).

Parks

Contact the following organizations for information on the many widely differing parks in Washington and its environs.

Alexandria Department of Recreation and Parks ☎ 838-4343

Arlington County Recreation Division ☎ *(703) 358-4747*

Fairfax County Park Authority ☎ *941-5000*

Maryland-National Capital Park and Planning Commission ☎ 565-7417

National Park Service ☎ 426-6700

Prince Georges County Parks and Recreation ☎ 699-2407

Rock Creek Park (☎ *426-6833*), which runs in a long strip through NW DC, has miles of leafy paths to explore, picnic places, playgrounds, a Nature Center and a Planetarium. **Battery Kemble Park** (*Chain Bridge Rd. NW, near American University* ☎ *426-6834*) is ideal for kite-flying and for tobogganing in snowy weather. **Fort Stevens Park** (*Piney Branch Rd. and Quakerbos St. NW* ☎ *426-6833*) has restored earthworks and gun emplacements from a Civil War fort. The Tidal Basin in West *Potomac Park* has pedal boats to rent (see *Boating* in **Sports and activities**).

Outside DC the attractions are richer. **Cabin John Regional Park** (*Rockville, Md.* ☎ *(301) 299-4555*) has train rides, a seasonal ice rink, a miniature zoo and a special playground for children under six. **Glen Echo Park** (*Bethesda, Md.* ☎ *(301) 492-6229*) has theater classes for children aged five and older, and free art workshops on Sun afternoons in spring and summer. **Wheaton Regional Park** (*Wheaton, Md.* ☎ *(301) 946-7071*) has train rides, a collection of animals called "Old MacDonald's Farm" and miles of wild country.

Zoos, nature centers and farms

In addition to the *National Zoological Park*, with its 165 acres (66ha) and superb cross-section of the animal kingdom, there are many other places where children can delight in animals, nature and wildlife. **The Audubon Naturalist Society** (*Chevy Chase, Md.* ☎ *652-5964*) has a nature trail and special programs for children aged four and older. **Potomac Overlook Regional Park** (*Marcey Rd., off Military Rd., Arlington, Va.* ☎ *(703) 528-5406*) has scheduled activities Fri at 4pm for youngsters of 6-8yrs, and Sun at 2pm for ages 9 and up. Wildlife and flora abound on *Theodore Roosevelt Island* (☎ *(703) 285-2600*), within sight of Kennedy Center. A distinctive, changing terrain of marsh and uplands is traversed by miles of nature trails. Ducks, deer and foxes can be sighted.

Turkey Run Farm (*McLean, Va.* ☎ *442-7557*) is a re-creation of a Colonial farm, which includes a family in period costume carrying out the farm chores. Other working farms that can be visited are **Frying Pan Farm Park** (*Herndon, Va.* ☎ *(703) 437-9101*), **National Colonial Farm** (*Accokeek, Md.* ☎ *(301) 283-2113*) and **Oxon Hill Farm** (*Oxon Hill, Md.* ☎ *(301) 839-1177*). Youngsters also enjoy **Carroll County Farm Museum** (*Westminster, Md.* ☎ *(301) 848-7775*) and **Pet Farm Park** (*Vienna, Va.* ☎ *(703) 759-3636*); the latter allow petting and feeding of their animals.

Nature centers and trails are always popular with children; the following are located in the Washington area.

Brookside Nature Center   *Wheaton Regional Park, Md.* ☎ *946-9071*

Clearwater Nature Center   *Cosca Regional Park, Thrift Rd., Clinton, Md.* ☎ *297-4575*

Gulf Branch Nature Center   *3608 N Military Rd., Arlington, Va.* ☎ *358-3403*

Hidden Oaks Nature Center   *4030 Hummer Rd., Annandale, Va.* ☎ *941-1065*

Hidden Pond Nature Center   *8511 Greeley Blvd., W Springfield, Va.* ☎ *451-9588*

Lathrop E. Smith Meadowside Nature Center   *5100 Meadowside Lane, Rockville, Md.* ☎ *924-2626*

Long Branch Nature Center   *625 S Carlin Springs Rd., Arlington, Va.* ☎ *358-6535*

Riverbend Nature Center   *8814 Jeffrey Rd., Great Falls, Va.* ☎ *759-3211*

Rock Creek Nature Center   *Rock Creek Park, 5200 Glover Rd. NW* ☎ *426-6829*

Remember too the *National Aquarium* in the basement of the Department of Commerce building.

Amusement parks

This form of attraction, which America has developed to an advanced degree, is a great hit with children. An old favorite is **Glen Echo Park Carousel** (*MacArthur Blvd. and Goldsboro Rd., Glen Echo, Md.* ☎ *492-6282*). **Kings Dominion** (☎ *(804) 876-5000; closed winter*), located 75 miles (120km) s of DC just N of Richmond, Va., on route 1-95, is a spectacular amusement park, complete with roller coaster, 33-story Eiffel Tower, steam train, safari park, fantasy rides, shops, restaurants and all kinds of live entertainment. It is possible to include nearby Colonial **Williamsburg** on the same trip (see *Excursions*).

In the same area is **Busch Gardens** (*Route 60, Williamsburg, Va.* ☎ *(703) 253-3000; closed winter*). One of the country's largest beer conglomerates, Anheuser-Busch, set up a brewery here and added walkabout replicas of European villages as they might have looked three centuries ago. Thrill rides, live entertainment, shops, restaurants, and a zoo of North American animals make for full days. Opening hours change frequently, according to season, so always call ahead. Closer to DC is **Wild World** (*Exit 15A off the Beltway*

☎ 249-1500), where the main attractions are water rides.
Bring swimsuits. There are shows, carnival rides and live
music, too. Opening hours change frequently; call ahead.

Museums and workshops

The only museum in Washington specifically for the young is
the *Capital Children's Museum*. But many other museums
are equally interesting for both adults and children. Examples
are the *National Geographic Society Explorers Hall* and
the *National Air and Space Museum*. Other places for
space buffs are the **Goddard Visitor Center and Museum**
(*Greenbelt, Md.* ☎ 334-8101), run by NASA, which has
exhibits on all aspects of the Space Program; the **Rock Creek
Nature Center Planetarium** (☎ 426-6829); and the *United
States Naval Observatory* (☎ 653-1543). Technologically-
minded children will also love the participatory exhibits at the
National Museum of American History. The *National
Museum of Natural History* is always a favorite too.

Many museums have special sections for children. The
Natural History Museum, for example, has a "hands-on"
Discovery Room, and the National Museum of American Art
has an **Explore Gallery**, a multimedia experience through
which children can explore different sensory effects. Children
interested in military matters will enjoy the **US Marine Corps
Museum** and **US Navy Memorial Museum** at *Navy Yard*,
and the **Fort Ward Museum** (☎ 838-4848 *for details*), which
has Civil War memorabilia and occasionally stages
re-enactments of events of the period. More peacefully-
minded youngsters will enjoy the *Dolls' House and Toy
Museum*, and transportation buffs will like the **National
Capital Trolley Museum** (*Northwest Branch Regional Park,
Bonifant Rd. between Layhill Rd. and New Hampshire Ave., N
of Wheaton, Md,* ☎ *(301) 384-9797* 🖼 *open noon-5pm, Wed
in July, Aug noon-4pm; closed mid-Dec to early Jan*). The
Wax Museum, with tableaux from the Bible and from
American history, is usually a great success with kids.

Movies, theater and music

Watch the periodicals listed in the introduction to this section
for children's performances of all kinds. For movie
enthusiasts there are many possibilities. The *Hirshhorn
Museum* and the *National Air and Space Museum* both
have lively movie shows. In theater the choice is even wider.
Listed below are some of the children's theater centers in the
DC area.
Adventure Theater (*Glen Echo Park, Glen Echo, Md.*
☎ 320-5331). Plays, music and puppetry, on weekends.
Theater of Arlington (*Arlington County Visual and
Performing Arts, 300 North Park Dr., Arlington, Va.*
☎ 548-1154).
Maryland Children's Theater (*4930 Cordell Ave., Bethesda,
Md.* ☎ 933-7999).
Programs for Children and Youth (*Education Office, John
F. Kennedy Center for the Performing Arts, New Hampshire
Ave. and Rock Creek Parkway* ☎ 254-7190).
The Round House Theater (*Montgomery County Recreation
Dept, 12210 Bushey Dr., Wheaton, Md.* ☎ 217-6850 *office,
468-4234 box office*). An adult theater that also has classes
and performances for children.
Smithsonian Discovery Theater (*Arts and Industries*

Building, 900 Jefferson Dr., SW ☎ *357-1500).*
Sylvan Theater (*Washington Monument grounds* ☎ *426-6975).* Outdoor plays, ballets, musicals and puppet shows in spring and summer.

For children who like to listen to music, numerous open-air concerts are given in Washington during the summer, such as the military concerts at the Jefferson Memorial or the Marine Corps Sunset Parade (see also p.34). The **National Symphony** also performs a series of young people's concerts at the Kennedy Center (☎ *785-8100*) in spring and fall.

Other ideas

A climb up the *Washington Monument*, a cruise on the Potomac or a barge up the *Chesapeake and Ohio Canal* all make ideal family outings, as does a visit to the *Federal Bureau of Investigation*. Budding racing drivers can try the **Skelterama Go-cart Track** (*4300 Kenilworth Ave., Bladensburg, Md.* ☎ *(301) 864-0110*). Practice sessions are organized for children at **Washington Youth Gardens** in the *National Arboretum*.

Check the *Calendar of events* in *Planning and walks* for other ideas. The following may appeal: **The Kite Festival**, held on a Sat in Mar or Apr near the Washington Monument (☎ *357-3244 for info.*); the Easter Monday **Easter Egg Roll**, when 24,000 wooden eggs are hidden away on the White House lawn; and free Sun afternoon concerts and the **International Children's Festival** of dance, theater and music, held on Labor Day weekend at **Wolf Trap Farm Park** (*Vienna, Va.* ☎ *(703) 941-1527*).

Toy stores and bookstores

Capital Children's Museum has a shop selling an interesting selection of books and toys. The only children's bookstore in Washington is **Cheshire Cat Book Store** (*5512 Connecticut Ave. NW* ☎ *244-3956*), which has a good selection for all ages.

Toy stores include the following:
Granny's Place　*303 Cameron St., Alexandria, Va.*
☎ *(703) 549-0119*
John Davy Toys　*301 Cameron St., Alexandria, Va.*
☎ *(703) 683-0079*
Little Caledonia　*1419 Wisconsin Ave. NW* ☎ *333-4700*
The Red Balloon　*1073 Wisconsin Ave. NW* ☎ *965-1200*
F.A.O. Schwarz　*Mazza Gallerie, 5300 Wisconsin Ave. NW*
☎ *363-8455, and Georgetown Park, 3222 M St. NW*
☎ *342-2285*
Sullivan's Toy Stores　*3412 Wisconsin Ave. NW*
☎ *362-1343, and other branches*
Treetop Toys　*3301 New Mexico Ave. NW* ☎ *244-3500*

For discount toy stores, try **Juvenile Sales** (*2321 University Blvd., Wheaton, Md.* ☎ *(301) 949-5157; 6612 Richmond Highway, Alexandria, Va.* ☎ *(703) 768-7500; and other branches*) or **Toys "R" Us** (*Tyson's Corner, Va.* ☎ *893-2223; Springfield, Va.* ☎ *922-7876; and other branches*), a chain of discount stores selling toys and children's furniture.

Babysitters

Assistants, Inc. (*2909 Wilson Blvd., Arlington, Va. 22201* ☎ *(703) 524-1131/0666*); **Child Care Agency** (*Woodward Building, 733 15th St. NW, DC 20005* ☎ *783-8573*); **Sitters Unlimited** (*DC and Va.* ☎ *823-0888*).

Sports and activities

The only large-scale general sports complex is run by the **YMCA** (*1711 Rhode Island Ave. NW* ☎ *862-9690*) and is open only to YMCA members. It gives access to, among other things, a swimming pool, squash courts, gymnasium and sauna. The only comparable facility open to the general public is the excellent **Watergate Health Club** (*2650 Virginia Ave. NW* ☎ *298-4460*), which offers a swimming pool, gymnasium, sauna, massage and exercise classes.

Otherwise, for the ordinary tourist there are limited facilities in the city for swimming (in a few hotels), golf and tennis, but very little else. The free *Recreation Guide Book* from the **DC Recreation Department** (*3149 16th St. NW, Room 22, DC 20010* ☎ *673-7660*) lists municipal facilities. Outside the city the choice becomes wider, especially in outdoor sports, but it can still be frustrating if you are not a member of a club.

In spectator sports, the prospect in DC is better. There are stadiums for professional games such as American football, soccer and ice-hockey. Interesting amateur events can be watched free in parks, including soccer, polo, rugby and hockey; for information call **National Capital Parks** (☎ *426-6700*) or **"dial-a-park"** (☎ *485-7275 daily bulletin*).

The following A-Z includes not only sports but also activities and facilities that come under the general heading of recreation.

Ballooning
Fly high on an introductory flight, with a glass of champagne to help you on your way up. There are several ballooning clubs in the vicinity of Washington. One commercial firm to try is **Maryland Balloon Adventures** (☎ *(301) 766-6434*). Or, check the *Weekend* section of the *Washington Post*.

Baseball
Washington no longer has its own major-league baseball team. The nearest is the Baltimore Orioles, who play in **Memorial Stadium** (*1,000 block of E 33rd St., Baltimore, Md.* ☎ *(301) 338-1300*). The season is Apr-Oct.

Basketball
The Washington Bullets play in the **Capital Centre Stadium** (*1 Harry S. Truman Dr., Landover, Md., off the Beltway from exit 15A or 17A* ☎ *350-3400*). The season is Oct-Apr.

Bicycling
In a land where the automobile is worshiped, cycling still holds its own, and there are many delightful cycle routes in and around Washington. For information contact the **Potomac Pedalers Touring Club** (*Box 23610, DC 20026* ☎ *363-8687*), which provides maps and advice. See also *Basic Information* for a list of bicycle rental firms.

Boating
You can rent pedal boats on the Tidal Basin, from the **Tidal Basin Boating Center** (*15th St. and Maine Ave, SW* ☎ *484-3475*). For the Potomac and/or the C&O Canal, try any one of the following: **Fletcher's Boat House** (*4940 Canal Rd. NW* ☎ *244-0461*) — canoes and rowboats on the canal and Potomac; **Jack's Boats** (*3500 K St. NW, Georgetown* ☎ *337-9642*) — canoes and rowboats on the

Potomac; **Thompson Boat Center** (*Rock Creek Parkway and Virginia Ave. NW* ☎ *333-4861*) — canoes on the Potomac.

Bowling

A classic American indoor sport and a good way to get a cheap evening's entertainment. Most of the bowling alleys are outside DC. The most pleasant and accessible is probably **Brunswick River Bowl** (*5225 River Rd., Bethesda, Md. 20816* ☎ *656-5531*). **Bowl America** (☎ *941-6300*) has more than a dozen facilities in and around the District.

Bridge

There are many clubs in and around Washington. Contact Charlotte Miller of the **Washington Bridge League** (*1111 University Blvd. W, Silver Spring, Md. 20902* ☎ *649-1812*).

Chess

On the open-air chess tables in Dupont Circle and on the w side of *Lafayette Park*, games of chess or checkers are played on fine days. For information on chess clubs, contact the **United States Chess Federation** (*186 Route 9W, New Windsor, NY 12550* ☎ *562-8350*).

Cricket

An amateur cricket league comprised primarily of British residents and those from Commonwealth nations holds matches on weekends during the summer. Practices are usually held in West Potomac Park, near the Lincoln Memorial Polo Field. (*For information* ☎ *636-7803*.)

Dance

In Washington you can cavort to music in any number of ways from classical ballet to clogging. Among a great many dance places, the following addresses might be useful.
High on Dance (*5207 Wisconsin Ave. NW* ☎ *362-3042*). Beginners and professionals, ballet, jazz, modern.
Joy of Motion Dance Center (*1643 Connecticut Ave. NW* ☎ *387-0911*). Jazz, tap, stretch, modern ballet.
Northeast Academy of Dance (*2011 Benning Rd. NE* ☎ *396-4661*) 50yrs' experience offering all forms of dance, beginner to advanced.
Washington School of the Ballet (*3515 Wisconsin Ave. NW* ☎ *362-1683*).

Fishing

Whether you want to charter a boat and go deep-sea fishing off the Maryland coast or try your luck upriver on the Potomac or the Shenandoah, there are endless opportunities. Read the regular feature called "Fish Lines" in the *Weekend* section of the *Washington Post*. Fishing maps of both fresh and saltwater fishing grounds are published by the **Alexandria Drafting Company** (*6440 General Green Way, Alexandria, Va. 22310* ☎ *750-0510*), obtainable from them or from bookstores.

Football

Washington's professional team, the Redskins, plays in **Robert F. Kennedy Stadium** (*E Capitol and 22nd St. SE* ☎ *543-6465*). The season runs approximately Sept-Dec. Tickets are rarely available but all games are televised.

Gardens

"A garden is a lovesome thing," especially on a hot day in Washington when you want to escape from the streets and enjoy the solace of trees and plants. See the *A to Z* entries for *Dumbarton Oaks, Franciscan Monastery, Hillwood, Lady Bird Johnson Park, Meridian Hill Park, National Arboretum, United States Botanic Gardens, Washington Cathedral* and *Mormon Temple*.

The following places also offer a green respite:

Brookside Gardens (*1500 Glenallan Ave., Wheaton, Md.* ☎ *949-8230*). 50 beautifully planted acres (20ha), including a herb, aquatic and Japanese garden.

Constitution Gardens (*in the Mall, just N of the Lincoln Memorial reflecting pool*). A lake, 5,000 trees and some 10,000 other plants.

Floral Library (*between the Tidal Basin and the Washington Monument*). A small but colorful array of many different flowers.

Gunston Hall (*Route 242, Lorton, Va.* ☎ *(703) 550-9220*). A Colonial garden, with a 200-year-old boxwood hedge.

Hillwood (*4155 Linnean Ave, NW* ☎ *636-5807*). 25 acres (10ha) of superb grounds, with Japanese and French formal gardens and a greenhouse with 5,000 orchids.

Japanese Embassy Gardens (*2500 Massachusetts Ave. NW* ☎ *234-2266*). An authentic Japanese garden, open May-Oct by appointment only.

Kenilworth Aquatic Gardens (*Anacostia Ave. and Douglas St. NE* ☎ *426-6905*). A delightful maze of ponds full of irises, lotuses and water-lilies — not to mention frogs, turtles, waterfowl, muskrats and other fauna.

Gliding (soaring)

Bay Soaring (*P.O. Box 257, Woodbine, Md. 21797* ☎ *(301) 731-6095*) organizes gliding.

Golf

The best courses in the Washington area are membership clubs, and the only way to play is either through a co-operative arrangement with one's own hometown club or as a guest of a member. Enthusiasts needn't despair, however, for there are scores of public greens throughout the region. Convenient to downtown DC are **Rock Creek Park** (☎ *723-9832*) and **East Potomac Park** (☎ *863-9007*), which in addition to its course has a driving range and miniature golf. Nearby suburban possibilities include **Hobbit's Glen** (*Columbia, Md.* ☎ *(301) 730-5980*), **South Wales** (*Jefferston, Va.* ☎ *(703) 451-1344*), **Reston Golf Course** (*Reston, Va.* ☎ *(703) 620-9333*) and **Montgomery Village** (*Gaithersburg, Md.* ☎ *(301) 948-6204*).

Health clubs and fitness centers

Washingtonians sweat themselves into shape in a variety of ways. One of the most popular is the muscle-conditioning equipment developed by the **Nautilus Fitness Centers** (*1901 Pennsylvania Ave., Md.* ☎ *887-0760 and 1101 Vermont Ave. NW* ☎ *289-0081*). Other centrally located health clubs are the excellent **Watergate Health Club** (*2650 Virginia Ave. NW* ☎ *298-4460*), with swimming pool, gymnasium, massage and exercise classes, **Holiday Spa** (*1750 K St* ☎ *296-0711*) and the **Office Health Center**

(*1990 M St. NW* ☎ *872-0222*); all these have saunas. The
Washington Hilton, (*1919 Connecticut Ave. NW*
☎ *483-3000*) has sauna, exercise room and outdoor
swimming pool, all open to the public. The **Washington
Marriott** (*22nd and M St. NW* ☎ *872-1500*) has indoor
swimming pool, sauna and whirlpool, but nonresidents must
join the hotel's club for at least one month.

Hiking, walking and rambling

Rock Creek Park and the *Chesapeake and Ohio Canal* provide
enjoyable walking. There are also good trails along the Potomac
around Great Falls, 15 miles (24km) upriver from Washington. In
addition to the **National Park Service** (☎ *426-6700*), the
following park authorities can provide further information about
trails under their jurisdiction:
Alexandria Department of Recreation and Parks
☎ *838-4343*
Arlington County Park Division   ☎ *558-2426*
Fairfax County Park Authority   ☎ *941-5000*
Maryland State Parks   ☎ *(301) 269-3761*
Prince Georges Park and Planning Commission
☎ *699-2407*
   Other sources of information are the **Appalachian Trail
Club** (*1718 N St. NW* ☎ *638-5306*) and the **Sierra Club**
(☎ *547-2326 for recorded info.*). Or, call **Dial-a-Hike**
(☎ *547-2326*).

Horseback-racing

In America, harness racing (where the horse is driven from a
cart or buggy) is popular. Races are run at **Rosecroft
Raceway** (*Oxon Hill, Md.* ☎ *567-4000*), **Ocean Downs**
(*Berlin, Md.* ☎ *541-0680*) and **Freestate Raceway** (*Laurel,
Md.* ☎ *(301) 725-2600*). Flat-racing, or steeplechasing, can
be watched at **Bowie Race Course** (*Bowie, Md.* ☎ *(301)
262-8111*), **Laurel Race Course** (*Laurel, Md.* ☎ *(301)
725-1800*), **Pimlico Race Course** (*Baltimore, Md.* ☎ *(301)
542-9400*) and **Shenandoah Downs** (*Charleston, W Va.*
☎ *(304) 725-2021*).

Hunting and shooting

Whether you prefer shooting at targets or live game, the
National Rifle Association (*1600 Rhode Island Ave. NW*
☎ *828-6000*) will be able to provide information.

Ice hockey

The local professional team, the Washington Capitals, plays in
the **Capital Centre** (*1 Harry S. Truman Dr., Landover, Md.*
☎ *350-3400*); tickets obtainable from **Ticket Center** outlets
(☎ *432-0200*). Season is Oct-Apr.

Ice-skating

When the ice is thick enough (☎ *426-6841 US Park Police for
an ice report*), skating is permitted on the C&O Canal or the
reflecting pools in front of the Lincoln Memorial and the w
steps of the Capitol. There are also numerous ice rinks in the
Washington area. Outdoor rinks: **Liberty Plaza** (*17th and G
St. NW* ☎ *377-6599*); **National Sculpture Garden Ice Rink**
(*Constitution Ave. between 7th and 9th St. NW* ☎ *289-7560*);
Pershing Park Ice Rink (*Pennsylvania Ave. between 14th
and 15th St.* ☎ *737-6938*). Indoor rinks open all year:

Fairfax Ice Arena (*3779 Pickett Rd. Fairfax, Va.*
☎ *323-1131*); **Fort Dupont** (*3779 Ely Pl. SE* ☎ *581-0199*);
Mount Vernon District Park (*2017 Bell Vue Blvd.,
Alexandria, Va.* ☎ *(703) 768-3222*). Skates are available for
rental at all of these rinks.

Polo
Polo matches — a good spectator sport that is free — are held
on Sun afternoons in spring, summer and fall on **Lincoln
Memorial Polo Field**, between the Memorial and the Tidal
Basin (☎ *972-7288 for info.*). There are also two polo clubs
within easy driving distance of DC: **Middleburg Polo Club**
(*on Route 50, 3 miles (5km) past Middleburg, Va.*), and
Potomac Polo Club (*Hughes and River Rd., 12 miles (19km)
past Potomac, Md.*).

Riding and equestrian events
Riding stables in the area:
Great Falls Horse Center   *Arnon Chapel Rd., Great Falls,
Va.* ☎ *(703) 759-3400*
Meadowbrook Stables   *Meadowbrook Lane, Chevy Chase,
Md.* ☎ *588-6935*
Rock Creek Park Horse Center   *Military and Glover Rd.
NW* ☎ *362-0117*
   The main equestrian event in the city is the Washington
International Horse Show, which takes place annually at the
end of Oct at the **Capital Centre** (*1 Harry S. Truman Dr.,
Landover, Md.*). For general information contact the
American Horse Council (*1700 K St. NW* ☎ *296-4031*).

Roller-skating
Roller-skating continues to gain popularity and seems to be
here to stay. Although one often sees roller-skaters on the city
sidewalks, there is only one roller-skating rink near DC:
Alexandria Roller-Skating Rink (*807 N and Asaph St.,
Alexandria, Va.* ☎ *(703) 836-6167*).

Rugby
Rugby has a relatively small but enthusiastic following in the
USA. It is occasionally played at **West Potomac Park**, near
the Lincoln Memorial. Contact the **National Park Service**
(☎ *426-6700*) for information about matches.

Running and jogging
Another national craze. For information and advice contact
the **American Running and Fitness Association** (*2420 K
St. NW* ☎ *897-0197*). The main running event is the Marine
Corps Marathon in Oct, but there are races year-round.

Sailing
Whether you plan to rent a dinghy for an afternoon or charter
a large boat for several days, there are abundant
opportunities for sailing near Washington. For a short sail on
the Potomac, try renting a boat from **Buzzard Point Marina**
(*at the foot of 1st St. SW* ☎ *488-8400*). Farther afield,
Annapolis on the splendid Chesapeake Bay has several boat
rental services, such as the **Annapolis Sailing School** (*601
6th St.* ☎ *(301) 261-1947*). At nearby Edgewater, **Pier Seven**
(*48 South River* ☎ *(301) 261-4555*) rents a wide variety of
boats, from 16ft (5m) upward. Charter firms at Annapolis

Sports and activities

include **Bay Yacht Agency** (*2nd St. and Spa Creek* ☎ *(301)
269-6772*) and **Dockside Yacht Charters** (*326 1st St.*
☎ *(301) 437-7190*). Chesapeake Bay Yacht Racing Week
takes place at Annapolis in early July, and the President's Cup
Regatta (hydroplanes, rowing and canoe races) in early June.

Soccer
The rest of the world calls it football, but efforts to establish
professional leagues here have failed repeatedly. However,
there is considerable enthusiasm at amateur and university
level. For information about joining or attending matches, call
the **Metropolitan DC-Virginia Soccer Association**
(☎ *(703) 321-7254 for men's teams, or* ☎ *484-0941 for
women's teams*).

Squash and racquetball
These two games, close relatives, can be played at many
places in the Washington area where entry is not restricted to
members. But court time can be expensive. Clubs include:
Capitol Hill Squash Club (*214 D St. SE* ☎ *547-2255*) —
squash; **Courts Royal Merrifield** (*2733 Merrilee Dr.,
Fairfax, Va.* ☎ *(703) 560-1215*) — squash and racquetball;
Courts Royal White Oak (*11313 Lockwood Dr., Silver
Spring, Md.* ☎ *(301) 593-7626*) — racquetball.

Swimming
Facilities in the city are not very extensive. The DC
government runs a number of pools (☎ *576-6436 for info.*),
as do the various suburban and county authorities. Among
the few hotels with a pool are the **Washington Hilton** (*1919
Connecticut Ave. NW* ☎ *483-3000*) and the **Washington
Marriott** (*22nd and M St. NW* ☎ *872-1500*), but at the latter
you must join the club for a month. The **Watergate Health
Club** (see introduction to this section) has an indoor pool
that nonmembers can use.
For other outdoor swimming avoid the local rivers, which
are polluted. The nearest good beach is about an hour's drive
away at **Sandy Point State Park**, by the w end of the
Chesapeake Bay Bridge. But the best beaches are on the
Delaware coast and a small part of the Virginia coast facing
the Atlantic, for example at **Dewey Beach, Ocean City** and
on **Assateague Island**, all having the disadvantage of being
at least a 3hr drive from DC.

Tennis
There are many public tennis courts run by DC and by the
surrounding county and suburban authorities (☎ *673-7660
for info.*). Some private tennis clubs allow nonmembers to
play, such as **Cabin John Indoor Tennis Court** (*7801
Democracy Blvd., Bethesda, Md.* ☎ *(301) 469-7300*) and
Courts Royal Annandale (*4317 Ravensworth Rd.,
Annandale, Va.* ☎ *(703) 256-6600*), which has indoor courts.
Spectator tennis events include the Women's Championship
in Jan and the DC National Bank Tennis Classic in July. For
further details contact the **Washington Area Tennis
Patrons** (*800 18th St. NW* ☎ *429-0661*).

Zoos
The *National Zoological Park* is the only zoo in DC. For
farms and nature centers, see *Washington for children*.

Excursions

It would be a pity to visit Washington and see only the
metropolitan area, for the city lies in a fascinating part of
America, full of natural beauty and historic interest. This section
describes five selected places within a day's excursion from the
capital; but first take a look at a map of the region and note some
of the other possibilities.

A couple of hours' drive to the E via the Chesapeake Bay Bridge
takes you to the eastern shore of Maryland, an area of quiet, rich
countryside, wooded inlets, charming old-world towns and an
abundance of excellent seafood. More accessible from
Washington is the peninsula that juts down into the Chesapeake
to the SE of the city, another deeply rural part of Maryland where
occasionally you will catch sight of the black-clad Amish in their
horse-drawn buggies.

To the SW lies Virginia, a state that is very conscious of its
importance in America's history and the many US presidents it
has produced. One of them, Thomas Jefferson, lived at
Monticello, just over 100 miles (150km) from Washington, a
beautiful hilltop house which he designed for himself, now a
museum. Nearby is the town of **Charlottesville**, where the
splendid university, also designed by Jefferson, can be toured.
Tobacco planting was one of the industries that made Virginia
rich, and many old plantation houses can be visited, a number
of them along the James River between Richmond, the state
capital, and Williamsburg.

Scenically, Virginia has much to be proud of in the
Shenandoah National Park, which extends for 85 miles
(127.5km) along the crest of the Blue Ridge Mountains. The
Skyline Drive through the park affords wonderful panoramas.

For those interested in military history there are many Civil War
battlefields within reach of Washington. Four of them lie in the
vicinity of **Fredericksburg**, 50 miles (75km) from Washington,
where there is a **Battlefield Park Museum**. Two more battles
took place at **Manassas**, some 25 miles (37.5km) W of
Washington, where there is also a battlefield park and museum.
Another Civil War site is **Harpers Ferry** in W Virginia, about 50
miles (75km) NW of the capital, a charming town and the scene
of much action, including John Brown's raid in 1859. The fort
where he was captured is now a museum. Not far away is the
Antietam battlefield, also known as Sharpsburg. But the most
famous of all Civil War battlefields is probably **Gettysburg** in
Pennsylvania, about 80 miles (120km) N of Washington. The vast
battle site, with its many relics and markers, is best toured with
a guide.

Note that many of these destinations can be visited on
organized bus tours.

Alexandria

6 miles (10km) s of Washington. Population: 103,000.
Getting there: By car, Route 1; by Metro to King Street or
Braddock Road; by Metrobus; or tour with Gray Line (333 E
St. SW ☎ 479-5900), which also includes Mount Vernon.
Although now part of the Washington metropolitan area and
a fashionable residential enclave for the city's professional
people, Alexandria is still very much a town in its own right,
with an old-world Virginian atmosphere which is entirely
different from DC. The spirit of the Confederacy lives on in
the old houses, the mellow, tree-lined streets and the twang

of the local accent. But Alexandria also has its chic, modern side. In and around its main artery, **King St.**, there are many smart stores and a proportionally richer selection of good restaurants than in the capital.

Allow an entire day if you want to appreciate Alexandria to the full. A good place to start your visit is the **Ramsay House Visitor's Center** (*221 King St.* ☎ *838-4200*), a small 18thC clapboard house, the oldest surviving Alexandria property, which was the home of William Ramsay, a Scottish merchant who was one of the founders of Alexandria and the town's first postmaster. Here you can obtain brochures, tourist advice and a free parking pass. Now walk along to Alexandria's heritage museum housed in the **Lyceum** (*201 S Washington St.* ☎ *838-4994* 🖬 *open 10am-5pm; closed major hols*), an imposing Greek revival building of 1839. In the Lyceum, Alexandria is reviving its first cultural center, with a museum of decorative arts and artifacts, plus free concerts and performances.

By now you will have become aware of Alexandria's strong sense of history. The town is named not after Alexander the Great but after a Scotsman named John Alexander who settled here in 1669. As Alexandria developed into an important port for tobacco and other goods, the Scottish connection continued. It was a Scotsman, John Carlyle, who built the grand stone building called **Carlyle House** (*121 N Fairfax St.* ☎ *549-2997* 🖬 *open Tues-Sat 10am-5pm, Sun noon-5pm; closed Mon, some major hols*). There is a guided tour of the interior, which has been restored as near to its original state as possible. Another reminder of the city's Scottish founders is the **Old Presbyterian Meeting House** (*321 S Fairfax St.* ☎ *549-6670* 🖬), a dignified, red-brick building.

There is a link with the town's Egyptian namesake in the form of the **George Washington National Masonic Memorial** on Old Shuter's Hill (*King St. and Callahan Dr.* ☎ *683-2007* 🖬 *open 9am-5pm; closed some major hols*). This 333ft-high (101.5m) edifice, built in the 1920s, is based on the Pharos Lighthouse at Alexandria in Egypt, one of the Seven Wonders of the World. It contains a replica of the lodge room of Alexandria Lodge No. 22, of which Washington was Worshipful Master. There are various memorabilia of Washington the man and the mason, both here and in the **George Washington Museum**, located on a higher floor. The observation floor at the top of the tower affords a fine view of the town, and children are always intrigued by the mechanical parade perpetually filing past a model of the Taj Mahal in one of the Shrine Rooms on the first floor.

Although Washington's main home was at Mount Vernon, he kept a house in Alexandria, where he was a leading citizen. A pew was reserved for him at **Christ Church** (★) (*Cameron and N Washington St.* ☎ *549-1450* 🖬).

Other prominent Alexandrians included General "Light Horse" Harry Lee, a hero of the Revolutionary War, and his son Robert E. Lee, the famous Confederate general in the Civil War. The Lee family is associated especially with two houses in Alexandria. The **Lee-Fendall House** (*614 Oronoco St., on the corner of N Washington St.* ☎ *548-1789* 🖬 *open Tues-Fri 10am-4pm, Sat, Sun by appt*) was built by Harry Lee's relative, Philip Richard Fendall. It was there that Harry Lee wrote the funeral oration for George Washington containing the famous words, "First in war, first in peace, and first in the hearts of his countrymen." Besides Lee heirlooms and furnishings, the house possesses a fine collection of antique dollhouses. Across the road stands Harry Lee's last residence, now known as the **Boyhood Home of Robert E. Lee** (*607 Oronoco St.* ☎ *548-8454* ▨ *open Mon-Sat 10am-4pm, Sun noon-4pm; closed mid-Dec to Jan*). Beautifully furnished, the house contains many Lee portraits and memorabilia.

It is pleasant just to stroll through the streets between the town center and the Potomac River, enjoying the street architecture and browsing in the stores and galleries. On the s side of Prince St. near its eastern end stand two charming groups of houses, **Gentry Row** and **Captain's Row**. On the opposite side of Prince St. at No. 201 is the **Athenaeum** (☎ *548-0035* ▨), a Greek revival building of about 1850, once a bank but now an art gallery showing temporary exhibitions. Around the corner at 101 N Union St. is the **Torpedo Factory** (☎ *838-4565*), a grim building from the outside, but imaginatively converted to a complex of artists' studios and craft shops where you can buy handicrafts or simply watch the artists at work.

The **Book Annex**, at 106 S Union St. in the next block, has a bright, welcoming tearoom at the back overlooking the river — a delightful spot for a tea, coffee or a light meal. For something more substantial in more traditional surroundings, go to **Gadsby's Tavern** ▰ (*138 N Royal St.* ☎ *548-1288*), a famous hostelry, once the haunt of many of the Founding Fathers. The older part of the tavern, next door to the restaurant at No. 134, is a museum (☎ *834-4242* ▨)

Many traditional events take place in Alexandria every year. In Aug, for example, a Civil War battle is re-enacted in costume at **Fort Ward** (*4301 W Braddock Rd.* ☎ *838-4848* ▨ *open Tues-Sat 9am-5pm, Sun noon-5pm; closed Mon, some major hols*), a partially restored Civil War Fort, now a park and museum. On the first Sat in Dec, the town's Scottish heritage is celebrated by the **Annual Scottish Christmas Walk**, when the pipes are played, the kilts twirl and Gaelic greetings are exchanged. Indeed, whenever you visit Alexandria, there is sure to be something going on. A calendar of events is available from the Visitor's Center.

Alexandria lies on the route to Mount Vernon, and the two can easily be combined in one excursion.

Annapolis
33 miles (53km) E of Washington. Population: 31,700. Getting there: By car, Route 50.

Annapolis, capital of Maryland, is one of those places where you can still catch a glimpse of the gracious, old-world face of America. On the Severn River close to where it meets Chesapeake Bay, the town's thriving economy is based on the sea and history. The sea brought Annapolis its early prosperity as a trading port; and today it retains its maritime image through its great Naval Academy and its fame as a sailing and fishing center. Many Washingtonians keep their weekend yachts here in the large marina. If you want to go out into the bay, sailboats can be rented or chartered (see *Sailing* in **Sports and activities**); or take a 40min narrated tour on the steamer *The Harbor Queen*.

There are few towns in the USA with so proud and well-presented a heritage. Originally settled in 1649 by

Puritans from Virginia, Annapolis was first laid out as a planned unit in 1694 when Washington was still a swamp. In the same year it became the capital of Maryland, and for a short period (Nov 1783-Aug 1784) it was actually the capital of the USA.

Today it is a charming town with quiet, brick-paved, tree-lined streets and an abundance of fine architecture. The best way to explore the small historic center is on foot; you may wish to follow one of the guided walks organized by **Historic Annapolis Tours** (*Old Treasury Building, State Circle, Annapolis* ☎ *(301) 267-8149*) or by **Three Centuries Tours** (*48 Maryland Ave., Annapolis* ☎ *(301) 263-5357*), whose guides dress in 18thC costume. The most significant old buildings are marked with plaques, color-coded according to period: terra cotta for pre-Revolutionary; blue for Federal (from the Revolution to about 1820); green for Greek revival (1820-40); mauve for Victorian (after 1840).

Annapolis brick is a beautiful soft red, and in the older buildings the mortar is made out of burned and crushed oyster shells.

Chase-Lloyd House
22 Maryland Ave. ☎ *(301) 263-2723* 🖭 *Open Tues-Sat 2-4pm. Closed Sun, Mon.*
In this fine 18thC building, across the road from the Hammond Harwood House and possessing a similar doorway, Mary Lloyd married Francis Scott Key, author of *The Star Spangled Banner*. It is now a ladies' retirement home.

City Dock
This is an attractive harbor, busy with pleasure craft and fishing boats and lined with historic buildings. **Middletown Tavern** (☎ *(301) 263-3323*) was established at No. 2 Market Pl. in 1750 and is still going strong. Washington, Jefferson and Franklin were among its patrons. You can dine or lunch here on such traditional fare as oysters or Maryland crab. Note also the 19thC **Market House**, which contains food stores.

Hammond Harwood House
Maryland Ave. and King George St. ☎ *(301) 269-1714* 🖭 *Open summer Tues-Sat 10am-5pm, Sun 2-5pm; winter Tues-Sat 10am-4pm, Sun 2-4pm. Closed Mon.*
This graceful Georgian house, now a museum, was designed by William Buckland, architect of Gunston Hall in Virginia and many other fine houses. It has a particularly elegant doorway with egg-and-dart moldings, Ionic columns and a fan window. The house is filled with 18thC furniture and *objets d'art*.

Maryland State House
State Circle ☎ *(301) 269-3400* 🖭 *Open 9am-5pm. Closed Christmas.*
This beautiful building is the oldest state capitol in the country that has remained in continuous use. Its dome, which dominates the town center, was built entirely without nails, using only wooden pegs. The building contains many portraits of men prominent in the history of Maryland, from the first Lord Baltimore onward. You can view the present **House of Delegates** and **Senate chambers** and also the **Old Senate chamber**, now a museum and preserved exactly as it was in 1783 when George Washington stood here to resign his commission as Commander-in-Chief of the Continental Army. The scene is depicted in a painting in the room.

Old Treasury Building

Grounds of Maryland State House (see p.148) 🔳

This small brick building is believed to be the oldest public building in Maryland. It was here that the country's first paper money, in the form of Bills of Credit, was kept. Restored in 1950, it now houses the tour offices of Historic Annapolis Inc. Exhibits relevant to the town's history are on display.

St John's College

60 College Ave. ☎ *(301) 263-2371* 🔳

This was one of the first public schools in America, opened in 1696 as King William's School, and the campus contains many historic buildings. In the grounds is the so-called **Liberty Tree**, under which many ceremonies have been held. In the mid-19thC some rowdy youths tried to blow the tree up with gunpowder, but in doing so they unwittingly saved the tree by killing all the vermin in it.

United States Naval Academy

Ricketts Hall USNA ☎ *(301) 267-3363* 🔳 *Open Mon-Sat 9am-4pm, Sun 11am-4pm ✗ in early spring and late fall every hr on the hr 10am-2pm; from June-Aug and on Sat and Sun until Dec every ½hr 9.30am-4pm.*

Founded in 1845, the US Naval Academy was designated a National Historic Site in 1963. It has beautiful grounds and some fine buildings, notably **Bancroft Hall**, a dormitory for the 4,400 midshipmen, and the **Chapel** with its crypt containing the remains of the naval hero John Paul Jones. Model ships, paintings, nautical relics and other items of naval history are on display in the museum, in **Preble Hall**.

The guided tours start from the **Visitor Information Center** in Ricketts Hall (☎ *(301) 263-6933; open 9am-4pm; closed some major hols*), reached via Gate 1 at the foot of King George St.

William Paca House

186 Prince George St. ☎ *263-5553* 🔳 *includes garden. Open Tues-Sat 10am-4pm, Sun noon-4pm. Closed Mon.*

Built in 1765 by William Paca, a signer of the Declaration of Independence and three times Governor of Maryland, this mansion is now beautifully restored. The delightful garden (*open year round Mon-Sat 10am-4pm, May-Oct Sun noon-5pm*), entered from 1 Martin St., also deserves a visit.

≈ Annapolis has hotels to suit most tastes, from the large and modern **Holiday Inn** (*Route US 50 going w* ☎ *(301) 224-3150* 💵) to **Gibson's Lodgings** (*110 Prince George St.* ☎ *(301) 268-5555* 💵), a charming old-world guest house.

🍴 The town also boasts numerous good restaurants, especially around the harbor area, where the specialties are seafood and other traditional Maryland fare. For something a little more European, try **Café Normande** (*195 Main St.* ☎ *(301) 263-3382* 💵), which is excellent for a coffee and croissant or a full meal.

Baltimore

35 miles (56km) NE *of Washington. Getting there: By car, Interstate 95; by train, from Union Station.*

Edgar Allan Poe, H. L. Mencken, Babe Ruth, Bromo-Seltzer, General Motors, Bethlehem Steel are all names associated with Baltimore, Md., second largest port on the E coast and a proud city whose history dates back to 1729. Although a working city, it possesses a strong sense of culture and a fine architectural heritage. Baltimore has had its ups and downs, but at present is very much enjoying an "up" phase, thanks in large measure to William Donald Schaefer, who became mayor in 1970 and initiated a program of development that has turned Baltimore into one of America's liveliest and best-run cities.

Epitomizing this transformation is the **Inner Harbor**, until the early 1970s a sad area of rotting buildings, ramshackle piers and rubbish tips, but now the site of one of the most stylish and imaginative urban developments in the world, an object lesson in combining modernity with grace, beauty and the human touch. One of its features is a smart shopping and restaurant complex called **Harbor Place**, comprising two separate pavilions. Sit here on a fine day under the awning of one of the open-air cafés, sipping a cool drink and looking out over the sparkling water as sailboats come and go, and you will feel that the Riviera has nothing over Baltimore.

The Inner Harbor is dominated by the tall, pentagonal **World Trade Center** (*401 E Pratt St.* ☎ *(301) 837-4515* 🖼), designed by I. M. Pei. Travel up to the 27th-floor **Top of the World** (*open Apr-Labor Day Mon-Fri 10am-5pm, Sat 10am-8pm, Sun noon-7pm; rest of yr Mon-Sat 10am-5pm, Sun noon-5pm*), where there is a superb panorama over the city, as well as a boutique, coffee shop and exhibits on Baltimore's history. There is another dramatic view from the 173ft (54m) **Washington Monument** (*N Charles St.* ☎ *(301) 752-9103* 🖼 *open Fri-Tues 10am-4pm; closed Wed, Thurs*). The **National Aquarium in Baltimore** (*Inner Harbor* ☎ *(301) 576-3810, open mid-May to mid-Sept Mon-Thurs 10am-5pm, Fri-Sun 10am-8pm; rest of yr Sat-Thurs 10am-5pm, Fri 10am-8pm*) is one of the most imaginative aquariums in the world. Youngsters will love the **Children's Cove**, where they can pick up fearsome-looking but harmless horseshoe crabs. At the top of the building, you walk through a re-creation of a tropical Amazon rain forest, with no glass between you and the iguanas and brightly colored birds. Another remarkable new museum on the Inner Harbor is the **Maryland Science Center and Planetarium** (☎ *(301) 685-2370* 🖼 *open Mon-Thurs 10am-5pm, Fri, Sat 10am-10pm, Sun noon-6pm; later hr in summer*), a kind of huge scientific adventure playground, where you can watch a show in the Planetarium, work on a computer, experiment with illusion-creating devices that tease your perception of reality, and learn about the ecology of the Chesapeake Bay.

The harbor also has three ships that can be visited. Moored on the N side is the graceful sailing ship, the US Frigate *Constellation*, launched in 1797 and the oldest American warship afloat (*open mid-May to mid-Oct 10am-6pm; rest of yr Mon-Sat 10am-4pm, Sun 10am-5pm*). Not far away, in the **Baltimore Maritime Museum** (☎ *(301) 396-3854* 🖼 *open Mon, Thurs-Sun 10am-4.30pm; closed Tues, Wed*), two more ships are open to the public, the US Submarine *Torsk* and Lightship *Chesapeake*. Another feature of the harbor is the warehouse of the **McCormick Spice Company** (*401 Light St.* ☎ *(301) 547-6166*), from which delicious aromas waft over the harbor. Visit their Colonial-style **Tea Room** (*by appt* 🖼), sample tea and coffee and learn about exotic spices.

As a change from sightseeing you can rent a paddleboat, or on certain days watch an open-air show at the NW corner of the harbor. You can also shop in the stylish new **Pratt St. Pavilion**, where there is a wide variety of merchandise and a café or two. The complementary building, the **Light St. Pavilion**, is devoted to a mouth-watering variety of food stores and restaurants. You can eat anything here from a sandwich to a high-class meal. Try the **American Café** or the upper floor of the **City Lights Restaurant**. Both have good food and open-air terraces commanding a fine view of the harbor. After lunch you could take a boat out to **Fort McHenry** on the end of a peninsula in the bay (*boats leave every ½hr 10.30am-5pm*). This fort successfully warded off a British attack during the War of 1812 and inspired Francis Scott Key to write *The Star Spangled Banner*, now the US national anthem. The fort is also accessible by land.

From the harbor a pedestrian walkway passes a fountain, where it is possible to walk behind the falling water and on to the award-winning **Convention Center** and the new Hyatt Regency Hotel. The city center to the N has been revitalized with new plazas, walkways and shopping areas. But the city also has some fine townscapes of an earlier period, notably the magnificent **Mount Vernon Pl.**, with its parks, statues and fountains, dominated by the Washington Monument and surrounded by such fine buildings as the **Peabody Institute of Music**. Unlike Washington, Baltimore has many skyscrapers, some charmingly whimsical, such as the **Bromo-Seltzer Tower**, based on the Palazzo Vecchio in Florence.

Sights of historical interest include the 246ft-high (75m) **Shot Tower** (*301 E Fayette St.* ☎ *(301) 396-8256* 🖾 *open 10am-4pm*); the **Star Spangled Banner Flag House** (*844 E Pratt St.* ☎ *(301) 837-1793* 🖾 *open Tues-Sat 10am-4pm, Sun 1-4pm; closed Mon*), where the famous flag was sewn by Mary Pickersgill; **Babe Ruth House** (*216 Emory St.* ☎ *(301) 727-1539* 🖾 *open Wed-Sun 10.30am-3.15pm; closed Mon, Tues*), birthplace of the great baseball player; and **Edgar Allan Poe House** (*203 Amity St.* ☎ *(301) 396-7932 for opening hrs* 🖾).

Baltimore has two very fine art galleries, the **Baltimore Museum of Art** (*Art Museum Dr. and 32nd St.* ☎ *(301) 396-7101* 🖾 *open Tues, Wed, Fri 10am-4pm, Thurs 10am-10pm, Sat, Sun 11am-6pm; closed Mon*), which includes a particularly good Impressionist collection, and **Walters Art Gallery** (*Charles and Centre St.* ☎ *(301) 547-9000 for opening times* 🖾), with works from ancient Egyptian times to the early 20thC. A nice feature of the Walters is that relevant books are placed in certain galleries so that you can read up the background to the objects on display.

For children, Baltimore has many attractions, including the **Zoo** (*Druid Hill Park* ☎ *(301) 396-7102* 🖾 *open 10am-4.20pm; closed Christmas*), which has more than 1,000 species of animals and includes a children's zoo with farm animals and playground equipment. Youngsters also love the **B&O Railroad Museum** (*Pratt and Poppleton St.* ☎ *(301) 237-2387* 🖾 *open Wed-Sun 10am-4pm; closed Mon, Tues*), with its superb collection of old locomotives and rolling stock.

An attractive aspect of Baltimore is the high number of ethnic traditions — Black, Hispanic, Polish, German, Greek, Irish and many more — represented in the city. The ongoing round of festivals and celebrations organized by several of these communities helps create the colorful and very human city that is Baltimore today (☎ *(301) 837-INFO for details of what's on*).

Mount Vernon and environs

*15 miles (24km) s of Washington. Getting there: By car,
George Washington Memorial Parkway or Route 1; by bus,
tour with Gray Line (333 E St. SW ☎ 479-5900), which also
includes Alexandria; by Tourmobile, from Washington
Monument or Arlington Cemetery; by boat, Mar-late fall
with Washington Boat Lines (Pier 4, 6th and Water St. SW
☎ 554-8000); by bicycle, on the Mount Vernon Bike Trail
along the Potomac.*

"No estate in United America is more pleasantly situated than
this," wrote George Washington to an English friend in 1793,
describing his house and farm at Mount Vernon. Now owned
and maintained by the Mount Vernon Ladies' Association, it is
a popular place of pilgrimage, not only because of its link
with America's great hero but because of its singular charm
and beauty.

Washington acquired the property in 1754, following the
death of his half-brother, and had the house enlarged and
redecorated. After an eventful career in the Virginia militia, he
settled down there in 1759 with his new wife Martha.
Washington adored Mount Vernon and hoped to spend the
rest of his life there as a hard-working farmer. But his plans
were interrupted first by the War of Independence, in which
he commanded the American forces, then by his two terms as
President of the United States. Throughout the momentous
events of his life he longed for the peace and solace of Mount
Vernon. After his final retirement from politics, he enjoyed
only a brief period of less than three years on his farm before
his death in 1799.

When you visit Mount Vernon today, it is clear why
Washington loved it so much. The house (☎ 780-2000 ▨
*open Mar-Oct 9am-5pm, Nov-Feb 9am-4pm; smoking, eating
and drinking are forbidden throughout house and grounds*)
is a gracefully proportioned building in a Neo-Georgian style
with a facade that looks like stone but is in fact painted
wood. Washington himself master-minded the alterations to
the house, which has many unusual features, such as the twin
open colonnades connecting with the dependencies on either
side, and the spacious porch at the back known as the
"piazza," two stories high and running the full length of the
house. Picture Washington sitting there with his friends on a
summer evening looking out over lawn and woodland to the
broad sweep of the Potomac.

The restrained, unpretentious dignity of the architecture is
in keeping with Washington's character. The interior has been
restored as closely as possible to the way it looked in his
time. The grandest room in the house is the **Large Dining
Room**, with its Hepplewhite and Sheraton furniture, its
delicate plaster moldings and marble mantelpiece carved with
agricultural motifs. Most evocative of Washington's spirit,
however, is the **Study**, from which he administered his estate.
Among the original items are his dressing-table, chair and
secretary-desk.

The many outbuildings surrounding the house deserve a
visit. The kitchen, smokehouse, coach-house, stable and
greenhouse have all been restored to their original state.
There is also a small **museum** containing portraits and
memorabilia of George and Martha Washington. Their bodies
lie in a brick tomb, ordered by Washington in his will, which
stands in a secluded part of the grounds to the w of the

house. About 50yds (46m) to the sw of this is an area where
the slaves of Mount Vernon were buried. Washington came to
oppose slavery and in his will provided for the freedom of his
slaves.

The formally laid-out **Flower Garden** and **Kitchen
Garden** are both delightful. By the Flower Garden is a shop
selling souvenirs and a variety of plants and seeds, many of
them taken from the garden itself. Along the driveway leading
up to the house can be seen elms, tulip poplars and other
trees planted by Washington himself: he was no armchair
gardener. Just by the estate's main entrance is a gift shop and
the pleasant **Mount Vernon Inn** ☎ (*☎ (703) 780-0011 ▥*).

There are a number of other places near Mount Vernon
worth visiting. **Woodlawn Plantation** (*3 miles (5km) to the
w via Route 235* ☎ *(703) 780-4000* ▨ **✗** *compulsory, open
9.30am-4.30pm; closed major hols*) was built in the early
1800s on land given by George Washington to his nephew,
Lawrence Lewis, and foster daughter, Eleanor Parke Custis,
when they married in 1799. The house, designed by the
versatile Dr William Thornton, first architect of the *Capitol*,
breathes the atmosphere of gracious Southern living. Set in
beautiful grounds, it is a center for courses in horticulture and
landscape architecture. In the grounds of Woodlawn is the
crisply modern **Pope-Leighey House** (☎ *(703) 780-4000* ▨
*at Woodlawn; open Mar-Oct Sat, Sun 9.30am-4.30pm and by
appt*), built by Frank Lloyd Wright in 1940 and considered a
pioneering design in small-scale domestic architecture. It was
moved in its entirety from Falls Church, Va., when it stood in
the way of highway construction.

Pohick Church (*3 miles (5km) to the* w via Route 1
☎ *(703) 550-9449; open 8am-4pm*) is a chaste, red-brick
structure dating from 1774. Washington attended here
regularly, sitting in pew No. 28. From Pohick Church continue
for about 1½ miles (2.5km) sw on Route 1, then double back
4 miles (6.5km) se down SR 242. This will bring you to
Gunston Hall (☎ *550-9220* ▨ *open 9.30am-5pm; closed
Christmas*), one of the most elegant Colonial homes in
Virginia, built by the Revolutionary statesman George Mason
(1725-92). Inside, note particularly the **Chinese
Chippendale** and **Palladian Rooms** with their fine wood
carvings. The house is set in beautiful grounds, with a grand
view over the Potomac.

Williamsburg

*150 miles (240km) S of Washington. Population: 10,000.
Getting there: By car, Interstate highways 95,295 and 64;
by bus, Greyhound or day tour with Gray Line (333 E St.
SW ☎ 479-5900).*

Williamsburg offers the visitor a uniquely vivid illusion of
stepping back into an 18thC American town. Capital of
Virginia in Colonial and Revolutionary times, Williamsburg
was superseded by Richmond as the capital, and for a century
and a half remained in obscurity until the 1920s when John D.
Rockefeller provided money for its restoration and
preservation. Run today by the nonprofit Colonial
Williamsburg Foundation, it is both a working town and a
living museum.

Before going into the center of Williamsburg, it is advisable
to report at the **Information Center** (*Colonial Williamsburg
Foundation, PO Box C, Williamsburg, Va. 23187* ☎ *(804)*

229-1000 or toll-free ☎ *1-800-447-8679*), on the outskirts to the N and, if you are driving, to leave your car here. You can buy a ticket here for the historic area, which will also entitle you to use the buses that run throughout the day from the Information Center and around the historic area. A conducted walking tour can also be arranged. The Information Center has a modern cafeteria and restaurant and a large store selling books, gifts and souvenirs. Before leaving the Center try to see the film *Williamsburg — The Story of a Patriot*, lasting 35mins, a superb semifictional re-creation of the town in the period leading up to Independence.

The film prepares you psychologically for the moment when you step off the bus in the historic center of Williamsburg. There, in the tranquil, tree-lined streets, with their white-painted houses, are men and women in Colonial costume. Occasionally a horse-drawn carriage passes, driven by a coachman in livery and filled with 20thC time-travelers. Other people in period costume are busy in workshops using traditional craft methods. They include a printer, a papermaker, a cooper, a gunsmith and a cabinet-maker, all actually working here for a living, though they tend to spend as much time explaining their crafts to visitors as they do working at them. An impromptu lecture from one of these craftsmen, dressed in stockings and breeches, is a fascinating experience. "This is how we do things in the 18thC," they explain patiently to their 20thC guests.

A number of stores in Williamsburg have merchandise typical of 18thC Virginia, from hand-printed books to three-cornered hats. And if in need of refreshment, you can repair to one of the taverns, such as **Chowning's** on Duke of Gloucester St., where the food is served on pewter plates by waiters in appropriate costumes. Williamsburg today is only a partially accurate reflection of 18thC life; at that time the streets would have been unpaved and unlit and the sidewalks made of mud instead of neat brick. The town would have been noisy and smelly, in contrast to the beautifully maintained place it is today. So Williamsburg is something of a charade, but one so brilliant that the visitor is bound to be charmed by it.

A ticket from the Information Center will admit you to most of the places of interest in the historic area. An exception is the **Governor's Palace** (*Palace Green* ▨ *open 9am-5pm*), but a visit to this building is well worth the extra fee. The palace seen today is a skillful 1930s replica of the original, which was destroyed by fire in 1781. Visitors pay an imaginary call on the Governor's secretary and are taught to bow and curtsey in 18thC manner. The beautiful gardens have also been meticulously reconstructed and make a delightful place to linger.

Another skillfully reconstructed building is the **Capitol** at the E end of Duke of Gloucester St., where many of the principles of American democracy were worked out. At the opposite end of Duke of Gloucester St. stand the buildings of **William and Mary College**, the second oldest college in the USA, which still functions as a respected place of higher education.

✍ If you wish to stay overnight in the town, **Williamsburg Inn** (*Francis St.* ☎ *(804)229-5000* ▥) is a pleasant hotel, offering modern comforts within a stone's throw of the 18thC charm of old Williamsburg.

Index

Excepting a few of the most notable, such as the Willard Hotel and Hecht's department store, individual hotels, restaurants and shops have not been indexed, because they appear in alphabetical order within their appropriate sections. However, the sections themselves have been indexed. Similarly, although most streets are listed in the gazetteer and not in the index, a few exceptions, such as the Mall, are indexed as well.

Page numbers in **bold** type indicate the main entry. *Italic* page numbers refer to the illustrations and plans.

Index

Index

158

Index

Gazetteer of street names

Numbers after the street refer to pages on which it is mentioned in the book. Map references refer to the maps that follow this gazetteer.

Numbered streets (1st St., 2nd St., etc) are listed in numerical sequence. Named streets are listed alphabetically.

It has not been possible to label every street drawn on the maps, although all major streets and most smaller ones have been named. Some streets that it has not been possible to label on the maps have been given map references in this gazetteer, however, because this serves as an approximate location, which will nearly always be sufficient for you to find your way.

WASHINGTON

1

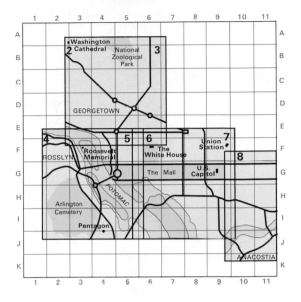

LEGEND

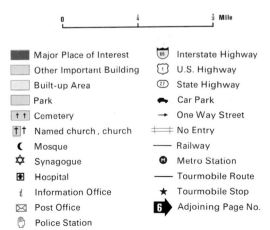

0   ¼   ½ Mile

Major Place of Interest	Interstate Highway
Other Important Building	U.S. Highway
Built-up Area	State Highway
Park	Car Park
Cemetery	One Way Street
Named church, church	No Entry
Mosque	Railway
Synagogue	Metro Station
Hospital	Tourmobile Route
Information Office	Tourmobile Stop
Post Office	Adjoining Page No.
Police Station	

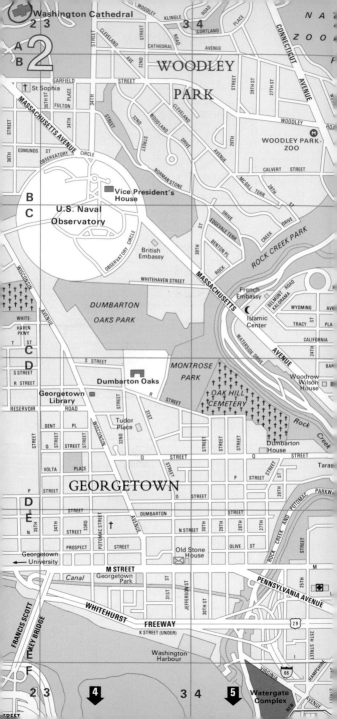

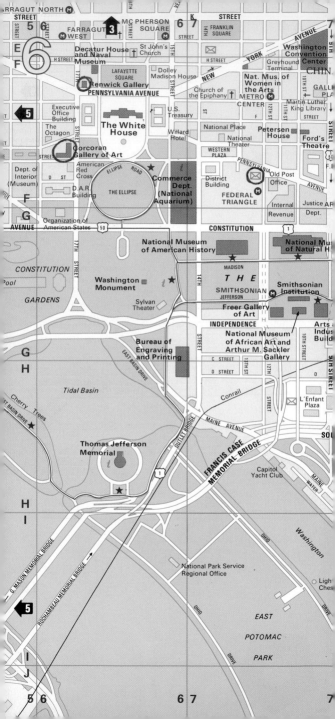

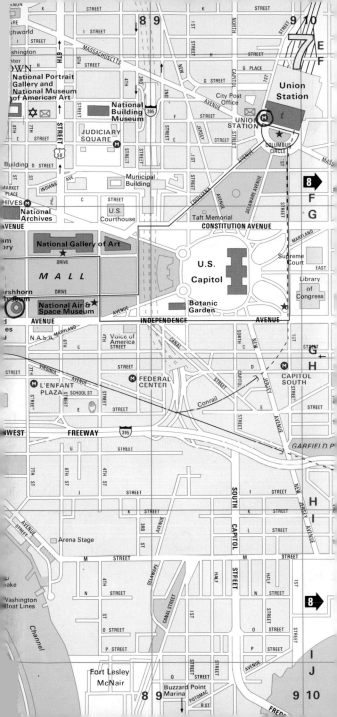

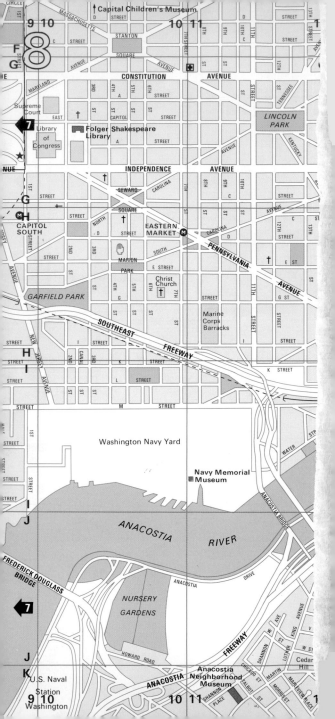